WHAT
AMERICA
DOES
RIGHT

OTHER BOOKS BY
ROBERT H. WATERMAN, JR.

*In Search of Excellence: Lessons
from America's Best-Run Companies*
(co-author: Thomas J. Peters)

*The Renewal Factor: How the Best
Get and Keep the Competitive Edge*

Adhocracy: The Power to Change

WHAT AMERICA DOES RIGHT

Learning from Companies That Put People First

Robert H. Waterman, Jr.

W. W. NORTON & COMPANY
New York London

Copyright © 1994 by Robert H. Waterman, Jr.
All rights reserved.
Printed in United States of America.

The text of this book is composed in Baskerville with the display set in Isbell.
Composition and manufacturing by the Haddon Craftsmen, Inc.
Book design by Charlotte Staub.

Library of Congress Cataloging-in-Publication Data

Waterman, Robert H.
    What America does right / Robert H. Waterman, Jr.
      p.   cm.
    Includes bibliographical references.
      1. Industrial management—United States—Case studies.
    2. Technological innovations—United States—Case studies.
    I. Title.
    HD70.U5W38   1994
    658.5—dc20   93-28837

ISBN 0-393-03597-2

W. W. Norton & Company, Inc., 500 Fifth Avenue, New York, N.Y. 10110
W. W. Norton & Company Ltd., 10 Coptic Street, London WC1A 1PU
  2 3 4 5 6 7 8 9 0

For Judy,
my love and inspiration

CONTENTS

ACKNOWLEDGMENTS

Though I take full responsibility for things said, unsaid, and ought-to-have-been said in this book, I owe endless thanks to the team of people who helped me put this work together. With four books under my belt, I keep thinking the next will be easy, which is probably what keeps me going. But none have been easy. This one has roughly ten person-years of research and writing in it. You'll have to judge whether that investment was justified.

The people who contributed can't help but think it was, and I owe particular thanks to the following four:

Jay Stuller—An author in his own right and savvy observer of the business scene from his perch in the corporate communications department of the Chevron Corporation, Jay joined this project early and had enormous faith and enthusiasm for it throughout. He helped with the research, brightened the prose, and frequently brightened my day with his wit and wry metaphor.

Evelyn Richards—Former business writer for the *Washington Post* and now world observer from her new home in Tokyo, Evelyn joined the project about the time Stuller had to put in more hours at Chevron. True to her training and professionalism as a journalist, Evelyn was the best of the lot of us at getting the full story, carefully checking the facts, challenging the flip answer, and getting down-line, as well as executive, points of view.

Sally Hudson—Long part of my staff, Sally joined my team while I was still at McKinsey & Company because she thought the work seemed fun, interesting, and important. I hope she has not been disappointed. It would be almost impossible for me to write a book like this without someone like Sally. She helps with the research, edits my prose, checks facts, and makes sure that suggestions from readers, comments from editors, corrections from sources, and afterthoughts from me—all of these things and more—come together as a cohesive whole.

Kay Dann—My extraordinary and able assistant since 1979, Kay, more than any of us, knows what it takes to put a book together and, at the same time, keep other aspects of my business in some semblance of order. With her unflagging (well, seldom flagging) good humor, Kay keeps the office in balance, my schedule in order, my writer's ego in check, and my friends happy when they probably shouldn't be, as for example when I get caught up in writing and forget to return their phone calls.

Among others who deserve credit for whatever success this book might have are the leaders and people—past and present—of all the companies I looked into. Without the good examples they set, I wouldn't have had much to write about. Many of them get a mention or are quoted in the text. Many others contributed mightily, but hit the cutting room floor so we could keep this a reasonably short book. I wish I could have quoted you all.

Some organizations contributed indirectly. In particular there is my old employer, McKinsey & Company, Inc., an excellent example in its own right and the springboard that launched Tom Peters and me on our continuing search for excellence. Others include the graduate business schools, particularly Stanford, but also Berkeley, Harvard, Dartmouth, USC, and Michigan, whose research is a touchstone for much of what I write.

Some special people also contributed from afar: Tom Peters, John Gardner, Tony Athos, Karl Weick, Jim Collins, Jerry

Porras, Jim Adams, Kirk Hansen, Charles O'Reilly, Sue McKibbin. One contributes in a different way—my sister, Susan Reed—who got me going as a serious artist. Painting keeps me both sane and refreshed.

My final thanks go to the person to whom I've dedicated this book, my love of a lifetime, Judy Waterman. She's my biggest supporter and toughest editor. Of more importance, her ideas, particularly on the subject of what motivates people and on matching people to work, heavily influence my own.

WHAT
AMERICA
DOES
RIGHT

1.

ORGANIZING FOR SUCCESS

Linking People, Strategy, Organization, and Customers

The purpose of this book is simple: to explore, in depth, the strategic and organizational reasons why a handful of widely admired American firms do so well. The theme is similar to that of everything I've written, starting with *In Search of Excellence:* learn from the best; find role models to emulate. It's the most powerful way humans learn, but it's still not done very well in business. Much more common is trial and error learning. Who messed up? Why? How do we fix it?

The *difference* between this and previous books is that it looks at fewer organizations but does so in much greater depth. Instead of relying mostly on the perspective of top managers, I spent a great deal of time trying to understand the viewpoint of middle managers and front-line people. The companies I studied gave me incredible freedom to interview, observe, and participate in discussions with people from all levels of the organization. As a result, there are many more stories, quotes, and comments from these folks throughout this book.

I picked this approach for several reasons. First, I wanted to get below the surface. Any look at top performers tends to find the same general themes—treat your own people and your customers well, and good results will follow. Most managers understand these themes. What many don't understand is how well the best firms manage the intricate interplay between people, strategy, organizational arrangements, and customers. Their ability and agility in this area separates them from the rest of the pack. Top firms do as well as they do because they constantly work hard at building coherence among widely diverse, often conflicting, interests. It's like a good marriage. A couple lives happily ever after because they work at making it work: a labor of love, but labor nonetheless.

Another reason for wanting to explore fewer companies in greater depth is that I'm mad as hell (for me) at most managers' short attention span and search for magic. Perfectly respectable ideas like "total quality" get turned into every person's bureaucratic nightmare because managers see these ideas working elsewhere but don't see the exquisite effort that went into making the ideas effective. As we'll see, decades of loving labor went into making true quality a reality at Motorola, to bringing self-direction to fruition in Procter & Gamble factories, or toward helping a noble set of aspirations come true at Levi Strauss & Company.

My last reason for studying firms in depth and over time is to sort out what is truly a sustainable advantage and what is ephemeral. Research on industrialized nations shows conclusively that American workers outproduce workers in Germany and France by about 20 percent, workers in Britain by over 30 percent, and Japanese workers by over 60 percent. What? You read it right. America leads; these days no country is closing the gap.* (See Appendix 1.)

Researchers from the McKinsey Global Institute, with help from Nobel laureate Robert Solow of MIT, and other university economists were so astounded by these findings that they wanted to know why. They concluded that the American lead could not

---

*The main reason the United States leads Japan by such a huge margin is service sector productivity. In both countries the service sector has stabilized at about 70 percent of the economy. American service productivity is roughly double that of Japan.

be attributed to differences in technology, capital availability, the marketplace, degree of unionization, economies of scale, production processes, capital intensity, or employee skill. Such factors are more or less the same across industrialized nations or, if not, quickly come into balance: Capital, technology and ideas, for instance, flow these days like quicksilver across national boundaries. Process of elimination led these researchers to conclude that the main reason America outperforms the others had to be differences in American organizational arrangements: less government regulation and ownership and greater flexibility in the way companies and people are managed in the United States. These researchers came to their conclusions not just by looking at the economy in general, but by looking at individual industries—banking, retailing, airlines, and so on—in depth.

There are some strong parallels between their approach and my own. The first, clearly, is the approach we both used: case studies and in-depth research. The second is the findings: I conclude that what makes the best firms the best cannot be attributed to such things as technology, a bright idea, a masterly strategy, the use of a tool, or the slavish following of guidelines laid out in a book like *In Search of Excellence*. These things are available to anyone who looks.

What makes top performing companies different, I would urge, is their organizational arrangements. Specifically:

- They are better organized to meet the needs of their *people*, so that they attract better people than their competitors do and their people are more greatly motivated to do a superior job, whatever it is they do.
- They are better organized to meet the needs of *customers* so that they are either more innovative in anticipating customer needs, more reliable in meeting customer expectations, better able to deliver their product or service more cheaply, or some combination of the above.

Organizing to meet your own people's needs seems a simple enough idea. It isn't. It means understanding what motivates people and aligning culture, systems, structure, people, and leadership attention toward things that are inherently motivating. It's a radical departure from management convention. The old (and still very pervasive) dictum says that the job of the manager is to tell people what to do. My research says that the manager's job is to lead. Leaders recognize and act on the idea, as people at Procter & Gamble would put it, that the needs of the business and the needs of people are inextricably linked.

ORGANIZING AROUND PEOPLE

So what does it mean to organize around the needs of your people? It means understanding those needs. A large part of *that* is something too few managers learn. They need to ask: What motivates people?

The answer is a lot of things. Each of us is unique, and what motivates me might be a complete turn-off for you. But in talking with workers, managers, top executives, psychologists, and career counselors, I found a number of common factors, including the need to feel in control, to believe in the value of their work, to be challenged, to engage in lifelong learning, and to be recognized for their achievements. Top-performing companies seem to honor these needs.

Control   People who feel in control of at least some part of their lives tend to be healthier, happier, and more effective. Old-style managers thought their job was to control others. Today's leaders understand that you have to give up control to get results. That's what all the talk of empowerment is about.

But we still don't go nearly as far as we could. In this book we'll examine how Procter & Gamble, for one, gets not only a happier workforce but an estimated 30 percent gain in productivity through plant workers who are essentially self-directed. These people have managers but no daily supervision in any conventional sense.

Putting control further down the line, even in the hands of the customer, is quite possibly the most radical departure from past management practice. It's also the most important. This theme will emerge over and over again in this book.

Something to Believe In   People report the need to feel that their organization stands for something important. They would like to believe that what they do forty hours every week makes a difference. The trouble is that although Wall Street, top executives, and business voyeurs like to talk "bottom line," most people in organizations don't relate to profit margins or return on investment. It's not visionary. It has none of the grab-you-by-the-heart quality that people find in the truly outstanding enterprise.

The once tiny AES Corporation seems to understand completely people's need to believe in the value of work. AES (formerly Applied Energy Services) is in the business of producing cheap, clean, non-nuclear power. In 1982 the company didn't exist. By 1992, shortly after it went public, the company had a stock-market valuation of over a billion dollars.

Great strategy? Partly, but the company's founders never set out to build a billion dollar company. Rather, they wanted to build an enterprise in which they and all their people could take pride. Social responsibility and having fun in work are among the values that have propelled this company since its beginning.

Levi Strauss also understands its people's need to believe in what the company stands for and the value of what they do. In this book we'll see in detail how this company tries to put what chief-executive Bob Haas calls "soul" into a company whose industry virtually defined the word "sweatshop." Through Levi Strauss we'll see what the word *vision* really means, and we'll see both the hard work and the exhilaration of getting a vision off a sheet of paper and into the fabric of a culture.

Challenge   Many of us thrive on challenges. In his book *Morale,* John Gardner put it nicely: "We are problem seekers. . . . When problems don't seem readily available, we invent them. Most games are invented problems, and a great many people fill their so-called leisure with activity indistinguishable from work except that it is self-initiated and uncompensated. Anyone who has pursued a little white ball around a golf course understands the principle."[1]

We will encounter this theme repeatedly with each company profiled. For the people at AES an obvious challenge was building a billion dollar business. Less obvious, but more important, was the challenge to make the business *both* profitable and socially responsible. For the people at Merck it's the thrill of discovering new drugs, and for those at Rubbermaid, the excitement of constant innovation.

Lifelong Learning   Closely related to the idea that people like to be challenged is the outrageous idea that people like to learn and can keep doing so throughout their careers. For a dramatically increasing number of those who populate the firms I studied, work no longer means merely manning your station on the assembly line or shuffling paper all day. For a Federal Express courier or package sorter, work could mean learning how to be a manager (most FedEx managers are people promoted from first-line positions—couriers, for example). For an AES operator, learning might mean moving to help start a new plant. For Motorola lifelong learning is woven into the cultural fabric. On their organization charts, commitment to learning shows up as Motorola University. What the charts don't say is that everyone at Motorola, no matter what their level, will spend at least one company-paid week a year back in school.

Recognition   Most of us want not only to stand out in some way as individuals, but to be appreciated for our contributions. Conversely, but very commonly, a big-time source of dissatisfaction is "attention only when I screw up." Money can be one source of recognition but shouldn't be the only one. Increases and special bonuses don't happen as often as people need recognition. And what people are paid has only partly to do with recognizing the value of individuals (the state of the economy, company financial health that year, and other factors also determine the size of the pay and bonus check). From organizations as different as Levi Strauss and P.S. 94 in the Bronx, we'll see the power of simple, non-cash recognition systems.

Except for a few fledgling programs at Sun Microsystems, Coors, and Apple Computer, one area of huge potential for individual recognition goes mainly untapped. That is the need to cotton on to the idea that, as much as all of us tend to be motivated by the same general things, each of us is also very different and that, over time, our interests change. Companies need programs that will help people understand their real interests and facilitate the process of matching their employees—not just new recruits—with jobs they can truly enjoy, of helping round pegs find their way into round holes. Take Apple's Marci Menconi, for example. She used to be a secretary, and she was good at her job, but she hated it. In most organizations she would have stayed put, but thanks to a chance encounter with a career counselor, Menconi is still with the company, now as an electrician. She bubbles with energy in her new role. She and Apple both benefit. We'll look at how the process of recognizing individual difference and enabling renewal worked for Menconi and others as a guide to what most companies ought to do.

ORGANIZATION AND STRATEGY

Organizing to anticipate and respond to customer needs—getting the customer to *want* you to succeed—seems like a simple idea. It's not, but it's at the heart of what we ought to mean by *strategy*. This idea, too, breaks sharply with much management convention. For many managers, strategy—a military metaphor—has meant either coming up with a brilliant idea or slamming the competition (or both). These kinds of strategic thinkers talk about strategy as "sustainable competitive advantage." Well, they are half right.

The companies I researched *do* look for sustainable advantage, but they *do not* do so by trying regularly to beat up on competitors. Instead, they look for advantages as perceived by the customer. What's more, they get a sustained advantage from the way they organize, not from the brilliant idea. Because they persist where others give up, they accomplish that most difficult part of strategy: implementation, that is, getting what is often a simple idea done and getting it done right.

Strategies that succeed are organic. They evolve. They wrap themselves around problems, challenges, and opportunities, make progress and move on.

The one part of conventional wisdom that has worked brilliantly in the past and will continue to do so is the market-based system for decision making. Not laissez faire: if the 1980s showed us anything it was the need for a market system with rules. But our winning the cold war wasn't so much a victory of capitalist might over communist determination as it was a victory of market-based economies over centrally planned economies. (No executive I know would argue that point, but I'm constantly amazed and amused by the number of managers who extol the market system while striving towards central planning for their own companies, and in doing so, setting themselves up for strategic failure.)

The research for this book suggests that there is both less and more to this strategy thing than meets the eye. Every successful company I looked at seems to sustain its success on the basis of one, or some combination, of three fundamentals: continuous innovation, customer satisfaction, and cost.

Continuous Innovation   Companies as different as Rubbermaid, Procter & Gamble, and Merck stay ahead strategically because they have the raw ability to out-innovate the competition. As we look at each we will see some very similar patterns in the way they manage innovation. We'll also see some differences that have to do mainly with the degree of technological difficulty facing each company.

Two patterns should not be missed. First, these companies are not merely inventing—coming up with new products for the sake of novelty; they are innovating—creating things that customers want or would want if they could only imagine them. Their drive stems more from this positive energy than from the inherently negative drive that comes from those out to kill the competition. They do beat competitors, but they do so, I'd argue, because they worry more about customers than about competition. The second pattern is their use of organization as a main strategic weapon. Others may decide to be innovative, get lucky, and actually invent something useful. Top companies sustain innovation. The reason they can lies deep within their organizational texture. They are better at innovating because they are better organized to be innovative. As we study each company we'll look at what their organizational arrangements are and why these arrangements make these companies reliably innovative.

Customer Satisfaction   Through years of working on quality, Motorola has saved billions and can deliver reliability at levels that would have been unimaginable a short decade ago. Federal Express has done roughly the same thing with the reliability of its service. Moreover, as companies like these work away at programs they call "total quality" or "total service," they find they can dramatically cut the time it takes to respond to the market, whether the request is as simple as an order or as complex as a design change.

Both Motorola and Federal Express have won the coveted Malcolm Baldrige Award for their extraordinary effort on the quality front. The point not to be missed, however, is that programs that result in total quality, total service, and fast cycle times are not, by themselves, strategic. Making them strategic means tightly coupling these programs to the needs of customers. That's why Motorola now calls its program "Total Customer Satisfaction."

Strategically, what these companies really do with total quality is build relationships with customers that are very difficult for competitors to match. A total-quality or total-service program might be either frivolous or strategic. The difference lies in how

focused the program is on the needs of the market and how
patient the company has been in adapting the tools and ideas to
their own idiosyncratic situation.

As with the innovators, the muscle behind the total-relationship strategists is the way they organize. As we'll see, Motorola
would have made little progress on its total-quality program
were it not for years of effort to push control as far down the line
as possible. Even that wouldn't have worked without a parallel
educational program. As many people at Motorola told me, you
can't empower without enabling, and by enabling they mean
educating.

At Federal Express the surface strategic advantage is also reliability; the underlying advantage—organization. In this case organization takes the form of systems that, in many ways, put the
employees in charge of the company.

Cost   Keeping customers happy also means keeping prices
competitive (although not necessarily the lowest). This means
sustained effort over time to keep costs low (although not necessarily the lowest). Again, we find a close link between a sustainable cost advantage and organizational arrangements. Procter &
Gamble gets cost advantages through the enormous productivity
gains of self-directed work. Motorola gets cost advantages
through the enormous savings generated by doing things right
the first time.

For most of the companies in this book, cost—while critically
important—doesn't take center stage in their strategic dance.
There's a reason for this. Customers who buy only according to
price, that is, from the lowest-cost competitor, are not loyal customers. So a low cost, low price strategy is a hard one to sustain.
Of course, some companies have no choice. These firms typically are in natural-resource businesses like mining where the
product sold is a straight commodity and customers' buying decisions are based mainly on price—copper is copper. The successful companies that do have a choice don't let the low cost,
low price strategy rule.

We'll look briefly at the cost dimension of strategy and explain how top companies think about it. The main idea they put forward is: keep cost in control but don't compete on price if you can possibly avoid it. For most of the companies profiled, cost competitiveness is a natural outgrowth of unusually productive organizational arrangements.

At this point I should be clear about what I mean by the words *organize, organizing,* and *organizational arrangements.* I don't mean charts, and I don't mean structure. Belgian surrealist René Magritte made the point in 1926 when he carefully rendered a pipe and under the drawing wrote the words: *"Ceci n'est pas une pipe."* This is not a pipe. A picture of something is not the thing.[2] Charts and structures are merely attempts to depict organization and, given the firms we look at in this book, they render a very poor depiction at that. By organizing I mean focusing on all the dimensions it takes to give an entity a sense of direction in fast-moving times. At a minimum this includes attention to systems and processes, the shared values in the culture, the way leadership shows what it deems important by what it chooses to pay attention to, the various sets of skills of the people employed, *and* the structure.*

AND PROFITS?

The conventional economic wisdom has it that the prime job of management is to maximize profits. But through my research and that of others, one message rings clear: Don't put profits first! Today's top enterprise does the best job for its shareholders by treating them as only one of the three main constituent groups essential to their success. The other two are quite clearly their people and their customers. This doesn't mean that shareholders get ignored. The point is that shareholder interests sit on the same plane as those of others who have a stake in the company.

*For further elaboration on this idea see the discussion of the "7S" framework in either *In Search of Excellence* or *The Renewal Factor.*

Recent research coming from the business schools strongly supports this theme. For example, over an eleven-year period, from 1977 to 1988, Harvard business professors John P. Kotter and James L. Heskett studied the nature of corporate values and culture as they related to company success. As they dug, they found one type of strong-culture company that outperforms all the rest. This is the company that values all *constituent groups*— employees, customers, shareholders. Kotter and Heskett found that companies which, perversely, *don't* put shareholders first did do better for their shareholders than organizations that *only* put shareholders first.[3] (See Appendix 2.)

Specifically, their sample of big, established companies that fit this category did 4 times better in revenue growth, almost 8 times better in job creation, 12 times better on stock prices, and an astounding 756 times better in net income growth. Kotter and Heskett's work, similar research conducted years ago at Johnson & Johnson, and research conducted by Jerry Porras, Jim Collins, and Kirk Hansen at the Stanford Business School all support this book's hypothesis. Organizing around the needs of people— your own and your customer's—pays off big.

— — —

MY EMPHASIS ON USING role models, catching great companies doing something right, is not to copy. Your style and culture is not theirs. Rather, my goal is to put forward enough examples so that you get a few good ideas, ones that you can adopt and adapt to fit your own pursuit of excellence in management.

A few words of caution: In choosing the firms studied in this book, I asked two main questions. Are they firms America can be proud of? Would we miss them if they were gone? My answer is a resounding yes to both, but it is a very personal answer. Many of your favorite companies may fit the criteria but have gotten left out. They may deserve to be studied too, but I can't cover all the deserving firms. Further, you might not miss some of the organizations that I would. Thus, despite all the work that went into this book, it's not sound research by the standards of most academics. For example, my basis for choice is unscientific, and, I didn't use formally paired comparisons.

On the other hand I've been around the management scene for over thirty years now. Through my consulting, board memberships, and own brand of research, I've seen the good, the bad, and the ugly. My own version of paired comparisons is to look at the organizations I've picked in comparison with all the not-so-hot others that I've seen and often studied closely. I can't prove the claims made in this book, but I'd be quite surprised if they are very far off the mark.

The big, well-known firms I look at in this book—Procter & Gamble, Levi Strauss, Federal Express, Rubbermaid, Merck, and Motorola—are not being held up as infallible paragons. Neither are the smaller, less well-known examples—the AES Corporation, P.S. 94 in the Bronx, and the Steadman Hawkins Clinic. All have their weaknesses. But each has performed with distinction. They have much to teach.

One last note: This book asserts that we are a productive nation and have vast potential to be more so. We can do it by investing in people. In doing so we create wealth—that's the definition of productivity—and that's good news.

But higher productivity often means fewer jobs. In looking at how a top enterprise now organizes itself to do work, one cannot help but be struck by the thought that we could be on the cusp of a revolution as profound as the one that took workers off farms and put them into factories. Just as we now produce all of America's farm products with a tiny fraction of the workforce, so we may be able to turn out much of the nation's manufactured goods (and a fair share of the services) with fewer people employed.

What would the rest do? America is not short of problems to solve and therefore potential work. How would we pay people to do these jobs? It shouldn't be too hard; for by definition productivity creates wealth. But how to get past the dislocations, how to match freed-up workers with America's (and the world's) pressing social issues, and how to do the above without massive gov-

ernment interference—those questions may be the most important and toughest we face as we move to the year 2000 and
beyond. This book doesn't begin to answer questions so large,
but the last chapter does attempt to put them in perspective.

2.

EVERYONE
A LEADER

**Giving Up Control
to Gain Control**

Twenty years ago, fresh from Cleveland's Case Western Reserve University with his chemical engineering degree in hand, Tom Tribone got a shock treatment in American management. A Pittsburgh native, he had spent summers during high school sweating in steel mills. Then he landed his first full-time job with a major oil company helping to develop the foamy plastic used for coffee cups and take-out food containers.

Today Tribone is a senior vice president of AES, a slender man with owlish glasses and a passion for both books and sports. But while Tribone's approach to managing at AES is light years ahead of his steel and oil company experiences, the same cannot be said, sadly, for much of American management. Tribone's first job stands as a metaphor for much of what is right and wrong with our nation's corporations.

Tribone's eye-opening experiences in management began a year after he joined the oil company, when he was promoted unexpectedly to manager of a small offshoot of the company's chemical operations, a Pittsburgh-area plant that made the latex used in carpet backings and as a medium for paint. "Here I was, all of twenty-four years old, and in charge of this plant and its 130 people, most of whom were much older and far more seasoned than I," Tribone recalls. "They looked at me like this was the most ridiculous thing they had ever seen—at least that's how it felt."

Tribone figures he got the job because there wasn't much risk for the company. The plant was a tiny part of a small division and had always lost money. The operation was so much a company backwater that the new manager got almost no attention or supervision. "It was," he now says, "the greatest opportunity for experimentation and learning that I've ever had."

The plant had never produced more than 2 million pounds of latex goo a month, despite its rated capacity of around 4 million pounds per month. In the early days, Tribone didn't do any better than his predecessors. "The way I did things was the way I saw everyone else running plants, by giving the folks detailed instructions—'add these ingredients to this batch, don't do this, transfer this, change the mix on this batch.' Managers did that because they were the engineers and smart; they understood the chemistry."

But Tom Tribone is one of those people who resists the *status quo*. He has a large chunk of what I call the "Columbo" factor: Like Detective Columbo on the old television show, if something doesn't make sense, Tribone asks why and keeps asking until he gets an answer that does make sense. In this case, what didn't make sense was the plant's output pattern. It ran twenty-four hours a day, seven days a week, and had its good days and bad, but it almost always did better on weekends. During a good weekend, in fact, the productivity rate came very close to the plant's 4 million pounds per month capacity.

To Tribone, this was an amazing statistic—the weekend blip. What was it about weekends? The conclusion was inescapable. The plant did better—two times better—*when he wasn't around*. Once he learned this the plant began setting production records. "The most effective direction I could give my people was simply to log the orders that came to the plant and convey that data," Tribone says. "These folks knew how to run the plant. If they knew what the customer wanted, and didn't have too much interference from me, they got it done."

Tribone had just learned today's most crucial lesson about managing: To be a true leader, you need to give up control in a narrow sense in order to get control in a much broader sense. As obvious as this now seems to some people, it flies in the face of centuries of conventional management wisdom that flatly states that the boss's job is to tell people what to do.

When Tribone's success earned recognition at the parent company, he was promptly put in charge of the main polystyrene plant. With the new job came close supervision from above. "My boss couldn't believe that I wasn't issuing detailed instructions," he laments. There was no way he could transfer his latex plant experience to the polystyrene plant. His supervisors wouldn't let him.

The incident that finally drove Tribone away from management was an egregious example of old-style management at its worst. His boss wanted him to write a letter to a man who had made a mistake. "Be sure to include the phrase 'subject to discipline up to and including discharge,' " he was told. Tribone looked into the incident and the individual. The worker had an excellent service record over his thirty years with the company; he had made one costly mistake. Tribone drafted a letter complimenting the man on past contributions, explaining his own analysis of the incident, and suggesting some corrective action.

"My superiors took that letter," says Tribone, "and they changed it completely. In effect it said, 'You did this wrong and will be disciplined *up to and including discharge* if you do it again.' " That sealed it for Tribone. He hated being controlled, hated doing something he knew was wrong, and hated being forced back into the command-and-control mode. For Tribone it was the Pittsburgh steel mill all over again. "When I saw that these guys were going to undermine whatever I wanted to do, I decided I better go back to engineering for awhile." He retreated from management and didn't touch it again until he joined AES.

Tribone's experiences mirror the struggle that almost all managers I know go through today. The problem is that few people know instinctively how to temper their desire for control. One of

the biggest challenges for would-be leaders these days is knowing
when to give direction and when to keep quiet.

EVERYONE'S NEED FOR CONTROL

One of the strongest needs each of us has is to feel that we
have at least a little control over what happens to us. Management literature is particularly rich in an area that the psychologists call "locus of control." This research shows that people who
believe they have a modicum of control over their lives are
healthier, happier, and more productive.

The best single illustration of this is the shut-off-the-noise experiments first reported by researcher Herbert M. Lefcourt in
1976 and since repeated always with the same results.[1] In the
experiment, a group of adults were assigned a series of tasks
including solving some puzzles (two of which were insoluble) and
proofreading. The only catch, and it was a big one, was that at
random times a loud and very distracting noise was played in the
background. The background "music" they had to work with
was a cacophony of two people speaking Spanish, one person
speaking Armenian, and clamorous sounds from a variety of
office equipment.

The subjects were split into two groups. People in the first
group were told to do their best to complete the task. People in
the second were given a button they could push, if they wanted
to shut off the noise. Not too surprisingly, the group with the
button did better, making almost five times the number of attempts at solving the insoluble puzzles as the other group and
making only a small fraction of the number of proofreading
errors. What was surprising was that none of the people who had
access to the switch ever used it. It was simply the knowledge that
they had control that made the difference.

Modern efforts to improve quality make extensive use of this
principle. At Motorola plants, for example, shut-down-the-line
buttons seem ubiquitous on the factory floor. One reason: the
assembly-line worker is the first one apt to spot a defect, and it is

far less costly for that person to shut down the line immediately than for an inspector to catch the defects later and either discard the product or send it back to be reworked. A more important reason: the operator is entrusted to make the decision. Given control over quality, the operator is much more apt to *care* about producing a quality product.

All of us, it appears, are happier and more productive when we have a "shut-off-the-noise" equivalent. It follows, then, that to build spirit, morale, and commitment in any organization, people should be given some influence over the things that affect them.

The quintessence of this idea is the self-managing team— groups of three to ten people who work without any direct super- vision. The concept is straightforward. Organize employees into teams that can cut across old boundaries. Train them. Put them in jobs that challenge their abilities. Give them the information they need. Tell them what they need to accomplish. Then turn them loose. Self-directed teams make decisions on the tasks of a given day, set their own goals, and take responsibility for quality control, purchasing, and the control of absenteeism and em- ployee behavior. Team members are also expected to learn all of the jobs that fall within their group's work area.[2]

The success of teams that are largely self-managing under- scores the power of giving up control over people to get control of results. Correctly implemented, such teams make enormous gains in productivity and morale. For example:

- Procter & Gamble reports anywhere from 30 to 40 percent higher productivity in plants that are team-based than in plants that are not.
- Self-directed teams at General Mills' plant in Covington, Georgia, produce cereal with quality that far exceeds that in other plants. The quality of the boxes themselves, measured by how well they are sealed, how legible the printing is, and so forth, is nearly 15 percent higher at Covington than at other plants. Covington's Big G cereals also generate the fewest number of consumer complaints.

- The mill-workers at Chaparral Steel, in Midlothian, Texas, form teams to do things like travel around the globe to select their own equipment. This has helped make Chaparral one of the world's most efficient steel producers.
- Tektronix Inc., in Beaverton, Oregon, says that one self-managed team turned out as many products in three days as a whole assembly line used to produce in fourteen days.[3]
- Roanoke, Virginia's Shenandoah Life found it could process 50 percent more paperwork with 10 percent fewer people after it began self-managed teams in the mid-1980s.
- In General Electric's Canadian operations, self-managed teams of four to twelve people have improved the productivity of the accounts payable, payroll, and other financial functions, while making the work more meaningful for employees.

Fortune magazine estimates that about half of America's large companies are experimenting with self-managing teams, which the magazine forecasts "may be *the* productivity breakthrough of the 1990s."[4] Variously named self-managing teams, self-directed teams, technician systems, high-commitment systems, or even super teams, these groups define one frontier of excellence. I have little doubt that self-directed teams will have an enormous impact in the future.

Unfortunately, according to a 1990 study by the American Productivity & Quality Center in Houston, only 7 percent of the American workforce is now organized into *true* self-managing teams.[5] Why so few? Why aren't self-directed teams the order of the day? As we shall see in this chapter, putting self-management into operation takes years of effort and enormous commitment. Most managers I know want to pull rabbits from hats to fix next quarter's earnings. It's a paradox, but in our everything's-changing, do-it-yesterday society, this strategic race is won by the plodders. Consider that to run a self-managed-team system successfully requires challenging *every* assumption and attitude about human motivation and the way work gets done. Old attitudes must go out the window. Information, systems, and access must become completely open to every individual.

Pioneers, such as Procter & Gamble, have been experimenting with and refining the self-managed-team concept for over thirty years. Looking at that company, we begin to see the tight link between strategy and organization. P&G's strategic success has much to do with its relentless drive to make self-direction a management reality.

SELF-DIRECTION PIONEERS

Procter & Gamble's innovative approach to business life, which we'll encounter again in the way they manage research, plays a major role in keeping this Cincinnati-based company vibrant.

The company is truly a phenomenon. Few companies achieve excellence, and many of those that do can't hang on to it for long. In fact, it's tough even to maintain success, let alone excellence. Not many that have made the *Fortune* 500 list stay there for more than a few decades. Defying the odds, P&G has not only stayed in business for more than one hundred fifty years, it continues to be one of the world's most respected companies, a consistent leader in consumer products with nearly $30 billion in global sales.

These days P&G officials talk openly about their long and successful history with self-directed teams. But when they first discovered the concept in the early 1960s, they found the results so astonishing that they deemed it a major competitive advantage and declared the approach a trade secret.

Attitudes Must Change The seeds of self-direction were sown at P&G when a young David Swanson joined the company in 1953. Swanson, who retired in May 1990 after a thirty-seven-year career, cuts an imposing figure. Tall, muscular, silver-haired, and silver-spectacled, he seems to be central casting's idea of the executive who ought to occupy that bastion of corporate America, the hallowed eleventh floor headquarters of P&G.

His credentials are right, too. On discharge from the military, Swanson went to Yale University for an undergraduate degree and then to the Massachusetts Institute of Technology for a master's in chemical engineering.

But in person Swanson is quick to call on his gentle smile and enthusiastic way of telling a story that he must have told thousands of times to others. One's reaction is: "I'd like to work for this guy." It's easy to see why he played such a key role in pioneering a way of manufacturing that probably will be the standard in the twenty-first century.

Swanson explains that the idea that led him to self-direction had its roots in the Korean War. The notion Swanson brought back from that war was much different than the ideas most managers took home. Many adopted the military model as their own. By contrast, when Swanson left the armed services in 1956, he wanted to leave behind the barked orders, the arbitrary constraints imposed by superior officers, and the rigid structure of military life. "A number of us who had just gotten out of the armed services joined Procter & Gamble," he recalls. "We were really surprised at the similarities between the structures and behaviors in the military service and what we found in industry. It was not what we expected, in a company that was, by reputation, as enlightened as Procter & Gamble." Structures and systems were designed, it seemed, primarily to constrain people. Elaborate procedures were written in policy manuals, contracts, and rule books. "The system," says Swanson, "didn't let people do what people could do; it put wraps on them."

To its credit, Procter & Gamble captured that dissatisfaction on film, long before the advent of the camcorder and long before corporations would tolerate the mildest grunt from a disgruntled employee. Swanson showed me some footage from a 1961 film in which workers described the prevailing attitudes. "We have to just be here and go home," said one. "We don't have to really put out. We don't add any ideas or anything extra. It's a big company and I can get away with not doing much."

But what really irritated this worker was the behavior of the typical manager. He (almost always it was a he) would join the plant fresh from college at around twenty-three years of age. Then the new manager, like Tribone, would start to make decisions and issue instructions. "Before you know it, he finds himself in a bind and he's hoping for fellows like me to bail him out. What I'm trying to say is that if he communicated before [he started making decisions], we would all have been a helluva lot better off." Another worker said simply: "When you make a suggestion, they think you're complaining." A sense of helplessness and utter loss of control drips from that comment.

Swanson recalls one plant in the Midwest that seemed to produce more charges of unfair labor practices, grievances, and arbitration proceedings than products. Swanson sighs, "The state of industrial relations there was measured by the number of fist-fights on the plant floor each week. During one of the many strikes we had at this fine plant," Swanson says with a touch of irony, "we flew in managers to run the production lines." But they never got beyond the local airport. Employees had surrounded it with pick-up trucks and shotguns. That same day someone fire bombed the warehouse. "It was war," says Swanson.*

What Swanson was seeing, of course, emanated straight from the command-and-control wisdom of the day. He says: "It seemed particularly at odds with the expectations of a group of young folks who were joining the workforce both as managers and hourly workers." All of them had just shaped a new world order in battle overseas, and now thought they would have something to say about shaping the world in peacetime at home.

*This wasn't the turn of the century, but P&G in the early 1960s. Lest even that example seem outdated, in 1982 I witnessed a similar situation. A well-regarded foods company had just acquired a subsidiary. Plant morale was low, so they investigated. The plant manager's approach to labor disputes was to take complainers out to the parking lot and beat them up. Even as recently as 1991 I watched a *Fortune* 500 company try to refurbish and streamline one of its major plants while ignoring labor's demands. Before the problems were resolved, violence, gunfire, and bombings had cost these people injury, near loss of life, and hundreds of millions in damage and lost time.

Theory X and Theory Y The evolution of self-direction at P&G is testimony to the impact one individual with a vision can make—even on a big organization like P&G and even from a fairly junior position. While at MIT, Swanson had been very taken by a professor at the Sloan School of Business. "He was espousing a theory that sounded kind of far out to us," says Swanson, "but also rather compatible with what we had in mind." This scholar called the conventional management wisdom of the day "the assumption of the mediocrity of the masses." Its main tenets:

- Most of us have an inherent dislike of work and will avoid it if at all possible.
- We need to be directed, want to avoid responsibility, have relatively little ambition, and want security above all.
- We need, therefore, to be coerced, controlled, directed, and threatened with punishment if we're to put forward adequate effort.

He called that set of assumptions Theory X. His own beliefs, which he labeled Theory Y, were the polar opposite:

- Putting forth physical and mental effort in work is as natural as play or rest.
- Most humans don't inherently dislike work, though they are often placed in jobs that give them plenty of cause for unhappiness.
- External control and threat of punishment are not the only means for getting us to work.
- Commitment to objectives is directly related to the rewards attached to achieving those objectives; the most important reward: satisfaction of our own ego needs.
- Under favorable conditions most of us learn not only to accept, but to seek, responsibility.
- The capacity to enact a fairly high degree of imagination, ingenuity, and creativity is widely, not narrowly, distributed in the population.

Swanson's teacher, of course, was Douglas McGregor, whose seminal book, *The Human Side of Enterprise*,[6] was a scathing attack on the command-and-control view of the world.

The stark contrast between Theory X and Theory Y reflects, quite simply, a very different view of the human being. If the kind of change McGregor preached, and Swanson believed in, were to take place, it would have to start with a change in the attitudes of both managers and workers.

An opportunity to experiment with such a change arrived in 1961. That year Swanson participated in the design of a new detergent plant in Augusta, Georgia. At the time P&G had only twenty U.S. plants; Swanson and his colleagues were sure that this was a once-in-a-decade chance to make a major difference, in his words "to do something quite different and quite a lot better than anything we had done in the past."

The new plant might be the *tabula rasa* on which Swanson's team would start to write the industrial model of the future.

Swanson brought McGregor to P&G. Together they visited plants, listened to the workers, and what they heard was a square fit with Theory X. Both were convinced that if any change were to occur, it would have to be in the new Augusta detergent plant.

Designing a Theory Y Plant   Swanson and McGregor went to work on plans for the Augusta plant. They had in mind a team-based organization that would encourage and allow every individual to make his or her maximum contribution to the business. "That meant it was going to be an open system," Swanson explains. It's not a new term now, but it was back then. What it implied was that communications would flow up, down, and sideways in a very easy, uninhibited way.

To facilitate this, conference rooms were designed into the Augusta plant so that people would have a place to meet. It seems a small step in retrospect, but none of the other plants had meeting places. In a command-and-control operation, who needed them? They also changed the shift rotation schedule so that there was a half-hour overlap between shifts. "Every plant employee, every working day of his or her life," says Swanson, "would start each shift at Augusta in a thirty-minute communications meeting." Conversations in these meetings would cover everything from what happened on the previous day's shift to current profit margins on detergents and plans for the next year's budget. That practice not only worked; it persists to this day in the majority of P&G plants.

And at Augusta the line employees, called "technicians," were given the whole story. At other P&G plants, Swanson says, it was traditional to give the employees mostly good news. This led them to conclude that they were part of a highly profitable, unassailable ship of success. "The result," says Swanson, "was the conviction that anything I do doesn't really make a difference." People thought to themselves: "Someone above me always knows best. They don't listen to me, they don't involve me, they don't need me." From there it is a short hop to tension and dissatisfaction, with themselves, their jobs, and the company. It showed at other P&G plants—especially the ones with the brawls. At Augusta they started sharing all the news with employees. Whether the information was good or bad, the idea was to build the technicians' knowledge of the business right up to that of the managers. Since they also wanted to make learning new skills a major emphasis, they arranged for a person's pay to go up as he or she gained knowledge. At Augusta, as at the other technician-run plants that were to follow, developing multiple skills—not seniority or moving up in the traditional hierarchy—became the way to improve pay and status. The objective was to push the Augusta plant to be as unstructured as possible. "We were trying to take away the rule book and substitute principle for mandate. The hypothesis here was that we wanted people to reach for responsibility," Swanson says.

Another way to achieve this was to have all employees work in teams organized around different parts of the detergent production process. For the most part, the teams, which usually numbered about a dozen people, were to manage themselves. Says Swanson: "There is virtually nothing that managers used to do in the old system that technicians don't do as a matter of routine today." They scheduled detergent production, hired peers, evaluated peers and managers, and interviewed prospective recruits.

Moreover, it was not the boss who decided on advancement. An employee was deemed qualified to move up (that is, move forward in the skill-based pay system) by a jury of peers, which also set up the training program and qualification system.

There are still managers at Augusta. But the atmosphere is egalitarian, with few tangible barriers. Managers and technicians wear the same uniforms and share the same parking spaces. Their benefits packages are almost identical, and workers are on salary instead of an hourly wage.

RESULTS AND ROADBLOCKS

Dave Swanson's experiment with the Augusta detergent plant quickly grew into a raging success. By the mid-1960s, and by almost any productivity measure Swanson and his colleagues could think of, Augusta was about 30 percent better than any other P&G plant. Even more important than the hard numbers, Swanson says, was the flexibility of the Augusta system. Expectation of change was built into the organization; its people were trained to think broadly and move quickly on any new developments in their business. (This aspect of P&G's form of self-management seems to me the most strategic benefit of self-direction. We'll learn more about how it works in the next chapter, on P&G's plant in Lima, Ohio.)

While the Augusta plant experiment was underway, Procter & Gamble was beginning to grow, purchasing the Charmin Paper Company and expanding into other businesses. Instead of adding a plant every ten years, it began erecting one every fifteen months for the next two decades. Moreover, these were plants built from scratch (known as "greenfield" plants), and each could build off the organizational knowledge gained from its predecessor. Augusta became P&G's first "college."

"We figured we were onto something," Swanson observes. "And if this was so good for the greenfield plants where you could do everything exactly right from day one, how about the rest of the system?" P&G knew that converting twenty old plants to the technician model wouldn't be quite as easy as starting fresh. Some of the facilities were a century old. Attitudes and behaviors of management and employees alike were frozen in traditional ideas about the specialization of work and lines of authority. To those people, the P&G pioneers, with their ideas about self-direction, must have looked like aliens from Andromeda. The job would be tough.

Still, the company invested heavily in both time and money trying to make the transition in old plants with old attitudes. "I wish I could say the effort paid off initially," says Swanson, "but we seemed to explore every blind alley in the book." The system frightened workers who felt that they wouldn't be able to learn broader skills. And it frightened managers who wondered what would be left for them if they systematically delegated most of what they'd previously done. P&G also frightened unions that saw the necessary commitment to training as a way to make workers feel they owned the business. If workers owned the business, why would they need a union?

That warring old-line plant in the Midwest posed a special challenge. Swanson sent for one of his most experienced plant managers and asked him to convert it to the technician system, adding, "You've got my permission to fail. Give it your best shot for two years and if it doesn't come around, we'll close the plant." The grievances and fist-fights that had plagued the plant for years continued for another year. Finally, the manager simply shut the place down and for two weeks met with employees, collecting as much information as he could about their attitudes. He laid out the scenario behind technician plants, starting with one compelling reason for change: the plant was near financial ruin. He then fed back to the workers a sampling of their attitudes, their clear dissatisfaction with the status quo, and told them how he'd help them change. When the plant restarted, it was with self-directed teams of technicians.

It took five years before all the wrinkles were ironed out and productivity rose by the expected 30 percent. But this was the first old plant to turn the corner, and its employees proudly participated in making the film about their experiences that I was to see years later. People at the plant wanted everyone in P&G to see that film. They knew they had been the company bad boys and wanted to change that image. It worked. Ironically, the worst plant in the system became the role model for all the other older plants.

The conversion process in the old plants took a solid decade of trial and error. Still today the operations at some of P&G's older plants don't match the effectiveness of greenfield start-ups, but they're close. Here again the close link between strategy and organization shows: For P&G, changing the psychology of work was the real barrier to progress.

LESSONS LEARNED

From the combined example of Augusta, the new plants modeled on Augusta, and the old plants converted to technician systems, P&G people have learned enough to write the definitive text on giving up narrow control over people to gain control of results. From their experiences and the experiences of others, several important lessons emerge. Just as Tribone found in the latex plant, P&G and a few others have learned that we don't need managers in the traditional sense. Technology, better educated workers, and sophisticated systems for getting work done (like the technician approach) have made the old tell-people-what-to-do boss obsolete.

We do need leaders, however. The technician system at P&G is not about fewer managers. It's about more leaders. Under this system everyone takes on managerial and leadership responsibilities. As we'll see in the next chapter, the numbers of people with the title "manager" doesn't change much. But their jobs do, and for the better. Technicians look to them as coaches, trainers, support people, and as resources. Headquarters looks to them to bring new strategy to life.

Despite the clear evidence that its day is done, the old boss model will die hard. As both Tribone and Swanson found, it hangs on like *eau de skunk*. The reason is clear: Though sometimes it doesn't seem so, bosses are people too. Their need for control is just as high as it is in the rest of the population, probably higher. And most bosses don't distinguish between controlling people and controlling results. Perversely, this phenomenon offers great strategic opportunity. Moving toward self-direction is hard, which also means that it's hard to copy. For P&G that means strategic advantage.

As P&G learned in its older plants, it is easier by one or two orders of magnitude to start something right than to try to change it later. I've spent a career in consulting ignoring that simple truth and am still not sure I know what to make of it. Are there situations where it's better to close something and start from scratch than to try to renew it? How would you work that into a financial analysis? Could you just "blow up" the old and build something new, but do it in a humane way? The benefits of starting fresh offer clear opportunity for small and medium-sized business. One good example is the AES Corporation (discussed in Chapter 5), which makes high-tech returns in a low-tech business. For AES, building and operating mainly new plants has been a clear advantage.

In these days of "continuous improvement," it may be well for all of us to think harder about discontinuous improvement. One step would be to rethink the assumptions behind the discounted cash flow analysis we use to judge the merit of capital spending. Such calculations rarely compare fixing up an old plant with simply tearing it down and rebuilding it from scratch. Traditional analysis always favors fixing up a facility that's old and fully depreciated, as opposed to creating something new. Another step would be a return to accelerated depreciation on new investment.

But we never will have the luxury of starting everything afresh. So we need to see what lessons P&G learned about changing the old. Says Swanson, "First, we learned that you need an articulate, logically presented, emotionally compelling reason for change." Change can't be presented as something that would be nice to do. It's got to be a survival issue. Swanson suggests that there isn't any business in the world that isn't two years from disaster. Making the case that a crisis is imminent if change doesn't happen is not that tough.

Another of P&G's major findings, obvious now but not then, is that you have to change the whole organization. "We had focused singularly around the design and structure of the non-management job. We kind of forgot about the management job," Swanson said. Fearful of the changes, supervisors still kept too much information to themselves and were unwilling to share power. They inhibited the growth of the process, the workers, and themselves. They needed just as much training as the technicians (albeit on different subjects, like how to coach rather than boss, when to intervene and when to give a problem back to the teams). Even with extensive education, some managers never could make the change, but P&G was pleased that the failure rate was not nearly as high as anticipated. P&G figures it lost only about 5 percent of its managers through their sheer inability to change.

In the beginning, P&G also kept people from the company's various plants apart, a practice that Swanson admits now makes him "a little red in the face." His fear was that workers from old plants would contaminate the thinking at the greenfield facilities, injecting archaic practices into a pure setting. "For a guy who had spent most of his life propagating these systems," he explains, "that was a classic lack of faith. Of course, what happened when I woke up and opened the gates was exactly the reverse." Indeed, P&G began sending workers from old plants to the new sites—not for walk-through visits, but for two- to three-week assignments. While given a project, the visitors were free to manage their own time, go anywhere in the plant day or night, and talk with anyone they wished. By actually living and working in the new system, they discovered people who really enjoyed coming to work. And there was another unanticipated benefit: Many of the greenfield technicians—who had never known anything different—earned a deeper appreciation for what they had.

Swanson's final discovery was how tenaciously old plant culture hangs on, particularly the element of mistrust that was endemic in the established facilities. "We just missed the fact that we had automatically built trust into the newer plants," he said. People believed in management. There were no we-they boundaries. Breaking down the entrenched barriers and building trust in the older plants was a trying process that required five to ten years. One of the most important aspects of it was to assure people that the new system was not designed to work them out of a job. P&G doesn't guarantee employment, but it does promise people that the new systems will make the firm more competitive—the only real security.

— — —

"NOT LONG AGO I had breakfast with a group of employees at our St. Louis plant," Swanson recalls. "It was one of our oldest and had been one of the stodgiest plants in the company. So, around the table, people were telling stories about their new lives under the new system, with each story better than the last. Finally, it came around to the woman who was running the session, whom I didn't think I'd ever met. "You may remember seeing me when you were here about five years ago, Mr. Swanson," she said. "I was the plant cook. Up to that point, the most creative thing I'd ever been allowed to do at Procter & Gamble was cook a fried omelet." When Swanson met her this time, she was one of P&G's most qualified trainers. Her new job has her traveling to company plants all over, giving seminars and hands-on instruction on total quality management!

From plant cook to worldwide corporate quality-guru, it happened under P&G's self-managing system, a system that gives people everywhere the control they need to feel and be their personal best.

3.

A LEARNING ORGANIZATION

The Team System at
P&G, Lima, Ohio

This may be the best managed plant I've ever seen," I remarked to some of my colleagues after spending several days there. I wasn't talking about the obvious skill of the young plant manager, Cathy Oxner, although she is very good at her job. What I had in mind was the system—started twenty-five years ago, it puts all of the plant's 350 people in a position of leadership. For me, the most revealing bit of evidence of everyone's involvement in leadership crystallized in my consciousness after I had attended about four meetings with both factory workers and factory managers. After every meeting I had to ask who the managers were! Usually it's obvious: Managers dress differently; often they are more articulate; people defer to them; they run the meetings. At this plant I could not tell, and that's because the workers take on so much management responsibility.

The plant that so astonished me is the Procter & Gamble facility in Lima, Ohio. There the Cincinnati-based company makes detergents, bleaches, and fabric softeners—products that Americans see regularly on television, in supermarkets, and near their washing machines, products such as Tide, Era, Downy, and Biz.

If pressed, Oxner can pull out a more or less standard organizational chart to show visitors the structure. Reporting to her are people responsible for the main product lines: heavy duty liquids (HDL), a category that includes P&G liquid laundry detergents like liquid Tide, liquid fabric conditioners (mainly various forms of Downy fabric softeners) and Biz bleach. Also reporting to her are people from a variety of functional specialties (personnel, finance, and logistics) and finally some people responsible for a special effort that they call organizational effectiveness. Looked at in terms of a classic framework there are only three layers— plant manager, managers, and technicians. But as Oxner is quick to point out: "We produce charts like that because outsiders ask for them. The charts don't even begin to depict the way the place works." She didn't need to tell me that. My inability to figure out who was who in meetings had already made her point.

TEAMS AT WORK

So how does the place work? To understand it, let's start where I did, at a 7:30 A.M. meeting of the Downy process team— sixteen people in all. The night shift was just ending and the day shift was just starting. Everyone from both shifts had gathered in a conference room. The first to speak was a technician from the night shift who reported a recurring problem with a control valve. The day shift took note.

Next, Barbae Avery, a day-shift technician, reminded everyone to stay current on their BOS (Behavioral Observation System). She was talking about a component of a plantwide safety program that reinforces a very fundamental belief in P&G manufacturing: Nothing employees do is important enough to risk injury. The philosophy and concern expressed by people like Avery go a long way toward explaining the Downy process department's record of four years' production without a single OSHA reportable accident.

The discussion then turned to other matters: the introduction of a technician who would be transferring into the team, some concerns over water-treatment measuring equipment, an announcement that some Allen Bradley people would be in that day to make a sales presentation. The meeting broke up: The night shift went home; and the day shift left to make, pack, and ship Downy.

Meetings like this, which last a half an hour and take place at every shift change, show more clearly than any organization chart how Lima really works. Nobody needs to be told what to do; the parameters are clear—the paramount importance of safety, the production targets, the quality goals, the need to improve customer service. How they organize themselves to get the job done on that particular shift, what they do about the control valve, whether they do something that day to respond to Avery's concerns about safety—all these activities and more are entirely up to them. In short, they manage themselves.

Jerry Schonhoft, a Cincinnati-based P&G executive who looks after the Lima operation among his other responsibilities, explains that he, Oxner, and the other managers talk a lot about "what needs to be done." For example, the need for speed in getting a new product to market. The need for better service to giant customers like Wal-Mart. The need to manage diversity more proactively. Managers communicate such needs quite clearly. *How* to meet those needs—or in some cases whether Schonhoft, Oxner, or even Chief Executive Edwin Artzt is right about these needs—is squarely in the hands of the technicians.

"Anytime we get into the 'hows,'" says Schonhoft, "we're asking for trouble." In other words, the system at Lima breaks down when managers get bossy. Former Lima-plant-manager Bob Tharp makes the same point with what he calls "Ouch!!!" stories. The theme of all the stories is the same: If, when the going gets rough—say, when they need to speed up a product roll out—ambitious management gets heavy handed and runs roughshod over the Lima system, it always backfires. Not only does this make the plant miss targets, but it also sows the seeds of distrust that begin to cut away at Lima's extraordinary productivity and the principles that underlie its success. That's why Tharp calls these stories "Ouch!!!"

THE LIMA CONCEPT

The phrase "Lima Concept" is used frequently by both managers and technicians as they try to explain how and why the place works. It is shorthand for a set of shared values that were put in place when Lima opened its doors twenty-five years ago and that have been polished and refined from time to time ever since. Several technicians patiently explained the Lima Concept to me. In its simplest form it means: "Get results. Do what's right. Work together."

In practice, however, the simple statement of shared values needs elaboration if it's to provide guidance to the 350 people who now staff the plant. Furthermore, things change. As the plant has grown, as customers have become more demanding, as new generations have joined the workforce, and as new priorities—like managing a diverse workforce better—have come to the fore, the people at Lima have needed to revisit and refresh the statement. This was last done in 1991, when a team (what else?) made up of both managers and technicians wrote a document entitled "Lima Organizational Premises." Here are the ten assumptions that underpin the Lima culture, as set forth in that document:

- We believe in an environment where people are allowed and expected to maximize their contribution as business owners and naturally contribute to the success of the business. [All employees own P&G stock, but by saying that they expect employees to act as "business owners," they mean they expect them to "act like this plant is yours." They all recognize that one of their most basic needs—getting the paycheck—won't be met unless the business does well.]
- A culture without barriers that allows for individual contribution will yield maximum business results. [The inextricable link between people's needs and business's needs is articulated both here and in many of the statements that follow.]

- We believe the organizational ability to make rapid changes is linked to our individual ability and desire to change. [Lima people recognize the demands of a highly competitive, fast-moving global market.]
- The long-term needs and success of the business and the employees are inseparable. The need of the business is long-term profits. The needs of the employees are: safety, security, growth, recognition, and income. [A combined emphasis on business needs and human needs, as we'll see with other companies, characterizes the best statements of vision.]
- For the success of the business and the employees, we need people to express their thoughts and ideas openly and constructively, while seeking diverse opinions and listening effectively.
- Value of self and other individuals is fundamental to the success of the work system.
- People who are trained, motivated, and rewarded to attain the business objective will maximize business results.
- Operating a safe plant and being a good corporate citizen are the best ways to do business.
- Organizational effectiveness can best be met by utilizing the diversity and creativity of our work force, leading to better solutions.
- For the success of the business and employees, a healthy organization has boundaries based on known principles that support the mission and will follow a standard process to change those that do not fit. [This somewhat enigmatic statement simply means that as autonomous as Lima people are in some ways, they are not free to "just do it." Safety, showing up for work, supporting other team members, meeting objectives, are all sensible bounds within which individuals can do things their way. If an established boundary no longer makes sense, there is a system for challenging it successfully.]

In revisiting the Lima Concept, the Lima team has shown remarkable insight into what makes for cultural success, understanding concepts that have eluded some of the brightest business thinkers. First, they demonstrate the importance of a written statement of beliefs. (Many organizations don't even get that far.) Second, as researchers on what makes a successful corporate culture, like Kotter and Heskett, would urge, their statement talks to the needs of multiple constituent groups. Third (and here's the elusive one), they show the will to revisit and reexamine beliefs. Others, most notably Thomas Watson, Jr., at IBM, stated that everything about a business should change except for its basic beliefs. Unwillingness to challenge beliefs in light of changing conditions seems to get companies, political parties, nations, and even organized religions in trouble.

QUALIFICATION AND PAY

In trying to understand Lima so far, we've looked at a statement of shared values and at one of the systems we discussed in the last chapter—the shift overlap. Now let's turn to some other systems that keep the place productive and the people happy. One that was instituted early on and that inevitably comes up early in conversations is the way technicians get paid. They call it a skill-based pay system. The idea is that people will get paid for what they know and what they are able to accomplish, as opposed to getting paid for seniority, or for position on an arbitrary pyramid, or even by tying special bonuses to productivity or outstanding contribution.

The compensation structure has five levels (and a range within each level). In theory, everyone in the plant can be in the top level; in practice about 185 technicians, which is 60 percent of the plant, are at the top. Each level is referred to as a "Q-block," or qualification block: In order to move to the next level you have to qualify. Gil Francis, a young technician who grew up in Downy processing, took me through the drill.

The entry level in the Downy process is called "operator B." That person starts off as part of a control-room work team and in essence learns how to make Downy. After a year or so, an operator B is ready to qualify as an operator A, the next Q-block level. To make the leap, technicians must be able to demonstrate to their fellow team members that they have a thorough knowledge of and ability in making Downy. For example, they must be able to diagram the system for making Downy and talk about each element in the system; draw a flow sheet for one batch of Downy, including raw material used at each step, temperatures, and cycle times; list the finished product quality parameters and variables that operators can control to keep quality within limits; describe the system for water treatment; describe the fire protection system—the list goes on.

Like everything else in the system, the team decides whether someone is qualified to move to the next level. For the Downy people, the group involved in the qualifying process includes, of course, the person being evaluated, the individual who has worked most closely with the candidate, another individual already qualified, the manager of that process department, and other already qualified individuals of the candidate's choosing. People in training may also attend a person's qualifying session for exposure to the process.

In another year or so, an operator A might be ready to qualify for the next level, called "General Tech." Again he or she would have to demonstrate knowledge and competence in making Downy, but this time at a much higher level. When I visited Lima, Gil Francis had just cleared the General Tech hurdle. To move to this level, he told me, requires skill and knowledge outside the day-to-day business of the team, in this case making nearly perfect batches of Downy. To qualify, Francis had moved to the boiler operation, the part of the Lima plant that provides process steam for all the products made there, recycles the steam, maintains the boilers, ensures that the water that gets into the boilers is pH-balanced and particle-free, and makes sure that any water discharged will not harm the environment.

OFF-LINE, ON-LINE, AND OWNERSHIP

Moving on to the top qualification level (and the highest pay level) usually means that the technician can work both "on-line" and "off-line." Translated, on-line work means anything directly connected to making the product, packing it, and shipping it. Off-line means everything else. Ron Fails, for example, pulled himself out of the Downy operation for two years to head a small team of full-time, off-line technicians to study, design, and then conduct a plantwide program on how to work with and manage an increasingly diverse workforce. By the time he had finished that assignment, every member of the Lima plant had been through his team's four-day offsite learning program on making diversity in the workplace an asset rather than a problem.

Brian Smith, another technician, temporarily left his on-line position in HDL packaging to take on an off-line job as a training coordinator. He and others felt that, despite a system that rewards skill, people's skills at Lima may not have been keeping up with the times in such areas as computer controls, pneumatic controls, and laser scanning. Heretofore, Lima had pretty much relied on the inherent mechanical skills of its farm-based work force, combined with on-the-job training, to keep individuals' technical skills current. That loose, comfortable approach no longer seemed adequate, and in Brian Smith the Lima plant found an enthusiastic, thoroughly motivated individual to champion the training cause.

Technician Tim Bible, an old hand in the Lima plant, says there's one word that explains Lima's success: *ownership*. He says that when someone like Ron takes on diversity or someone like Brian takes on training, the programs will almost inevitably be effective because they were developed by people rich in on-line experience. Technicians at Lima, or anywhere else, are not likely to take real ownership of a program dictated by management, developed by outside staff, or put forward by an outside consultant.

On the other hand, when off-line programs are put together by on-line people, employees' sense of ownership is very high. First, the program developers are thoroughly familiar with the needs of Lima operators, having just come from operations themselves. Second, they inspire confidence in the programs, since their co-workers know that these programs were developed by some of their own. Finally, they have a stake in making sure the programs work—the off-line developers will eventually find themselves back on-line having to live with whatever they created.

Nobody embodies the concept of ownership more than Bible. On November 15, 1991, he was put in charge of a team responsible for the "Downy rebuild." This was a project to make most Downy in a concentrated form to save on packaging and respond to environmental concerns. Though this sounds easy, the guts of the Downy production process would have to be torn out and replaced by new equipment to make it work. The total budget for the project would be just under $5,000,000.

When he told me the figure, I did my first of several double takes. How often do you find first-line, nonmanagement people managing projects, let alone projects that large and central to a company's success? If Bible were somehow to mess up, the cost to the company in lost sales, customers, and market share would be a heck of a lot more than $5,000,000.

Even in the steps leading up to Bible's appointment, we see something quite extraordinary about the Lima system. For example, the technicians at Downy are encouraged to "push-back," that is, if they don't agree with management decisions, they are expected to challenge authority even if the authority is Chief Executive Artzt. ("In reality," said Jane Ballard, the first Lima employee when the plant opened in 1968, "we are much more likely to push back on decisions made by Cathy [Oxner] or Jerry [Schonhoft] than ones made by Mr. Artzt.")

In the case of concentrated Downy, the technicians pushed back. They weren't sure that the concentrate was a good idea. P&G had tried something similar about ten years earlier. The product had failed in the marketplace, and people like Bible vividly remembered being stuck with useless equipment, lost business, and possible layoffs as a result. "We had to present all our marketing data and reasoning," says Schonhoft. Even then the technicians balked until management agreed to leave one regular line open as a fallback position in case the concentrated product didn't sell. (It turned out to be a good thing they did.

Even though concentrated Downy has been an enormous success, there still is an important segment of the market that will only buy the original.)

Once convinced that concentrated Downy could be a success, Bible and his cohorts went to work. Their first problem was to find space for the team and, not being able to find any in the factory, Bible rented and outfitted a trailer that would become mission control for the rebuild. At roughly the same time, he and his team, working with P&G engineers from Cincinnati, interviewed several different contractors and picked the one they believed was best suited to the job. (Here again, note the stark contrast from convention: In most companies, headquarters engineers and managers—not the technicians—would pick the contractor.

At that time the team decided that to complete rebuilding as quickly as possible, they would need outside help in two areas: computer modeling and technical writing, the former to speed up the design process and the latter to write training manuals for the new line even as the line was being built. The team interviewed and hired one person for each role. By early December, just a few weeks after Bible took on the project, the whole team (including outsiders) was ensconced in its trailer headquarters, designing the new line and planning the conversion.

The design phase lasted less than three months, from early December through the middle of February. During that period the team members were not just working with paper and computer, they were also working on a mock up of certain key elements of the new line. For example, they had Teflon piping installed early on, because Lima people had no experience with this relatively new product, so it was important to test it as quickly as possible. New heat exchangers were also ordered, but wouldn't get there as quickly as the team needed them. So they improvised, building mock heat exchangers from plywood. This let them get going on other construction, while still letting them make sure the piping would fit once the real heat exchangers arrived.

With no small sense of accomplishment, Bible and Oxner

announced that the project, from the start of construction to the time that Downy concentrate hit the supermarket shelves, took just sixteen weeks.

Sixteen weeks! I had already written "sixteen months" on my notepad when I did a double take and crossed out "months." Not only was the speed with which this project was completed testimony to the power of technician-run teams, it showed something else. The technicians seemed to comprehend fully the importance of what the business press, theorists, consultants, and executives call "time to market." Cutting the time between recognition of market opportunity and delivering product that meets that opportunity makes for a real source of competitive advantage.

While most companies are still talking about time to market, the Lima people, enacting the new version of the Lima Concept (with its assertion of the need for rapid change), have made it happen. As "business owners" and people who believe "the needs and success of the business and employees are inseparable," the Lima management system and its people have built fast response right into the way technicians behave.

Clearly, Bible is more than the run-of-the-mill exceptional technician at Lima. He has been there for 22 years and, during that time, has worked a variety of on-line jobs, qualified at the top level several times over, and run other projects. However, alongside Bible stand plenty of others with project experience, some who are relatively new and others who are old hands at line rebuilding and conversion.

By looking at the Downy concentrate example, we begin to understand the importance Bible puts on ownership. If, say, management had just said "do it," without the room for push back, technicians would have felt it was Cincinnati's project, not Lima's; the will to make it work would have been diminished. If the project had been managed by Oxner, with, say, outside contractors, it probably would have been full of start-up glitches (as projects of this sort usually are) with technicians looking for every excuse not to make it work. If Bible and his cohorts were merely off-line people, with none of the on-line experience they all share, such things as the need for early development of training manuals might have been overlooked.

Ownership also implies something else at Lima. You can't make a career of off-line work. At some point, even project managers as experienced as Bible will rotate back to the line. Everyone I talked to at Lima seems to believe this piece of the system is crucial. Otherwise, off-liners, despite their grounding in on-line work, will eventually forget their roots, start acting more like staff, become (or seem to become) increasingly divorced from operations, and start to cause we/they conflicts that defeat the whole idea of ownership.

Oxner and others warn that maintaining the on-line/off-line balance is no mean management task. The problem is twofold: At Lima all on-line technicians are expected to rotate among shifts—working several weeks on day shift, several weeks on night shift, and so on. Project work usually doesn't require shift rotation, and that can lead to an easier lifestyle and reluctance to move back on-line. Second, and more serious, many of the technicians really have fun on their special off-line assignments. While such assignments are not everyone's dish of tea, they can be invigorating. Going back to on-line work can seem a little tame by comparison.

Most of the technicians I talked with, however, don't see returning to the line as a problem. At least part of the reason is that for many of them there is no such thing as purely on-line work. The contrast is this: At most factories in the world, a technician would come to work, take his or her position on the line, and pretty much do the same thing day in and out. At Lima, however, most technicians are involved in a variety of special projects that require them to spend time working in what amounts to part-time, off-line roles.

ON-LINE AND OFF-LINE
AT THE SAME TIME

For example, a technician may be a member of the hiring committee. This is a group of eighteen people who represent all the various teams in the Lima plant. When the need arises, people get on the hiring committee in different ways. Some volunteer for the duty. Others are elected by their fellow department members. Some may have pulled that duty before. Others may be new.

The first step is to spend a couple of days training all members of the committee on hiring practices: how to interview, when to ask questions, how to listen, and legal vs. illegal practices in interviewing and screening. Then the committee breaks up and starts to screen resumes.

"Last time around we were looking to fill a hiring pool for the next several years," reflected Sherolyn Deaton, a technician from the finance and accounting area. "We started with over three thousand applicants." Working against a set of criteria that the committee had agreed on, the pool of potential workers was narrowed down to two hundred who were selected to be interviewed. The committee split itself into nine groups of two to do the interviewing. If candidates passed the first round with their two interviewers, they would go on to a different team of two for one more round.

As the process went forward, the committee would meet as a whole to discuss the candidates and decide which applicants might be "qualified" to be hired. Next, the candidate would take the routine physical and receive a formal job offer. Even then the candidate was not through the process. If someone, for instance, was hired to fill an entry-level position in Downy packaging, she would meet her prospective team to make sure she and the team felt the fit would be good.

Hiring is only one example of the off-line activities the on-line people might be engaged in. When I visited the plant, I sat in for about a half an hour on a special meeting, one of a series, made up of Downy shipping technicians. They were wrestling with problems of introducing a new product, what changes that would necessitate in their operating area and what case volumes they could realistically commit themselves to.

Later, I watched as another group of technicians wrestled with plantwide logistical problems. The corporation, working with big customers like Wal-Mart and Safeway, had found capacious opportunity to improve service—better approaches to packing, more accuracy in billing, faster delivery, fewer short shipments, and so on. The work of the Lima logistics team was to turn the general, corporatewide opportunity to reality, in the form of better service on shipments from the Lima plant.

Armed with statistics, trend data, bar charts and line charts, the team had carefully studied and communicated their progress over the last eight months or so. Every aspect of logistics was under review—customer complaints, damaged shipments, billing errors, missed delivery dates, orders not completely filled. So far, their progress had been remarkable, compared both to their own history and to other plants in what P&G calls "the soap sector." Still, there were problem areas, and they were duly noted and discussed. Everyone had complete access to the information.

BOS, KEA, AND CQV

Even when Lima people are not assigned to special teams, they still do a fair amount of work individually that is off-line in the sense that it is not related directly to daily output. One of the most striking is the Behavioral Observation System (or BOS) process that I first heard about when Barbae Avery brought it up in the Downy shift-change meeting, reminding everyone to get it done.

As she and others explained to me, the BOS process is a direct outgrowth of a P&G finding that roughly 85 percent of injury-causing accidents are related to operator error rather than to design flaws in machines. That's what the "B"—the behavior—

part of the process means. The idea is for each employee in the Lima plant to take time at least once a month to wander through the plant with a safety check list. On the list are all the kinds of behavior that might lead to accidents. Avery says that whenever she sees someone doing something that seems unsafe, she makes a note of it and most of the time she approaches the person directly to talk it over. Clearly, the system has a double whammy effect. Every day someone is likely to be cruising through the plant looking for unsafe activity; knowing that, people will be less likely to violate the guidelines. Of equal importance is the fact that, by going through the BOS drill each month, everyone in the plant is constantly reminding themselves of the importance of safety and the causes of injury.

Several other individual "off-line" processes affect everyone in Lima and are integral to the way this plant runs. One is called "KEA," for Key Element Assessment. Like BOS, KEA is a checklist. The key element on the list might vary depending on the job to be done, but the areas covered should be thought about when any change is being made. Risk is one example, and questions in that category include the risk of fire and the risk of harm to the environment. Concern about the environment is another area unto itself; items here include training needs, documentation needs, EPA compliance, air-quality and water-quality analysis. Safety is another area: Is additional training required? Should the BOS checklist be modified? Should a special safety committee be established?

Yet another system, and one fairly new to the Lima operation, is CQV (you can't get very far in Lima without a manual explaining the acronyms). CQV stands for Commissioning, Qualification, and Verification. This is a procedure that applies to any change in the production process, and it is designed to find out, before the plant gears up for a longer run, whether new equipment can produce a limited quantity of a quality product. If that limited quantity is produced successfully, then the plant can gear up for a longer-run with confidence; if the short run fails, then there's an opportunity to find out what is going wrong and fix it before moving forward. It sounds sensible, but new production processes are often ramped up more quickly and less deliberately; then, when problems occur, they are big ones.

Take the Downy conversion to concentrate. "Commissioning" meant one three-hour run on each of two products they would be making: April Fresh Downy and Sun Rinse Fresh Downy. "Both had to meet all finished product quality standards," says Bible. There were a few problems in those early runs, and the team ended up with a series of nine three-hour runs before they were satisfied and the line was "commissioned."

The next step is qualification. What's being tested here is whether the line, processing continuously and working around the clock, can make a quality product. In the Downy case that meant running multiple shifts, producing huge quantities of Downy, and then holding it in storage tanks so that its quality could be thoroughly tested. Here is where we can see the importance of the previous step. Had the first multiple-shift run been unsuccessful, Lima would have had thousands of pounds of worthless product to destroy. Fortunately, the first commission run was successful and the product could be bottled and shipped to market. (Even had there been something wrong with it, far better to catch it in the holding tanks than bottle it, only to have to destroy it, or worse—send bad product to market.)

The last step is verification. With these new Downy products, this stage lasted from April 19, 1992, when the first product went to market, until September 1, 1992. During verification, Bible and his team, who got the line up and running, continually checked on the process and the quality of the final product. Satisfied, they gradually turned Downy concentrate manufacturing over to the department technicians who would be making the new product day in and day out.

Processes such as BOS, KEA, and CQV are developed partly by P&G people like Cincinnati executive Jerry Schonhoft and partly by managers and technicians in Lima. They form the guidelines or boundaries without which the self-direction idea would not be nearly as successful.

In *In Search of Excellence* we talked about the importance of managing ambiguity and paradox. In particular, we urged the "loose-tight" properties of excellent companies—tightly central-ized around a few things of importance, radically decentralized on everything else. Since then I've seen the idea at work at all levels of organizations and called it "directed autonomy." Lead-ers need to define the game, the rules, the playing field, and the boundaries. Then they can leave it to a well-chosen and trained team to do things their own way (including challenging the boundaries).

Without calling it "directed autonomy," the Lima people seemed to be completely at ease with just the kind of tight and loose properties that the phrase implies. It's this combination of carefully worked out system and the freedom to do things their own way that makes technicians and their teams so effective in Lima.

WHAT DO MANAGERS DO?

The question now is what could possibly be left for managers to do? The answer is a lot, but the work is different from the way we usually see the boss.

Eric Westley, an engineer by training, joined P&G about eight years ago. (One thing that separates most managers from techni-cians is an engineering degree, although Oxner is not an engi-neer, and some technicians do get promoted to manager.) Before joining P&G, Westley was a manager in operations for a big steel company. He says the contrast with his current job is like night and day. "In some ways it's more difficult to work in this type of environment," he comments. "It definitely takes a different style." He elaborates that in the steel mill everyone has rule books and tight job descriptions. If you or someone working for you doesn't know what to do, you consult the rule book. At Lima, he elaborates, echoing what others have said, it's princi-ples, not rules, that guide the process. That can make it more frustrating at times. It also makes it more challenging, interest-ing, . . . and human.

Westley, Lea Ann Patrick (manager for Downy shipping), and

Larry Robbins (a heavy-duty liquid manager) seem to spend most of their time on two main activities: working with people and developing strategy. Close interaction with people is far more important in the Lima system than it was in the steel company, Westley told me. When you're operating on general principles, not rule books, technicians need plenty of access to managers to help them work their way through decisions. In describing how they spend time, managers use words and phrases like "listening," "coaching," "meeting with individuals and small groups," and "building relationships." Westley says that a Lima manager's work is done through influencing, not telling. Building strong, trust-based relationships with individuals and groups is crucial.

Patrick amplifies: "A boss tells you what you're going to do and how you're going to do it." That wouldn't work at Lima. Her style fits Westley's remarks on influencing: "Let's talk about what we want to accomplish. What's your input? Here's my advice." She clearly understands that different people have different needs. Some of her people are highly motivated, experienced, and self confident. "With them you mainly stay in touch, provide encouragement, direction if they seem to need it or ask for it." Others may be coasting, less sure of themselves, or honestly puzzled by how to approach a new challenge. In that case she probably spends more time, does more listening, and may well be more directive.

The strategic part of the manager's job is to make sure headquarters', Lima's, or their own strategic initiatives get nudged forward. Such strategic initiatives would include steady improvement in the plant's total-quality program, getting new products more quickly and reliably to market with systems like CQV, working with other managers to make sure they are, what Westley calls, "aligned"—taking care that the teams at Lima are not working at cross purposes.

One thing that managers clearly avoid is making day-to-day decisions. Oxner loves to tell the story of coming to work one morning and finding the concrete steps to the plant being torn out to be replaced by a ramp. "I had no idea we were going to do that," she says. The technicians responsible for making sure Lima is in compliance with ADA (Americans with Disabilities Act) knew what was required, had the budget, and just did it. Patrick emphasizes the point. "I have no need to get involved in the details. In fact, if [my people] try to involve me, it's usually because they want to abdicate some kind of responsibility. Usually I know darn well they can do the job, and if I wasn't here, it would get done."

AN ORGANIZATION THAT LEARNS

What the whole system adds up to is an organization that learns. The phrase "learning organization" is so catchy that I keep thinking there must be something to the idea. But before Lima, I'd never seen one. It may well be the exception: Change and learning are built right into its fabric. What might it take for a whole organization to learn? First, I think, would be the ability of all individuals to change and learn. With the Q-block system and the ease with which people move from on-line to off-line and back again, the Lima system supports and encourages individuals who take on new challenges. Ron Fails with his diversity program and Brian Smith with his training challenge are but a few examples. Remember that 60 percent of the Lima technicians are in the top qualification category.

A second factor might be the willingness to take risks and to fail, but to do it in a safe way (in other words, support experimentation but don't bet the business on it). Systems like KEA and CQV help Bible and others make radical changes to, say, a Lima manufacturing process, but in a way that minimizes the chance of disaster. The pay structure helps here also. When Gil Francis was showing me around the Downy control room, the crew was talking about a technician who would be joining them from BIZ. The new man would have to start as an operator B just like any other new employee, but as a fully qualified individual from another part of the organization, his pay would not be cut. Schonhoft says they try to encourage more of this kind of rotation. It breaks down potential we/they walls and makes the plant less dependent on the one or two fully qualified people.

P&G's pay system takes much of the worry about pay out of the picture. This also aids learning. For starters, as Swanson and McGregor had envisioned, everyone is on salary. There is no artificial distinction between technicians and managers, with the one exception that technicians do get paid for overtime. Another factor: Lima people, like others in P&G, are paid in the top range of competitive pay for their jobs. Compensation levels in Lima get surveyed every year to ensure that they stay competitive. Here's the real kicker: Every year (as long as P&G is successful, which it almost always is) each employee gets a generous chunk of his or her compensation tucked away in a profit-sharing program, mainly but not necessarily invested in P&G stock. According to Schonhoft, this means that most long-time P&G employees will retire with enough wealth that they will take no cut in annual income! Interestingly, people like Tim Bible, who have made extraordinary contributions, get no extra compensation. They don't seem to mind; they believe that special bonuses would destroy the sense of teamwork and camaraderie they so cherish.*

Another part of learning is breaking complex tasks down into steps that are simple and understandable. Everything from the Q-block system to the BOS process has extensive guidelines and long checklists. When you first see these procedures, they have a "rule book" look about them. But that's only on the surface. The only rules are that safety is the top priority and operator behavior is the first place to look for potential accidents. It's up to teams and individuals to tailor the checklists to fit their own situation.

---

*This doesn't mean that special bonuses and programs like gainsharing don't work elsewhere. Lincoln Electric, for example, a highly successful and people-oriented manufacturer of welding equipment and electric motors, thrives on piecework pay systems and individual bonuses. This point only highlights the need for integrity if cultures are to function smoothly. What I think Bible's comment really means is that special pay would be so disruptive *in P&G's culture* that the deficits would outweigh the benefits.

Learning also means motivation to change behavior. It means understanding why something that doesn't seem to be broken needs fixing. That's where David Swanson's original concept of sharing all news and information—good and bad—plays such a key role. Lima people are not "protected" from market and competitive realities. Technicians know what their market share is. They know the strengths and weaknesses of their major competitors. They know the importance of quality, service, and just-in-time production. They even listen regularly to taped consumer comments about their product from the 800 number. (At the Duncan Hines facility in Jackson, Tennessee, P&G takes this one step further: calls from customers about, say, a cake that isn't rising sometimes go straight to technicians.)

Finally, learning means using role models. Because managers see their role as coach, rather than boss, there is no shortage of good role models around Lima. The importance of manager as coach rather than boss needs special emphasis. On the surface it seems a little wimpy; who wants to coach and influence when you can just tell people what to do? But we'll see how effective this management style can be as we turn to the next chapter and meet Sheldon Salzberg at P.S. 94.

— — —

THINK ABOUT THE LIMA CONCEPT in terms of the motivating factors mentioned in the introduction. The fit is nearly perfect. The match with need for control is exact. The technician system was designed around that. More subtly, the system also fits neatly with people's need to believe in the value of work. Part of it is pride in the product (a point we'll come back to when I discuss P&G's approach to innovation). The other part is belief in the Lima Concept itself, an approach to work that everyone knows is almost without parallel.

How about challenge and lifelong learning? They're there in spades. Nobody checks their brains at the gate of this plant. The Q-block system and management's wish that more than "only" 60 percent of the technicians will be qualified at the highest level helps ensure that challenge and learning are merely business as usual. Add to that the off-line duties, the free flow of information, and self-designed training programs, and you have a system that seems singularly well designed to offer everyone constant challenge and opportunity to learn.

Recognition? The place is awash in badges, buttons, T-shirts, and special awards. Further, and of most importance, by being free of normal supervisory responsibilities, managers have far more time to pay attention to the needs of each individual. Time and attention from managers—in both quality and quantity— make for the most powerful form of recognition.

Swanson and McGregor should be very pleased. What has happened at Lima is better than even these visionaries would have imagined. Try to argue for the distinction between organization and strategy at the Lima plant—you can't. The great strategic secret at Lima is the way it's organized to let people learn and change. They've been at it for over twenty-five years. Even if would-be competitors understand the system, and few really do, it's nearly impossible to copy.

4.

TWO GREAT
COACHES

Management Lessons from
the Bronx and Vail, Colorado

P.S. 94 shouldn't work. For starters it's an inner-city K through 6 public school in the Bronx. Admittedly it's in one of the better parts of the Bronx, but it's still the Bronx, and a security guard must always be present during school hours. The guard is there not so much to prevent trouble in the school as to keep older children from disrupting classes or threatening physical harm to the children or teachers. P.S. 94 is massively over-crowded. Built to house 650 children, the school now bursts at its brick seams with an enrollment of 1,300. For a time the school's library served as a classroom, and the gym was turned into four classrooms. There is no science room, no art room. P.S. 94 doesn't even have a cafeteria. The children eat in a big hallway that doubles as a lunchroom around the noon hour. The student population is roughly 65 percent Hispanic, 25 percent African-American, and the remaining 10 percent a seeming Heinz mixture of every other race. The odds definitely don't favor success at P.S. 94.

But reading, writing, and math scores are above national averages, and absentee rates are low. What seemed most striking on the day I visited was that most of the people I met were having fun. In fact, more laughter, good natured banter, and smiles filled the atmosphere there than at any enterprise, public or private, that I can recall. A good deal of that was a direct reflection of P.S. 94's Sheldon Salzberg.* During his tenure as P.S. 94's principal, Salzberg called himself, "just a middle manager." He has much to teach us about the future of middle management.

MENTORING AND COACHING

When I asked P&G managers at the Lima plant just what it is they do, the word "coaching" came up frequently. Having said that, however, they seemed less clear on what it really means to be a coach. It's not that they don't fill that role. It's just that there is so little written on what good coaches do that even the people who seem to do it well have trouble describing the role. (This is no different than any other form of expertise; people who are good in their field often have trouble explaining to others exactly what it is that they do.)

What does it mean to be a coach? My dictionary says that coaching could mean several things. One is driving people around in a limousine or bus; the P&G managers don't mean that. Another definition is training teams, especially athletic teams, like John Madden or Bill Walsh did. They don't really mean that either, even though they do work with teams. The difference is that they are not coaching teams in a win-lose environment. What they do mean is helping individuals develop; in other words, they fill the mentoring role. I use the words "coach" and "mentor" interchangeably here. What I intend by both is the person who develops others or the act of developing others.

Tony Athos, former professor at the Harvard Business School, and my mentor on many things, puts it nicely. "A mentor helps young men or women *find* and *word* their dream." Athos goes on to say that the mentor then applauds that dream as "really worth

*Sheldon Salzberg moved on to become the district's supervisor of principals.

living for." The mentor may even go on to help the young person develop the skills, technique, expertise, and attitudes—whatever is necessary to achieve the dream. There's another part, too, says Athos. "I think the older person often stands as example in part of what the young person will be like if he or she achieves the dream." In short, in addition to being the coach, the mentor acts as a role model. (Athos talks mainly of the older person's relationship to the young because that's the usual mentor-student relationship in society.)

My first encounter with Athos as a coach and mentor goes back about twelve years. Athos was working with about sixty of us in an exercise that helped us understand what good mentors do. He asked us first to think back on who had been good coaches in our lives. Athos deliberately chose the word "coach" instead of "mentor" because he felt that with this group of McKinsey partners, the word "mentor" would be too soft and squishy. (It's probably for similar reason that I never heard the word "mentor" at Lima while I heard the word "coach" frequently.)

Our first surprise was how many of us listed the same McKinsey partner as having been a coach to us, someone whom most of us thought of as a superb consultant first and only secondarily as a manager. The next surprise was in how few partners, whose roles were primarily managing, appeared on the list. Clearly coaching and managing were different.

Next Athos had each of us list, as specifically as we could, what our coaches did that set them apart. Here are some attributes we came up with:

- The gift of time: They spent more time with us than any of us would have expected, given the difference in our relative status. "Just by paying attention to people," says Athos, "you give them information about themselves." It tells them they're important.
- High expectations: Mentors see and articulate more of their protégés' potential than the protégés would ever dream of for themselves.

- Genuine concern and interest: The mentor seems truly to care about the person and what interests him or her.
- Approachability: Mentors are easy to get close to, though there may be a great difference in status as defined by the usual hierarchy.
- Informality: The mentoring process takes place outside any formal hierarchy. It cuts across functions, layers, and even organizations.
- Competence: Protégés view mentors as people worth listening to. Their advice is sound. Often they are experts in the field where guidance is wanted.
- Protection: Mentors act as buffer between their protégés and the whims of both the bureaucracy and an overbearing boss.
- A sense of fun and humor: The good mentors seem to take their jobs very seriously, but they don't take themselves too seriously. Frequently this shows up as a fine sense of humor, as we'll see with Salzberg at P.S. 94.

When I read that list to Oxner and other Lima managers and employees they agreed quickly that it did capture what their best managers do. Then they added a few parallel points:

- Safe zones: Mentors help people to learn by encouraging people to take risks and protecting them when they fail. They give people guidance on what kinds of risk taking and failure is acceptable and what is not.
- Supporting champions: They help people advance their ideas when the rest of the organization thinks they are nuts. The best single example is Jack Craig, a mentor to one P&G technician who believed that there was a way to fill Downy bottles, which are packaged a dozen to a box, all at once instead of individually. When everyone, from engineers to equipment suppliers told the technician it was impossible, Craig arranged for the idea to be presented to the engineering hierarchy at corporate headquarters. The technician's idea was accepted and ended up saving P&G millions of dollars.
- Shared values: The best coaches at Lima, as Athos pointed out in his comment on role modeling, behave in ways that reflect

and radiate the organization's shared values as, for example, expressed in the Lima Concept.

SHELDON SALZBERG AND P.S. 94

When I visited Sheldon Salzberg and P.S. 94, I honestly could not figure out how he made the place work. If he had to rely on traditional organizational arrangements, he couldn't have gotten anything done. Too many teachers reported to him to make any conventional organizational chart work. Other individuals critical to his success, like the janitors, didn't report to him at all. Finally, P.S. 94 sits under the combined thumbs of a 6,000 person-strong head office in Brooklyn. Then it dawned on me. What I was observing in Salzberg's management style while I was at P.S. 94 was a neat fit with what we ought to mean by mentor or coach.

Time, Concern, Approachability   It starts with the way Salzberg would spend time. He began his day at about 7:00 A.M. by getting administrative chores out of the way—desk work, scheduling substitute teachers, rearranging classes if necessary. Then he would walk around the neighborhood. He told me, "Storekeepers know me, parents know me. It has a nice effect. People have problems on their way to work, they stop and talk to me in the street. I smile; they feel like someone cares."

Sometimes Salzberg would act as a crossing guard. The Brooklyn office took a dim view of that, but Salzberg continued to do it. It's one of the main ways he had of staying in touch with the parents, visiting with them as they dropped their children off for school. It's another way he let parents and the local merchant community around P.S. 94 know that he cared.

Having made his rounds outside the school, Salzberg would wander around the school itself. He told me, "I go over and visit the mini-school for awhile and see if things are okay over there. [The mini-school is a separate, "temporary" structure built in the parking lot to help alleviate crowding in the main building.]

Then I walk through the main building. Finally, I'll come in here and see what the messages are and so on. That's usually after 10:00 A.M. I try to get around again in the afternoon. They have to see me. Visibility is the whole thing."

Counselors who worked with P.S. 94 and other schools were effusive about what Salzberg called "visibility." One told me about another school where "the principal is always behind a closed door. I never see her." That school reflected the principal's apparent lack of concern. "Classrooms were in disarray, bulletin boards were down, everything was a mess." The counselor went on to say that in her opinion this principal was the norm, Salzberg the exception. In these tough times in inner-city schools most (understandably) hide from the hostility and chaos around them behind the closed door of the principal's office.

When I first saw it, Salzberg's office looked like it, too, might make a good refuge. Just like a principal's office anywhere in the country, it had a high ceiling, spacious, large, old-style windows, walls partly plastered and painted in pastel green and partly paneled in light, scuffed wood.

The difference was that it was the principal's office in name only; during most of the day, it seemed, everyone was using that office. Throughout the day, Salzberg's office was a beehive of noise and activity. His desk sat diagonally in one corner of the 30-by-30 foot space. Plunked near the center was a conference table at which I never saw less than three people—and more typically five—working and talking. A few were program coordinators, others were teachers on special assignment, another was an intern, on assignment from another school for six months to help and learn from Salzberg. Salzberg explained that there simply wasn't any place else to put them. Privacy didn't exist.

I spent most of one day talking with Salzberg and following him around. In theory he had blocked his office hours to talk with me. What this really meant was that there were fewer people than usual standing in front of his desk, people who "had" to see him on one urgent matter or another. While I was there, the queue was seldom shorter than three people and often longer. The large anteroom through which one gains access to the office was always packed with people who had business with the principal's office, if not with Salzberg himself. The whole scene in and around his office reminded me of nothing so much as the set from "Hill Street Blues," minus the violence.

Sheldon would guard his availability, not his privacy, like the crown jewels. "Take a day like today: It's a half day [for the children] but I still had three different sets of parents in here this morning, all with valid reasons to talk. One mother wanted to know if her kid's class was going to be held in the gym next year. I told her yes and she was unhappy. I'm unhappy too. I wish there were a way we could get another school in this community. We need it; we need it desperately." Salzberg couldn't do anything about this mother's child being in a class held in the gym. On the other hand he did something that was very important. He was there and he listened.

Through raw accessibility—wandering around the neighborhood, greeting parents in the morning in his role as crossing guard, wandering through the school and the mini school, permitting his office to be a gathering spot—Salzberg was doing several things that characterize the good mentor and coach. Like the P&G managers at Lima, he was approachable and concerned, and he gave that most precious gift of all—time.

Sound Counsel Salzberg has another quality that seems to characterize the good mentor. Through his seventeen years in the principal's job, and a lifetime in education, he's grown wise. People seek and respect his guidance. Take a simple but important example. Janice Sills, a long-time teacher, and now someone who teaches teachers remembers her job interview with Salzberg. "He told me, 'I just want you to remember where your priorities are. You still have two children. Don't think twice about it if you have to stay home or come in a little late or leave a little early. We'll take care of it for you.' " With that touch of sage advice and humanity, Salzberg won her undying admiration.

Or take a more complicated situation. On an afternoon walk around the school, a sixth grade girl approached Salzberg in tears. He comforted her and then asked what was wrong. A teacher had confiscated her umbrella during the noon hour, she sobbed, and she knew that she'd be in big trouble at home if she went home without it. He promised to look into it. About an hour later we were back in the office with the girl's homeroom teacher and the teacher who had lunchroom duty that day. The youngster, it seemed, had taken a swing at another child with the umbrella and the teacher on lunch duty had confiscated it. The homeroom teacher was irate, arguing that the girl was his responsibility and that the other teacher should have alerted him so that he could take whatever disciplinary measure he deemed appropriate. Salzberg asked both what should be done. They agreed that the homeroom teacher should return the umbrella and reprimand the girl. Later Salzberg told me that the whole thing had little to do with the umbrella or the girl. "Those two teachers fight all the time," he said. "If one says, 'up' the other says 'down.' "

The real point of the incident—Salzberg's open door and wise management style—became clear. An issue that could have smoldered was quickly dampened. Everyone had his or her say; everyone felt better; the girl went home with a big smile under her umbrella.

Bureaucracy Buffer   Like other good coaches, Salzberg doesn't let the bureaucracy get in the way of his people's or team's performance. One area of constant friction in the New York system is the gulf between the schools and the janitorial staff. The custodial staff does not report to the principal, and it has its own strong union. In January 1990, then newly appointed New York City schools' superintendent Joseph Fernandez drove by an elementary school with graffiti on it. He went on a rampage, deciding that the graffiti was a symbol of the low standards plaguing the school district he'd vowed to change when he took office. He called the principal of the school and told her to clean off the graffiti.

In a kind of Catch-22, the principal explained that during the daytime, people parked cars in front of the wall and the janitors couldn't get to the graffiti. When people drove the cars away, the janitors were off work. To get the money needed for someone to come in and clean the offending wall after hours, the principal would have to apply to the district and then wait six months for the application to work its way through the system.[1]

To avoid this kind of stand-off, Salzberg would drop in on the janitorial staff as part of his normal walk around P.S. 94, meeting them in their office, not his. When I was there, Jim Burke, the head janitor, and his assistant obviously seemed pleased to have Salzberg come by. Burke, an Irishman who used his brogue with good and humorous effect, waxed eloquent on the virtues of Salzberg's style. He said his job would be impossible without the cooperation of teachers. "If they don't keep their rooms neat, no amount of custodial help is going to keep the school looking tidy." And Salzberg's style encouraged that kind of cooperation and personal responsibility. (During another part of the day several teachers marveled at what good support they were getting from Burke.)

Salzberg's "management" of the janitorial staff bears no relationship to the old command-and-control ethic. He would give both the teachers and the janitors control over the relatively spotless look of the school, and he wouldn't do it by mandate. He did it by demonstrating that he cared about individuals and the standards of the school.

Near the end of our conversation, and before I had heard anything about the famous Fernandez incident, Salzberg brought up the only piece of graffiti I had seen on the school walls. Burke said he had noticed it too; someone must have sprayed it on a day or two before. He promised Salzberg that it would be gone as soon as the cars near it were out of the lot.

Exceeding Expectations Another quality in mentors is their ability to bring out the best in people, a "best" that often exceeds what the people would have had in mind for themselves. This is certainly the effect Salzberg had on Doris Budow. During my day at P.S. 94, I talked at length with Ms. Budow, a pleasant woman in her mid-thirties who had been a teacher and was

serving as intern under Salzberg's guidance so that she might
become a school principal one day. Said Budow, "The first day I
came to the school I began to understand something was very
different here. Shelly took me to every classroom and introduced
me. Immediately he set the tone that I was someone the children
and the teachers should take seriously."

Budow continued, "I like to joke that my job description is
'streetwalker.'" She had only been on the job a few days when
Salzberg had her busily engaged in the activity he holds most
dear: walking the streets in the mornings and afternoons to show
the merchants, neighbors, and parents that he cares. She told me
that everyone in the neighborhood knew Salzberg, wanted to
shake his hand and ask how he was doing. "Now that I've
worked the streets," Budow said, "I get the same kind of response."

Even something as seemingly small as Salzberg's strict dress
code for faculty would send out the signal that the teachers were
there to teach and the students were there to learn. "It's not a
day-care center in disguise," one teacher told me. I walked into
Salzberg's office on a hot day in late May. He was wearing a
newly pressed light gray suit, a white shirt, and a silk tie; I was in
jeans and a casual sweater. Salzberg was nice enough not to
comment on my attire, but throughout the conversation he emphasized that the basic business of P.S. 94 is education. It's a
learning environment. The business of learning is serious and
behind the seeming chaos lie rules, decorum, and dress codes
that constantly remind the children that they are there to learn.

Budow had a similar experience on her first day at P.S. 94:
"As we walked the halls, kids would say, 'Nice tie, Mr. Salzberg',
or 'Nice suit.' This is an inner-city school, not the kind of place
where you usually hear that sort of thing." A few days later, and
dressed to the Salzberg standard, Budow laughed, "One kid said
to me, 'Are you important?' I said, 'I guess so.' The kid said,
'Well, you look important.'"

This story conveys precisely the message Salzberg would try to
get across to children, parents, and teachers. Children today will
be adults tomorrow. They need role models. They need higher

self-expectations than they might normally get in a public school in the Bronx. Salzberg firmly believed that you have to draw the line somewhere. Being overly strict won't work, especially for Salzberg, who describes himself as a person with a big sense of fun and humor. But you can't be totally loose either. Children need to know there is a difference between being an adult and being a child. They need people and institutions they can respect.

"Teachers have to be recognized as professionals," Salzberg commented. "Years ago, they were treated with respect. I think the 1960s changed that. We began to talk about rights, but we left off the second part and that was responsibility. With every right that we get there's a responsibility. That idea was put down in the 1960s. I think the school system is still paying the penalty"—no dress code, lack of respect for the adult, but perhaps even more important, lack of self-respect and self-esteem among the teachers.

Salzberg told me that an inch of respect goes a long way. All the staff called him by first name [most of them called him "Shelly"]. But the children called him "Mr. Salzberg." He also insisted that the children address the teachers, the custodians, the assistant—all the adults—formally.

Humor   When I was there, P.S. 94 was a place filled with laughter and fun. I'm sure part of it was the "M*A*S*H" kind of humor; the situation was so awful in many respects that all you could do was laugh. But there's another part. Salzberg said that lots happens in the daily life at P.S. 94, but that it helps to keep a sense of fun and humor. He illustrated with just one incident. "Sometimes in June we get these 95 degree days with humidity to match, and I'll send someone out to buy ice cream for the staff. "It's a little thing, but it goes a long way. Then you get the odd individual—the first time I got ice cream for everybody, this person came storming into my office and said, 'What about the people who are on diets?' " All he could do was laugh.

A sense of humor—in this case a sense of the absurd—helps.

AND IN MEDICINE?

Sheldon Salzberg and Richard Steadman are two very different people. They work in entirely different surroundings. Yet
there are strong parallels in the way the duo brings out the best
in their followers. Many think Dr. Steadman, now practicing in
the Steadman Hawkins Clinic in Vail, Colorado, is the best knee
surgeon in the world. What I believe is that his success and
reputation have at least as much to do with the way his clinic is
managed as his clear technical skill as a surgeon. He is not only
mentor to his staff (unusual enough in medicine) but mentor to
his patients as well. Steadman takes the idea of empowerment—
transferring control—to its limits. He empowers his patients.

Around mid-day Steadman's waiting room is as crowded as
Salzberg's classrooms, a reflection of Steadman's reputation.
Among his patients are tennis star Martina Navratilova and
World Cup–winning ski racer Marc Girardelli. Walking into
Steadman's private office gives one a sense of near reverence.
Every wall is covered with large, framed photographs of athletes
in action. Each photograph is signed with a very personal and
private tribute to Steadman. Under a beaming picture of Mar-
tina Navratilova, the inscription reads: "To Dr. Steadman—
Thanks for putting a smile on my face, my heart, and my knees."
A picture of Girardelli is inscribed: "For the man who saved my
career." And seasoned ski racer Cindy Nelson has three of her
World Cup medals hanging in his office. The plaque underneath
reads: "A part of each of these medals belongs to you. Thank
you for helping these dreams come true."

Steadman himself takes quiet pride in pointing out that many
of his patients have done *better* in competition since their injuries.
Girardelli, from Luxembourg, may be the best example. In 1983
he crashed in a ski race and dislocated his knee, tore every ligament in it, and did serious cartilage damage to boot. In 1985 he
dislocated his shoulder, and in 1988 he severed a tendon in his
elbow. Steadman is the only orthopedic surgeon he will see. And

with good reason. Since the knee injury in 1983, an injury that was so severe you wonder that he can even walk, he has won the World Cup combined title—an annual compilation of points accumulated by racers over the season—five times. In the 1992–1993 season, he won it again.

Steadman's size almost matches his reputation. He is six feet three inches tall and tips the scale at about 230 pounds. His reputation and size are daunting as he walks toward you to shake hands. But his reassuring smile and manner, which somehow come across as a singular and marvelous mixture of warm, shy, and competent, put you immediately at ease. You wonder if he always maintains the equanimity he exudes. Perhaps not, but none of his staff can remember his using a cross word with them.

That same mien probably plays a large part in his success as a physician. It certainly does in his leadership of the 30-person Steadman Hawkins Clinic. Shirley Carlson, a nurse who has worked with him for more than ten years, says: "When I first worked with him, I wasn't an employee of the clinic. I was a surgery supervisor, and he was one of several doctors that I helped in surgery. There was something different in the way he handled himself as a surgeon and in the way he treated the people he worked with. He wasn't the tyrant or egotist that so many surgeons can be. He had a very quiet demeanor and no need to be the center of attention."

An Inspiring Vision   Like other leaders, Steadman understands the importance of individual control. He empowers his staff—and most important, his patients—through a simple vision, a very personal view of the way he wants to practice medicine. His dream developed partly from a negative reaction to what he has seen in practice elsewhere. Steadman believes that too many doctors look at their work as fixing a knee, a shoulder, a gall bladder, a stomach, or what have you. Steadman treats people. He questions patients about their lifestyles, sports interests, plans for the future, what the patient wants to achieve after the operation. Answers to all these questions could influence the

extent of the surgery or whether surgery is needed at all. Answers
to these questions will certainly influence the prescribed rehabilitation program, which Steadman points out, is just as important
as the surgery itself.

The Doctor's Time   Behind these discussions and Steadman's demeanor lies another very important part of his philosophy of treating people. I've talked with a host of Steadman patients; I've been one myself. We all have the same reaction: As
busy as he is, when you are in Steadman's office, you feel like you
are the most important person in the world.

It's not an act. Spending time with the patient is a vital part of
the Steadman philosophy. He particularly believes in the importance of gaining a patient's confidence. The more confidence the
patient has in the doctor, the better the patient's chances of
healing and recovery. Also, and just as important, the more confidence the patient has in his or her ability to recover, the better
the chances are of full recovery. Steadman wants patients to
understand exactly what and what not to expect from surgery
and rehabilitation, what is possible through physical therapy and
why post-operative therapy is important.

Steadman's intense curiosity strongly reinforces this part of his
vision. He was deeply influenced, for example, by the post-
operative success rates he had read about in East Germany. In
science and physical equipment, the East German's lagged behind the United States and other countries. But East German
orthopedic surgeons reported astonishingly high records of long-
term success. What made the difference? Steadman traveled
there to find out. His conclusion: The disparity was mainly in the
doctor-patient relationship. Patients there had more faith in the
doctor and spent more time in rehab.

Optimism without illusions is central to Steadman's view of
effective medicine. It's the quality of mentors that gets people to
see possibilities instead of problems. Writes the *Wall Street Journal*:
"When he examines patients, Dr. Steadman is relentlessly cheerful, saving his warmest remarks for frightened children. 'I'm real

optimistic, and you should be too,' he tells a teenage boy with severe cartilage damage."[2]

He seems to understand completely the importance of personal ownership and control that we saw in P&G's Lima factory. Writing for a professional journal, he says: "The effect of the dramatic change in lifestyle from being a competitive athlete to being a patient has implications that are both psychological and physiologic. It seems important to [address both] problems in the immediate postoperative stage."[3]

After a knee-shattering accident, a patient has suddenly lost control—a particularly acute problem for athletes. The feeling of control starts to return with the first visit to Steadman, when the patient encounters his reassuring manner and confidence. Steadman wants to get that feeling of control transferred to the patient as quickly as possible. He says: "Starting to exercise almost immediately after the operation replaces that feeling of hopelessness with 'something to shoot for.' " By "almost immediately," Steadman means as soon as the anesthesia has worn off. He's not talking, of course, about exercise that would negate the surgery. He is talking about exercising whatever is not injured: stomach muscles, arm muscles. He even suggests the use of a stationary bicycle as soon as the patient can move the uninjured leg comfortably.

My case is a good example. While skiing at Vail, I had taken a spill and completely severed my left knee's anterior cruciate ligament. The accident happened on Monday; Steadman operated Wednesday. Before the operation Steadman's nurses had me shave my own leg, scrub it with antiseptic soap, and make a big mark with permanent ink on the knee that was to be treated. Saved a little time for them? Probably. But more important, it was an early step toward getting me to take control. The unstated but clear message was: It's your knee; Steadman can do great surgery, but if you want to ski or play tennis again, you own the problem—the responsibility for physical therapy, exercise, keeping leg muscles in shape.

To help with the process of ownership, members of the clinic

helped develop the Sport Cord, a heavy-duty, six-foot length of
rubber tubing with handles and straps attached. The clinic had
not been satisfied with the standard approach to therapy, where
the patient has to work out a regular schedule to rendezvous with
the therapist. It's often inconvenient and many give it short shrift
or skip it. With the easily portable Sport Cord, the patient can do
a broad range of exercises just about anywhere, so there is
damned little excuse not to do regular therapy.

Of the clinic's staff, Steadman says: "In each area I just tried
to choose someone who would be better in that area than I was."
Though he and Hawkins are clearly the core of the practice,
much of the day-to-day activity is run by a team like those in a
P&G factory. "Teamwork" is a big word for Dick Steadman.
Steadman does several things to build his team. For starters he
picks people who are compatible with his style. All seem to share
his approach: treating the "total patient."

The first staff member added was Shirley Carlson. When she
started at the clinic in 1982, she mainly helped with general office
administration. Now, she is Steadman's key assistant in the operating room. With the kind of support Carlson provides, Steadman can spend more time outside the operating room, engaged
in the activity he deems so important—talking with patients.
The most recent addition to the team is Dr. Richard Hawkins.
Steadman felt he needed another dimension to the practice. As
time went by, Steadman had gotten more and more focused on
the lower extremities. But athletes also break arms and do damage to their shoulders. Steadman says: "I found the guy who I
thought was the best anywhere on the shoulder [and whose style
and philosophy were compatible]. Now, when I see somebody
with a shoulder problem I have no hesitation. I know the best
place to go is in the office next door."

His need to build teamwork also applies when he picks "fellows," young doctors who believe a year's training with Steadman and Hawkins at a relatively low $42,000 salary will more
than pay off in the added skill and luster that they will take back
to their own practice. When I last talked with Steadman, one of
his main management problems was choosing the five finalists to

fill the available fellowship spots from the more than two hundred highly qualified applicants. About twenty-five had been chosen to visit the clinic. He made it clear that compatibility of style was a big consideration in his final choice.

Like other great leaders, Steadman encourages his team to cross boundaries. Cristal Adams joined him in 1985. She is another skilled nurse who took over much of the office administration and brace fitting work from Carlson. When needed, however, Adams helps out with operations by doing pre-op and post-op, and Carlson can still fit a brace. Steadman also invites his staff to take over where they are just as competent, or more competent, than he. Annette Fulstone, who leads clinical research in a nonprofit sports-medicine foundation partly funded by Steadman, reports: "He really relies on the people around him and their good judgment. He trusts us to make decisions. Often I'll go to him and ask, 'What do you want me to do here? We have choice A, B, and C.' He always asks me, 'What do you think is the best choice? Why?' I like that . . . so much better than someone saying, 'We need to do this or that.' "

Finally, like Shelly at P.S. 94, Steadman empowers staff and patients alike by being very accessible. His clinic, laid out by his wife Gay, another member of the team, makes it easy for him to wander around and see the patients or interact with Cristal, Shirley, Topper, John and the rest of the staff.* If you're a patient, it's easy to catch him in the hallway, and he will spend time if he has it or return later if he's busy at that moment. The staff all know that if they have a problem they don't feel comfortable

---

*The importance of physical layout on effective team management cries out for more research. The subject comes up indirectly but repeatedly in my research. For example, many of those successful at working as teams have convenient meeting places—the extra conference rooms at P&G factories, the easy access to Salzberg's office, and the design of the Steadman Hawkins clinic. By contrast, I've recently worked with a large group of professionals who want to work in teams but for a variety of reasons never have. One reason, I'm convinced, is their new building, an architectural wonder that spreads everyone out and puts them behind closed doors.

solving on their own, they can find him. He enables the rest simply by being as available as his schedule permits.

— — —

IN THIS ERA OF paring down, when the middle manager seems to be an endangered species, we all might learn a lot from people outside the mainstream of business like Salzberg and Steadman. Each personifies what it means to be a mentor. That lesson alone is worth the small price of looking at the way they lead. More subtly, though, there is another lesson. Salzberg and Steadman aren't just managers. They are professionals with a mission in life that includes management but goes well beyond it. Management by itself may well be a position ripe for elimination. That, indeed, could be what makes radical delayering possible. When management works, as at P&G's Lima plant, the managers aren't there just to manage. They're there to help make high-quality products like Tide and Downy. Managing well is a means to that end.

So far in this book, we've looked at how motivating factors like giving employees control get passed down in team settings. What happens in situations that don't lend themselves as naturally to teamwork? Control, belief in work, and learning still can be pushed further down the line than previous management theories ever would have allowed. For a prime example of that, let's turn to Federal Express.

5.

SYSTEMS THAT SET US FREE

People First at Federal Express

$\mathbf{A}$t 8:10 each morning, in every corner of the United States, 25,000 Federal Express couriers hop into their purple-and-orange vans and begin their daily race against deadlines. Back in the office, the couriers' desk-bound bosses can, if they want to, peer onto computer screens and track them, almost minute by minute, as they wend their way through city streets and disappear into office buildings. And when they return to home base after the afternoon rush, the couriers can get a snap-shot of how they fared that day compared to a precise "expected" efficiency as measured by the distance they traveled, the number of stops they made, and the number of packages they handled.

Meanwhile, any customer concerned about the whereabouts of a package can phone Federal Express at any time to get an update, within thirty minutes, on where the parcel is located in the company's maze of planes, vans, handlers, and sorters. It's all done electronically, with the help of a huge computer system and hand-held scanners, called SuperTrackers, that record the movements of packages and employees.

Whew! It sounds like Federal Express, the world renowned overnight delivery service company dubbed FedEx, is an oppres-

sive operation that marches to the tyranny of time schedules and
electronic systems. It's not the kind of place, you'd think, that
would dare put mere mortals in control. Yet everyone I talked to
at FedEx—from couriers to middle managers to people at the
top—say the thing they like most about the company is the *freedom to do things their way*. Managing this delicate balance—the
balance between potentially oppressive systems and the cheerful
attitudes of a clearly enthusiastic workforce—turns out to be the
key to FedEx's success. That's why they lay claim to a U.S.
market position that is twice that of archrival UPS.

To see how it works, let's jump inside the FedEx system.

ONE DAY IN MEMPHIS

During the day at the giant FedEx terminal in Memphis,
things are relatively calm. Employees here and there are cleaning up, a few maintenance operations are in progress. Overall,
though, the facility seems quiet and strangely empty. At
9:30 P.M., as the rest of the city gets ready for bed, the first trickle
of what will become a wave of part-time employees starts to fill
the parking lots. By 10:00 P.M. 6,000 employees have arrived and
turned the peaceful scene into what seems like chaos to an outsider. By 10:30 the first plane, winging in from Orlando, has
landed. From then until 1:30 A.M., when the last plane comes in
from the West Coast, 98 jets will be landing at the rate of slightly
more than one every two minutes at the Federal Express airport
in Memphis. As the planes unload their crush of packets, packages, and large boxes, the conveyor belts in the labyrinthine
heart of the building start to fill with 750,000 packages. Each
package has to be sorted, routed, and rerouted until it, along
with thousands of others, is loaded onto one of the more than 100
jets. The first will take off at 2:45 A.M., the last, headed back to
the West Coast, at 5:45 A.M. As dawn approaches, the package
handlers, sorters, and aircraft maintenance crews head home.
The facility begins another sleepy day.

For the other 82,000 FedEx U.S. employees, the day is just

starting. As planes land in the early morning hours in Orlando, Seattle, Boston, or Los Angeles, the 25,000 U.S. couriers spring into action. Their first job is to make sure that all priority items will be delivered by 10:30 A.M. local time. Unless the couriers are out of the doors of the 600 main stations across the United States by 8:10, FedEx figures the chances of priority items being delivered late increase exponentially. By 8:00 A.M., thousands of Federal Express offices around the nation are in action. Their job is to ensure that every customer sending a letter or package is getting all the help that he or she needs, whether the package is just going across town (perhaps via a detour to Memphis) or on its way to do battle with the customs officials in Moscow or Tokyo.

Before I saw the action in Memphis, I knew that there must be something "absolutely, positively" special about the way Federal Express manages its affairs. But like many, I suspect, who tour the nightly fray in Memphis, I was mystified. The only thing I "saw" was a mind-numbing array of moving boxes, packages, and envelopes, whizzing conveyor belts, bustling electric carts, and busy people. The only thing I didn't see in this apparent frenzy was a glitch. And that's the point. There isn't much to see. At least "see" in the sense of understanding how it works. In a service company like FedEx, systems are crucial but, unlike manufacturing operation, the systems are largely invisible. They are no less powerful and precise, however, than the pipes, conveyors, machinery, and computers that help make Downy or Liquid Tide.

At Federal Express the systems infrastructure has the effect of putting its own people in charge of the company. Behind that lies a philosophy that says: *people first.*

PEOPLE FIRST

I didn't really think deeply about how FedEx manages its affairs until the winter of 1990. I was late for a lunch date. The trouble was I couldn't find the restaurant. Though I knew I was in the right neighborhood, nobody I asked seemed to know where it was and there were no phone booths in sight. In desperation, I wandered into a Federal Express office, one of those small ones that are typically staffed by just a single person. The fellow behind the counter was clearly busy, but he looked up cheerfully when I walked through the door and said: "How can I help you?"

I told him about my dilemma. He didn't know where the restaurant was either, but said: "Wait a minute." He rummaged around, found the San Francisco telephone directory, looked up the restaurant, and called them for me to verify the address. Then he made sure I knew how to get there.

By itself, the incident might not have been unusual: Every city has the occasional helpful stranger. The odd thing is that I can't think of a time that I have been in a Federal Express office that the people have not been friendly, helpful, and courteous. The combination of this and their unflagging reliability makes me, at least, a loyal customer. There must be plenty of others like me, and that's what gives them a powerful strategic edge. How do they do it?

A few days after I'd gotten lost I found my way to Chief Executive Fred Smith's office. I told him about that incident and I asked him the question: How? How do you get such uniformity of cheerfulness and helpfulness? How, especially, do you get that when so many offices are staffed with only one or two people? Surely they must get lonely, feel overworked at times, bored at other times, grumpy sometimes. And why would that man have gone out of his way to help me find my lunch date? I wasn't there to do business with Federal Express. I had already stopped in a few other establishments. Their people had offered nothing like the same kind of help. The answer, it turns out, is not a simple one. But it does boil down to a single theme: Put people in charge—first your own people, then customers.

In Memphis, Tennessee, Fred Smith and the rest of the crew at Federal Express keep stressing that they are a "people-first" outfit. Yes, they want to be known for their extraordinary service. Yes, they want to be the leader in reliability. Yes, they want to grow and make a decent profit in the process. But at Federal Express people come first. Smith says: "We discovered a long time ago that customer satisfaction really begins with employee satisfaction. That belief is incorporated in our corporate philosophy statement. People—Service—Profit." Three very simple words, easy to remember, hard to act upon.

Many know the now legendary story of how Federal Express got its start. In the mid 1960s, Smith wrote a paper for an undergraduate economics course at Yale University. In it he outlined the basic concept: overnight delivery service with near-100 percent reliability using a hub somewhere near the center of population in the United States. Even if the package went only from Baltimore to Washington, D.C., it would still go through the hub. Outrageous, right? That's what his professor thought, and Smith got a C. The idea stuck with him, however, and after two tours in Vietnam, a large inheritance from his father, some help from venture capitalists, and $4 million of his own money, he started just such a company.

What many don't know is that Federal Express works so effectively for its customers because the workforce understands the concept well. As one station manager told me: "Federal Express's philosophy is that if you take care of the people, they provide the service which gives you good returns and your profits." She added that that's easy to forget in the day-to-day crunch. But the best FedEx managers take the time to treat their people right. "It actually, really works," she said. In 1990, FedEx won a Malcolm Baldrige Award for quality, the first service company to do so.

John West, who had general charge of quality at FedEx when I talked with him, believes that what it took to win the Baldrige was more a matter of tidying up what the company already had in place—starting with its "people-first" approach—than mounting a major new program. What's wrong with most of the quality-assurance programs of American companies, West believes, is that they leave out the human factor, which he calls the very bedrock of any effective quality or service system. He argues that too many quality programs rely on tools; if you leave out the human factor, the program is quicksand. "Treating people well, and having people feel the genuine care from the company, results in a natural service attitude that you can't buy for all the gold in the world," West explains. He claims that you can go out and spend all the money you want on communicating, on training, on whatever, but if employees don't feel good about themselves, about their job, about the place where they work, you're not going to have good service.

Smith believes that his people-first philosophy is nothing more than consistent with present and historic trends. He argues that, since the American Revolution, protecting the rights and respecting the value of each human life, regardless of a person's heritage, have become the dominant concern of social evolution. The Federal Express *Manager's Guide* puts it this way:

> The U.S. Constitution, Bill of Rights, Civil Rights Act, and [other] important legislation—particularly in the United States since the Depression—mark steady progress in the elevation of human dignity. Modern behavioral scientists such as Abraham Maslow and Frederick Herzberg have shown that virtually every person has a hierarchy of emotional needs from basic safety, shelter, and sustenance to the desire for respect, satisfaction, and a sense of accomplishment.
>
> Slowly these values have appeared as the centerpiece of progressive company policies, always with remarkable results. Simultaneous improvement in the laws protecting individual rights, combined with improved education and mass communications, have created a work force that must be led rather than 'bossed.' . . . Energies formerly wasted by workforce strife have been redirected towards satisfying the only real boss—the customer.[1]

While it sounds advanced, the FedEx people-first manifesto could easily be just so much pap from an enthusiastic chief executive and a smooth-talking P.R. department. Do they really put these lofty ideals into practice? Well, yes. One way they do so is by matching people and jobs. Fred Smith believes strongly that it's important to get the right people into the right positions and to start that process on the front line.

Over the years Federal Express has developed a pretty fair profile of the person who will be good at, and enjoy, working closely with customers. He adds: "We all know people who are introspective and not very amiable. You can't imagine putting them into jobs that require lots of customer contact. Yet it happens all the time [in other service companies]." He speculates that this is one of the major problems in the service industry.

Much of the work of couriers, and almost all the work of customer service agents, requires direct customer contact, often under strained conditions. One of the couriers I interviewed was even more direct: "If you didn't like people you wouldn't last a day in this job." Another added: "What do I like about this job? My customers. They're more important to me than Federal Express." (She adds, "Of course without Federal Express I wouldn't have the same great customers, so it's kind of a circle.") A package handler had a different perspective: "You have to be crazy to want that [customer service] job. Frantic, upset, or just plain chatty customers come in during busy times. You have to be nice even though you know the more they talk or yell, the greater the chance is that their package will be late."

FedEx also not only understands but implements the seemingly obvious but oft violated idea that the definition of the "right person for the job" changes with one's level within the organization. Promotion is not used as routine reward for those who have proved best at one of the many frontline jobs. As we'll see presently, Federal Express has a very rigorous screening process for those who will fill leadership positions. The company puts as much or more care into understanding the characteristics of those who make good leaders as they do understanding the qualities of top service personnel.

Clearly, FedEx does a better job than most in putting the right people in the right jobs. The major challenge still remains: bringing out the best in those people. At FedEx there are two mechanisms that put muscle behind the people-first idea: first, a survey with a twist and, second, a program that virtually guarantees fair treatment to all employees.

SURVEY-FEEDBACK-ACTION

Each spring, FedEx employees take an attitude survey made up of twenty-nine questions. The first ten questions ask about the atmosphere in one's immediate work group. Is there favoritism in this work group? Does your manager treat you with respect? Does your manager listen to your ideas? Does your manager help you do your job better? The next set of questions asks the employee to consider the management beyond his or her immediate manager. The remaining questions ask about the company's atmosphere in general. The last question asks how well FedEx responded to last year's concerns. The results are tabulated by group. Each manager receives a score, question by question, for each of the twenty-nine questions as well as a total score. Combined scores on the first ten questions comprise what FedEx calls the "leadership index."

Each year a goal is set for the leadership index. If the company doesn't make that goal, the top three hundred managers in the company don't get a bonus—simple as that. The bonus, which normally is about 40 percent of base salary for a senior vice-president, doesn't just drop to 30 percent or 20 percent. It falls to zero, zip, nothing. What this says to FedEx managers is that they'd better work with their people and treat them right. What it says to each FedEx employee is: You count. You have control over the way this place is run.

A similar program has existed for years at Hyatt Hotels, another service operation. The way all of us experience a hotel is in the way we are treated by the people at the check-in counter, the type of service we get in the restaurant, and so on. It's critically important, therefore, that employees feel good about the place where they work. Otherwise we won't get good service, no matter how many service quality programs the chain has in place or how many "smiley face" buttons are passed out. Like FedEx, Hyatt does an annual attitude survey, and it's the one thing that can make or break a hotel manager's career. A manager whose career is dogged by several less-than-satisfactory scores is going nowhere at Hyatt, except probably out.

At FedEx the survey gets done every spring. What about the feedback-action part of the system? Once the surveys are tabulated, managers receive a score sheet, not only for the work group that reports to them but for work groups throughout the corporation as well, so they can compare their results. Shortly thereafter, the manager calls a meeting of his or her work group and together they review the results. The idea is that the group as a whole should delve into the problems and come up with a plan for doing better. This plan, then, guides the manager's objectives for the coming year and is submitted, not only to that manager's boss, but also to a handful of top executives at what FedEx calls its "managing-director" level.

FedEx's 500-person billing department in Memphis illustrates the system in action. About five years ago, management in the department was scoring about 70 percent on the leadership index, considerably below expectations. There were surveys, all right, but little action. "It was kind of like a joke," recalls Mike Lauderdale. "Everything was the same the next year as it was the last year." Doris Elder, another member of the customer invoicing department, agrees: "You talked but nobody listened."

Several levels up from Lauderdale, however, customer invoicing director Cyndi Henson was getting the message. What grabbed her attention was her own low score—14 percent—on a question people two levels below her were asked: Does your manager's boss give you the support you need? Henson had been trying to juggle pressures at work with the demands posed by a sick child at home. "I had to do a lot of looking within," she says. Henson called an off-site, all-day meeting of several managers. "They told me all the things I had done wrong in the last two years. To be quite honest I was scared to death because they had rated me low. I listened to seven hours of all the things I had screwed up."

Henson vowed to change, and the managers vowed to help. They did, and she did. She met more regularly with them, often away from the building so they would feel free to talk about more than just work. She changed her body language, in response to their comments that she was reacting to them much like she would to a child. She started wandering through the department more, listening to employees' concerns. At the same time, Henson made it clear to mid-level managers that the survey-feedback-action process had to start resulting in some action on their part, too. The managers began to meet quarterly with their groups and gave them the leeway to draw up plans to solve one of their biggest concerns—inflexible working hours, a particular problem for single parents. Over three years, employees and their bosses worked hard together to implement new ideas. They started flexible working hours that permit people to come in anywhere between 5:00 A.M. and 10:00 A.M. and to work different numbers of hours on different days. They also launched an unusual program that allows workers to make up time they miss unexpectedly, usually because a child gets sick. Morale picked up, and so did productivity. "The flexible shifts added the motivation to get people going to get the work done," Lauderdale says. Federal Express figures it saved $2 million over two years from decreased overtime and staff reductions made possible by the flexible hours.

Other things changed, too. In one group, employees thought managers were playing favorites and asked for a more precise, scientific way of being evaluated in correcting errors in customer invoices. They formed a quality team and devised a statistical rating system now used to evaluate the workers more fairly. "Things have improved dramatically," Doris Elder says. "We are anxious to [speak up] because we know something will be done." Within three years, the leadership index in the invoicing department was up to 90 percent.

Finally, and as if all the rest were not enough, FedEx sets a baseline for the leadership index every year. Those souls whose score falls below that line spend time in a kind of purgatory that FedEx calls a "critical concern" group. That means your work group takes the survey again in six months and loops once again through the feedback and action drill.

GUARANTEED FAIR TREATMENT

Federal Express calls the survey-feedback-action program the mainstay of its people-first philosophy. And if that's all they did, they would already have outstripped most organizations by ten or twelve light years in eradicating the dichotomy between the individual and the organization. But there's more: FedEx's guaranteed fair treatment policy. You can't help but notice its importance. Plaques and posters hang on walls everywhere at FedEx describing and explaining this program.

Like the survey-feedback-action policy, this program is straightforward, easy to grasp, and seemingly well understood by every FedEx employee. It's designed so that anyone who has a grievance can take it right to top management if necessary, and get it resolved within twenty-one days.

Under normal circumstances, when FedEx employees have a complaint or problem, they take it right to their manager and get it resolved on the spot. But if that doesn't work to the employee's satisfaction, then that person's manager, that manager's manager, and a managing director convene to consider the issue. They have seven days to respond. "What they're looking for is, 'Can we solve this person's problem?' " says human resources vice-president Larry McMahan. If they can, then that's the end of it. If the employee still isn't satisfied, the grievance then goes to the division vice-presidents and senior vice-presidents. They go through the same kind of deliberation that took place between the managers and the managing director. Like the first group, they have seven days to respond.

Now suppose that both stage one and stage two reach the conclusion that management was right, but the employee still doesn't see it that way. The grievance then goes to a board of appeals, a group made up of the chief executive, the chief operating officer, the senior personnel officer, and two senior vice-presidents. At this point, the board, which meets every other week, has three choices. It can decide on the spot that the facts support the earlier decision and let it stand. Or it might alter the manager's action (possibly hearing the case personally to clarify the facts and the circumstances). Or it could convene a board of review, made up of a couple members of management and several peers that the aggrieved employee chooses. The board of review pretty much has carte blanche to hear the case as a jury would and to decide what ought to be done.

West tells of being on a board of review that decided to reinstate an employee who felt he was unjustly fired. "But we didn't stop there," West says. "We determined that the person shouldn't go back to his former job. We had to decide whether he should get back pay, what new job he would be doing, what pay level would be appropriate, and so on."

With survey-feedback-action and guaranteed fair treatment, Federal Express goes way beyond the norm in backing its people-first philosophy. In the philosophy itself, and in the systems that make it believable, we once again see the tight links between a company's people, its organizational arrangements, and its sustainable strategic success.

SUPERTRACKER AND SQI

"With all this emphasis on employees," one might ask, "isn't there some danger of losing touch with the customer?" In a word, no. Two more systems—called SuperTracker and SQI—help keep customers in the forefront.

FedEx made what may have been its biggest breakthrough in technology with its SuperTracker system. This is how it works: Each time a package changes hands, employees pass a small, hand-held scanner over the package's bar code. With some regularity the scanner is "shoed," or plugged, into a unit in, say, the courier's van, which sucks all the accumulated data from the scanner and flashes it, via an 800 megahertz radio beam, to a nearby station. The station then transmits the new data via satellite to a huge computing complex in Memphis.

SuperTracker makes SQI (Service Quality Indicator), a measure of customer service, possible, bringing FedEx closer to Fred Smith's original dream for the company: 100 percent customer satisfaction. Before SuperTracker was introduced in 1988, the company could aspire to that goal but couldn't tell accurately how close they had come to achieving it. Now SuperTracker lets the company measure customer service precisely. SuperTracker brings new life and vitality to an old FedEx dictum: Everyone works for the customer.

SQI tracks service within the whole system daily. In fact, much of the data on service is available as the last plane takes off from Memphis at 5:45 A.M. It works by providing a composite score on a dozen elements that FedEx considers crucial to customer service. For example:

- Wrong day late—the package got there but was late by a day or more.
- Right day late—the package was delivered on the day it was supposed to arrive, but instead of arriving at 10:30 A.M., it got there at, say, 10:45.
- Invoice adjustments—something was wrong with the way the customer was billed.
- Missed pickups—the package wasn't picked up or it was picked up late.
- Damaged package—it arrived but got banged up in shipment.
- Lost package—the package never arrived and nobody can find it.

Some errors, obviously, are worse than others, and this fact is taken into account through a point system. For example, one "right day late" would cost the system 1 point. A "wrong day late" would cost 5 points. A "damaged package," a "missed pickup," or a "lost package" would cost 10 points. At the end of the each work day, the points are added, and everyone—from Smith to the part-time sorter in the Memphis hub to the courier in Minneapolis—knows how the company has performed. The day I visited Memphis the SQI point total was about 130,000. FedEx people told me that number was typical and that they were doing about 15 percent better than they had in the last fiscal year, despite continuing volume growth.

The company's aim is to cut the SQI to one-tenth of its current score—that would be 13,000 daily points—within the next five years. Notice that the number is absolute. It's not measured relative to volume. Assuming FedEx volume continues to grow, achieving that aim seems nearly impossible. (Yet as we'll see later, Motorola has hit equally ambitious-sounding targets in its total-quality program.)

A second use of technology that helps improve SQI scores is Federal Express's own broadcast television network: FXTV. With monitors in almost all locations, the station is used for everything from letting employees know the status of the company's mercurial attempts to penetrate overseas markets (before that news is broadcast elsewhere) to live question-and-answer programs with top management. One main use of the station is to flash daily SQI results to every FedEx employee.

Before we get too enthusiastic about these gee-whiz systems, however, it's important to note that the SuperTracker system can be, and sometimes is, used to track the movements of couriers. One courier I met was only half joking when she called it "little big brother." Combined with FXTV, FedEx does sound like something straight out of Orwell's *1984*. The crucial question is why systems like SuperTracker, SQI, and FXTV are liberating and not oppressive.

First, just like the best of today's automated factories, they are designed to meet the needs of customers and to make life easier for those serving customers. This is in sharp contrast to systems that support bureaucracies, systems designed to serve the needs of inside administrators. Their focus is on pleasing the boss, not on pleasing the customer. (This, in fact, is one of the best definitions of bureaucracy I've heard. It's a simple, yet comprehensive, test that anyone can use to judge the state of bureaucracy in a company or department.) Nonbureaucratic systems are just the reverse; at a minimum they serve up customer satisfaction—and sometimes customer delight. They make life easier for those who are on the front line trying to serve the customer.

Second, FedEx's systems give people astonishing flexibility to do things their own way. Take Nora Rooney, for example. She is senior manager of station operations at a huge center on Harrison Street in San Francisco. The center collects, sorts, and dispatches packages from a good part of San Francisco, including its bustling financial district. She is responsible for more than $3 million in annual revenues and supervises close to 200 employees who handle 5,000 packages a day.

Rooney joined FedEx as a courier in 1978; before that she was an art major at California State University. I asked her why she liked Federal Express well enough to stick around for fourteen years. She mentioned a number of factors: money, the challenge, the caliber of the people she works with. But the main thing she talked about was "creativity—a lot of freedom in how you do your job." As a former art student this is especially important to her. During her five years as a courier, what she liked most about her work was freedom and variety. "You have complete control over your day. How you manage it is up to you, and I think that gives people a lot of power."

Now that she's a senior manager, Rooney feels the greater weight of responsibility, but despite the multiplicity of systems and the reams of data that flow in her direction almost daily, she still feels relatively independent. Her goals are very clear. Once she and her boss agree upon them, how she does her job, she feels, is pretty much up to her. "My boss doesn't come in here and say, 'not enough people on the morning sort,' or 'you don't have your routes organized right.' I develop my own training programs, quality teams, route structure, and so on. It's really up to me to put the focus where I think it needs to be." This could be just another manager seeing things through slightly rose-colored glasses but comments from first-line operators were similar. "I like the freedom of being out there, interacting with people, being the customer contact, which I think I'm good at," one courier told me. Another said, "If you're doing your job, they leave you alone." And from a third: "It's not boring; time flies."

Despite all the systems in place to regulate what they do, FedEx couriers have considerable freedom in deciding how to get their jobs done. For example, they decide their route from building to building, negotiate special pick-up arrangements with customers, and organize their trucks in whatever way works best for them.

People in other positions seemed to feel the same degree of freedom—even "tracers," the people whose job it is to help customers find out the status of packages. On the surface of it, the job seems very controlled. Two tracers in San Francisco told me that one of their jobs is to take account each evening of every one of the roughly 5,000 packages that moved through the Harrison Street location that day. One said: "We have to be 100 percent before we go home, so we're very conscious of [the control imposed by the system]." But then she added: "I always feel pretty free. That's probably the best part of this job." The tracers are in frequent phone contact with anxious customers, but there is no manual "telling us what to say on the phone or anything like that. They pretty much trust you." The other tracer chimed in: "We have seven managers here, including Nora. Most people would find that intimidating. But they don't hang over your back. They let you know what's expected. If you're not doing what's expected, they let you know that, too. But they don't rule with an iron hand by any means."

People in Federal Express's vast administrative operations in Memphis seem to feel the same way. Mike Lauderdale works at FedEx while attending school to study television and film production. He has worked in two billing departments, where attention to detail is of utmost importance. Still, he says, "I never look at things being a rule. I look at them as a guideline. I always have the freedom to take guidelines and [adjust them] to best suit me."

Clearly things are relative in life. FedEx does have standards for courier performance, which include the number of packages that should be picked up or delivered per mile and per hour on different routes, certain dress and appearance codes, and, most demanding of all, deadlines—especially for early morning deliveries and during the late afternoon crunch when couriers are sandwiched between customers who wait until the last minute to send the package and the airplane that is scheduled to take off and whisk the parcels to Memphis. But the Federal Express couriers look at their own jobs in relation to jobs they have held in the past, jobs that their friends do, and the job of couriers in rival organizations (where they say that supervisors ride the routes with couriers and time activities with stop watches).

In fairness, roses have thorns. During a two-hour session with eight San Francisco couriers, at least 80 percent of the discussion centered on various gripes. Discounting for the fact that any session like that is likely to tend more toward what's wrong than what's right, some legitimate beefs did emerge. For one, many feel far more pressured now, in tight financial times, than they did in the days of nonstop growth, when the corporation was staffed more liberally. They also complained that FedEx didn't have a satisfactory promotional route for "aging" couriers. A few had been at the same job for fifteen years. The job is physically demanding, and more and more couriers report injuries resulting from repeated muscle stress. On the other hand, they still have some control. Anyone who chooses can try to get into management, as we'll see presently. One individual said: "If you want something bigger and better [than a courier job], that's up to you." In his mind neither the company, its systems, nor its pressures stood in the way of individual renewal. Some agreed. Others didn't.

The couriers I spoke with seemed surprisingly blasé about all the measurement systems that mean so much in Memphis. What do they think about SQI and the other ratings? Speaking for the group gathered around a table, one courier ventured: "It's in one ear and out the other." Yet couriers understand the SQI system and its importance to management. What they seem to really be saying is: Trust us to use our skills and judgment to produce the numbers that please the higher-ups at headquarters.

TWEAKING THE SYSTEMS

Another reason why FedEx people feel free, rather than op-
pressed, is that they have considerable ability to tweak the systems that govern operations. One way to do that is through what
FedEx calls the "Quality Action Team," or QAT (pronounced
"Qwat").

All top managers at FedEx not only fulfill their normal role in
the hierarchy, they also run a QAT—a problem-solving team
that cuts horizontally across divisions. As an illustration, when I
met with the people at FedEx in Memphis, they had a whole
network of teams working on just two issues: wrong day late and
right day late. Five of the ten senior vice-presidents made up a
steering board to lend muscle to the effort. Reporting to the
steering board were eleven "root cause" teams. Their job was to
don a detective's mantle and find out the most common of the
hundreds of possible causes of, say, a wrong day late.

In the field, one first-line manager in each of the thirty-five
operating districts was taken off his or her regular job and put to
work on the late delivery problems. Supporting these people in
turn was a service team from each of the six-hundred-plus main
stations that dot the United States, such as the Harrison Street
office in San Francisco. At these stations a manager, several
couriers, and a customer service agent met periodically to focus
on the late delivery problem, to look especially hard at the root
causes, and to brainstorm—then implement—ideas for corrective action. For example, one of the most frequent causes of a
wrong day late has now been corrected through SuperTracker.
Customers would sometimes misdate their airbills, and FedEx
agents and couriers would miss the error. Then, even though
the package arrived on the date the customer intended, the delivery would be categorized as a "wrong day late" because of
the discrepancy. Now SuperTracker dates each item and calcu-
lates delivery from its internal clock, so such discrepancies don't
arise.

Harrison Street's Nora Rooney took QATs a step further. In her operation four couriers and a customer service agent were trained to preside over small teams formed to attack problems as they arise. She made a pact with the participants: Whatever they come up with will be implemented. One QAT team, made up mainly of package handlers, addressed a hitch in the way packages were loaded each morning into the courier vans.

Inside the station, which resembles a colossal garage, parcels pour out of a huge truck and down a conveyor belt, which is bordered on each side by empty vans. Eagle-eyed couriers pluck the packages off the conveyor and load them into the appropriate vans. Too often, though, packages are missed, then stacked up at a holding area at the end of the conveyor, to be picked up and recycled down the line.

The team identified one source of the problem: The instructions on what packages should travel down which side of the belt weren't clear. Among other things, the team suggested better training and clearer charts that spell out what goes where. Because the people who found the problem and suggested solutions were mainly the same folks who would implement it, their ideas went into effect immediately and with salutary results.

LEAP TO LEADERSHIP

The pattern is all too common in America: A super salesperson is promoted to sales manager; a super teacher becomes a school administrator. And at FedEx in the old days, a super courier or customer service rep was first in line to join the ranks of management. The problem with that pattern, of course, is that people who excel at a job don't necessarily make good bosses. When they're promoted, they're often unhappy, and the people who work for them are miserable. Rooney, our San Francisco boss, remembers the way things used to be at the company. "Senior managers would have an opening and would say, 'Whoever wants to be a manager, raise your hand.' It was unstructured for sure and there were probably a lot of people promoted

who never should have been managers. A lot of people got into
management who weren't successful." These days there's nothing serendipitous about how FedEx picks its bosses. A process
put in place in January 1989 helps match the right people with
leadership jobs. Once again, it's a first-class marriage of systems
and people-first.

Like other top companies, FedEx promotes mainly from
within. But further, it promotes in a way that attempts to ensure
that the people doing the managing will keep the people-first
philosophy bright and shiny. Of singular importance, the FedEx
system helps assure people at all levels that they will get good
leaders. FedEx started by defining—in the context of its people-
service-profit philosophy—what makes a great leader. A team
from personnel began several years ago with more than two
hundred characteristics that might define a good leader. With
considerable effort, the list was boiled down to nine (see Appendix 3), which form the nucleus of what FedEx calls its "Leadership, Evaluation, and Awareness Process," dubbed LEAP.

A next step was to develop a highly unusual one-day class
called, "Is Management for Me?" This is the place where the
wannabe managers at FedEx discover some of the nuances of
really being one. The class is taught by first-line managers, the
people who have gone through the transition to management.
For many attendees, the mystique of managing vanishes over the
course of the day—the job may not have as much freedom or
power as they think, it may not pay as much as they had expected, or it may simply be too much hassle and pressure. After
this session about 60 percent of the would-be managers drop out
of the program. (However, some of those who do drop out wait
awhile and then continue; they can try to LEAP at anytime in
their career.)

For the 40 percent who continue, the next step—and it's a big
one—begins with an exhaustive review. First, the candidates fill
out a questionnaire so management can find out how they think
they measure up on each of the nine key leadership traits. The
candidates' managers then fill out a similar evaluation of the

nascent leaders' skills and begin a program to help them work on any weak areas. Managers may, for example, ask candidates to lead part of a departmental meeting, if this seems like an area where they might need practice. During this time, managers will also select a handful of the candidates' peers—people who have worked with them for some time—to fill out confidential, anonymous evaluations of their colleagues' leadership potential.

Finally, these would-be managers are scheduled for a day-long review by a panel of senior managers. In the morning they are presented with questions describing typical management dilemmas and asked to write on how best to handle these situations. In the afternoon they are grilled on their morning's answers and asked to do a five-minute presentation on a topic they previously selected. The panel is looking for the ability to respond quickly and keep a cool, clear head. At day's end, the panel will review the written assessments by managers and peers and decide whether to endorse the candidates officially as management-ready. If the panel votes no on a candidate, that person has six months to work on his or her weaknesses before trying again.

LEADERSHIP INSTITUTE

Once candidates have been "LEAP endorsed," as the Federal Express people say, they're free to begin applying for management jobs within the firm. And once they're selected, the real training begins. It starts with a one-week course at the Leadership Institute in Memphis, where students learn of the values, philosophy, expectations, and guidelines for the would-be FedEx manager. Some of the staff is permanent; others are seasoned FedEx managers on leave from their regular jobs for a minimum of two years to serve as institute staff and instructors. "Hardly any of [the Leadership Institute] talks about the profit side of the equation," Smith says. "It talks mostly about the other things we want to do inside the company: why we spend a lot of time on employee issues and why we have put such big stock in our guaranteed fair treatment. We tell people we want to give them a foundation."

In fact, the first day of the Institute is devoted to a topic some might consider "soft"—the stress involved with moving into management. Participants talk about what it will be like to manage people who were their peers and about potential stress at home as their hours and income change. The rest of the week is grounded a bit more in the nuts and bolts, focusing on such topics as globalization of business, reading financial reports, and FedEx's vision, as well as its people-first tenet.

Following their week at the Institute, some candidates go on to spend several weeks on a sort of training sabbatical. The managers-to-be alternate between taking formal classes and working as mock managers in the field, where they get actual experience working under the close tutelage of a senior manager even though they aren't officially supervising people. They might, for example, sit in on a performance review and see how a seasoned manager handles the session. It's as if they were pilots, operating simulators, but not yet flying planes.

During these sabbatical weeks, or later in their careers, managers can take classes such as:

- "Coaching," where the relationship of coaching to managing and leading is explained and modeled.
- "Beyond Unions," which takes a philosophical look at the reasons for unionization and offers tips on what to do if unionization efforts begin. (The company isn't anti-union; the intent of the course is to explain that if management is doing its job, unions ought not to be needed.)
- "Diversity," which raises awareness and skills on how to make the most of a workplace filled with people of different heritage, sex, beliefs, and physical capabilities.
- "Ethics," an intriguing class that uses a mock prison to explore value systems (and how they are influenced), the abuse of power and trust, and the importance of treating others with respect.

- "Interpersonal Dynamics," where the spotlight gets turned on how to be flexible and how to handle conflict.

All managers, including executives, take similar courses when they get promoted or take on new assignments.

Through this process of alternating between classroom and field work, FedEx is adapting a classic and well-tested model of learning. First you explain why the new behavior is important; then you break it down into understandable steps (as the Leadership Institute does); next you model that behavior; and finally you give the learner the opportunity to practice in a safe environment (as the novice manager in the field does).

All in all, in a very important way, Federal Express is developing managers, not just training them. In one sense it's a huge investment on the company's part, because the people are not doing "real work" during the training sabbatical. Roger Podwoski, vice-president of service systems ground operations (perhaps the longest title in Federal Express and certainly the largest division) raves about FedEx's educational programs, one of which he recently went through himself: "I can't prove this, but I believe it's one of the highest-return investments we could make." The obvious objective of the program is to improve the performance of first-line managers. "And for this," McMahan says, "it works well. The people who make it through are really more serious about going into management. They don't try it on a fluke, to see how it works out. These are people who really are interested in being managers."

Less obvious is that the entire program—from the "Is Management for Me?" session, through the peer panels, to the carefully crafted leadership education—is designed to keep putting people first. The words sound trite, but the actions are only too rare. In a very fundamental sense, Federal Express has taken the traditional organizational pyramid and turned it upside down. Leadership sets direction—after all, the systems we just talked about exist because of management—but the systems are designed to give the front-line folks, the people at the top of this upside down structure, a very strong voice in the way the place runs.

— — —

NOW WE KNOW how Federal Express can have it both ways: Its systems do set people free; its systems also serve strategy by helping make the organization highly responsive to the market. Keeping these systems workable requires maintaining a very delicate balance. The sophisticated set of infrastructure systems that make FedEx work could easily become an employee's bureaucratic jungle. On the other hand, lack of infrastructure in a complex service business would be the same as lack of automated equipment in Procter & Gamble's factories. Just as high-volume manufacturing these days requires heavy investment in automated equipment and control systems, high-volume service requires heavy investment in systems technology.

Federal Express has found what author John Gardner calls the "simplicity beyond complexity." Gardner points out that the world is indeed a complex place and that just to function from day to day, most of us need to make simplifying assumptions. The acronym KISS (Keep It Simple, Stupid) is a useful idea but may be misleading in a complex world. Simplifying before you really understand the situation leads to the "stupid" part, more often than not. True genius is to understand complexity so fully that it becomes simple. That is the simplicity beyond complexity, and that is the power of FedEx's straightforward systems for enacting its people-first philosophy.

6.

VALUES FROM THE START

**Culture *Is* Strategy at
the AES Corporation**

The two people who started Applied Energy Services (AES) in 1982 launched their venture with a modest-sounding goal. They weren't out to make millions, or to change the world with a new product, or to see their names in the headlines. They simply wanted to build an enterprise they could be proud of. They were clear about that even before they knew exactly what the company would do. The founders wanted a company that valued people and acted responsibly, that was fair and honest in its approach not only to customers, suppliers, and employees, but to the greater society in which we live. If they happened to make good profits, so much the better. But that wasn't their goal—they cared more about the kind of company they could build than its bottom line.

To the mild surprise of some and the amazement of many, they have been able to achieve both. Today, the AES Corporation is a highly profitable independent power producer with $500 million in annual sales, a stock-market value of $1.5 billion, and a return to shareholders that rivals any of the best high-tech venture-capital deals. At the same time, the company treats its people well and is far ahead of many companies in sensitivity to the environment. As we'll see, AES people continuously strive for fairness and integrity, and in so doing they break the rules of conventional, everyday business. At AES, values have always been more important and constant than strategy.

Do their values guarantee financial success? Of course not. But the value focus at the company attracts exceptional people who enjoy their work. In turn, they are energized to do a good job. AES's leaders, however, resist making a direct connection between values and profitability. In fact, they constantly hammer at the point that trade-offs between values and profits should always favor values. (Levi Strauss encourages the same kind of thinking.) This has been a tough proposition for many—including some top execs—to buy into, since it goes against at least two hundred years of business culture that puts profit first. So enacting this values-first philosophy has not always been easy—keeping values in focus is hard work, especially in a fast growing company. But AES's people and its constituents will tell you it's worth the struggle. Because of its values, and the entrepreneurial challenge, AES makes exciting a business as potentially mundane as power generation.

SHARED VALUES

I've been closely associated with the company since 1982, first as an advisor to the board and, since early 1986, as a full board member. Because of this relationship, I have had a rare opportunity to observe carefully the company's progress, setbacks, near misses, and successes from start-up to prosperity. In the eleven years since its birth, almost everything about AES has changed—everything, that is, except a few key people and a few basic values that they, and in turn the company, uphold. The importance of AES is that its founders have shown that a noble culture can be created by leadership from the top and then sustained by leadership from every cranny in the organization. There is no understanding AES without understanding its culture—in other words, the shared values that give its people a sense of purpose.

AES's written value statement addresses fairness, integrity, social responsibility, and fun. But there is no way the written statement can convey the power of the company's value-driven culture. From AES here are some of the lessons we can learn about the values that combine to build a noble culture:

- They often precede and drive strategy.
- They have a grab-you-by-the-heart quality that speaks to everyone associated with the company and brings the whole enterprise truly to life.
- They are put in place by living them—not through a written statement, a weekend retreat, or use of the executive bully pulpit. Moreover, though they seem more constant than strategy, they continue to evolve as everyone in the company gains experience, grows, changes, and matures.
- They enable people at every level to become leaders in their own right because those people are clear on what the company, and they as individuals, stand for. In doing that, the values greatly reduce the need for written policy, directives, staff jobs, and organization charts.
- They are consistent with the everyday values most of us aspire to in our home and personal lives. What's more, they help individuals find balance between the dual, but often conflicting needs to feel personal freedom and yet be part of a larger purpose.
- They get managed as proactively as strategies, plans, and budgets do in this or any other company.

APPEAL TO THE HEART, CONVEYED BY ACTIONS

At AES, as at other top organizations, the shared values have both intellectual and emotional appeal. The latter is crucial. The reason: most statements of business vision, strategy, or mission, speak to the needs of the business—not to the needs of people. These "visions" are, in a word, dull. They don't grab anyone's

heart and soul and stir them to action. AES is different. Take, for
example, the emphasis placed on social responsibility. The written value statement reads: "The company has acted on its belief
that AES has a responsibility to be involved in projects that
provide social benefits—lower costs to customers, a high degree
of safety and reliability, increased employment and a cleaner
environment." The words aren't bad, but they're not especially
stirring either. It's the way this value gets enacted that really
makes it special.

The roots of this manifesto go way back in AES history. Company founders Roger Sant and Dennis Bakke and several other
key AES executives had all worked together in the federal government long before AES got its start. What brought all the
company founders to government in the first place was the feeling that they could have a greater social impact there than in the
private sector. Thus when they started AES, making social responsibility a central part of their written values was only natural. Of the early days at AES, Sant now says: "We really did
want to do the right thing. All of us who had been in government
together saw business repeatedly fight any socially responsible
thing every step of the way. We knew we wanted to be different."

In his government days Sant headed the office of Conservation and the Environment working directly for John Sawhill,
then the head of the new Federal Energy Administration (now
the Department of Energy), and now chief executive of The
Nature Conservancy, a nonprofit organization that is a leader in
land conservation. About the time that Sant joined the federal
government in 1974, OPEC imposed its first embargo. In America, oil was in desperately short supply. Both Sant and Sawhill
believed that conservation was just as much an energy "source"
as new supply, but Sant was getting nowhere with that argument. Political sentiment at the time favored new supply. But
Sant dug in, switched tactics, and, with the aid of talented analysts, was able to show that various conservation measures could
mean saving 25 to 50 percent of the oil then used, or the equivalent of $3 to $6 per barrel—not bad, since the going price for oil
at the time was close to $11 per barrel.

Sant's analysis made it all the way to Camp David and a
meeting with key members of President Gerald Ford's cabinet.
The cost-per-barrel argument got their attention, and the discussion quickly switched from *whether* to pursue conservation to
"how do we get it done?" This led to automobile efficiency standards, tax credits for home insulation, and similar legislation—
the first U.S. efforts ever to save energy.

In late 1977, Carnegie Mellon University recruited Sant to
organize and run the Mellon Institute Energy Productivity Center. Its *raison d'être* was to keep pressing the conservation-makes-
economic-sense issue. Joined by Dennis Bakke, the group of experts there studied everything from industrial processes to
refrigerators. In so doing, they became convinced that energy
was nothing but a commodity and a means to other ends. Later
they wrote: "The main departure from more traditional approaches was the decision to regard energy only as a means of
providing the services that a modern economy requires."[1] They
reasoned that consumers and industrial users of energy don't
care about the source of energy (unless it's obviously polluting or
unsafe). What they are buying is mobility, comfort, heat or productivity. Whatever source can provide that in a clean, safe,
economical way is the source that customers will prefer.

For Sant and Bakke, the Mellon Center was at most a four-
year proposition, a think tank that would pursue the conserva-
tion-costs-least idea and then disband. "We always intended to
close down and start our own business," says Bakke. Sant and
Bakke wanted to do more than just think and consult; they
wanted a hand in making a low-cost, conservation-oriented energy business happen. Although "making it happen" doesn't appear in any of their written value statements, it is a deeply held
belief within the AES culture. Making it happen quite clearly
galvanized the small group who started AES and still challenges
everyone there today.

In early 1982, they closed an equity placement that capped
their initial $1.2 million financing. With that AES was on its way.
Not long after, and eager to get some projects off the ground,
Roger Sant found himself in Los Angeles talking with Jim Morri-

son, who then headed refining operations for the Atlantic Rich-
field Company (ARCO). Sant started talking about possible uses
of the coke pile at ARCO's Houston refinery, though as he now
admits, he didn't really know coke from mashed potatoes. (Coke
in this sense doesn't mean the soft drink but a high-carbon,
high-sulfur by-product of the oil refining process.) Sant wondered aloud if somehow the coke couldn't be pulverized and
used as fuel for a giant diesel engine with what he now calls
"pistons the size of airplane hangers." The diesel would turn the
waste coke into electricity. The idea intrigued Morrison, who
gave Sant's new company $25,000 to study the idea further.

AES executive vice-president Bob Hemphill minces no words
about Sant's diesel brainstorm. "It was the screwiest idea the
world had ever heard. We were going to try to grind petroleum
coke, mix it with oil and water, inject it into . . . diesels, and then
try to clean up the exhaust in something called a fluidized bed
boiler. How we ever got ARCO to suspend disbelief is to Roger's
credit. Even in Waring blenders, we couldn't have mixed that
fuel." So much for the idea that clear strategic thinking must
precede action! (University of Michigan organizational theorist
Karl Weick contends that much of strategy is "retrospective
sensemaking," and that certainly seems to be the case at AES:
Ready—fire—aim.)

The appeal of the idea stemmed from the fact that diesel
engines are inherently energy efficient. But the idea's fatal flaw
was that additional coke would have to be burned to fire the
boilers to get rid of the noxious emissions from the diesel. Otherwise the plant would pollute heavily. Burning the extra coke
would negate any savings generated from using diesel technology. Nonetheless, the problem was intriguing. How *could* the
kernel of Sant's idea be made to work? Wasn't there some way to
use that waste coke to make clean energy? As AES and ARCO
people struggled for an answer, the right idea suddenly hit them:
forget the diesel; use boilers. The Deepwater project was born.

The idea was to burn the coke in a large cogeneration facility
that would, in effect, use the heat twice: once to turn turbines to
produce electric power that could be sold to Houston Lighting

and Power and again, as the hot gas left the turbines, to produce industrial steam that ARCO could use in its oil refinery. The concept made sense. ARCO could not only get rid of, but get paid for, its waste coke. For AES, the savings made through cogeneration would more than pay for a very heavy investment it would have to make in "scrubbers"—devices that mix the sulfurous emissions from burning coke with limestone to take out the sulfur dioxide that causes acid rain.

In this case the investment in scrubbing would be especially heavy. The coke contained six to eight percent sulfur. By contrast, some of the dirtiest coal used by other power plants around the world contains from a half to two percent sulfur. It was at this point that the AES commitment to social responsibility got its first true test. While perfectly legal and permissible under even the strictest Environmental Protection Agency guidelines, the scrubbing operation had one serious drawback: It would produce a steady stream of wet, dirty calcium sulfate. Not a hazardous substance, but still an addition, albeit a relatively small one, to the nation's solid waste problem. My guess is that most companies, especially in the early 1980s, would have simply ignored the issue and built the plant. The small but noble band at AES took on the issue with relish. One person had heard about a process developed, he thought, by Hitachi that would dry, clean, and turn the dirty calcium sulfate into very pure gypsum. If the process really worked, they could sell the gypsum by-product to a nearby U.S. Gypsum plant that made wallboard. Then the plant would be its own, complete ecosystem. Waste coke coming in; electricity, steam, clean air, clean water, and gypsum going out. Perfect!

Well, almost. As the AES people looked into the Hitachi process, they learned that it would cost more than they could make on the gypsum. By then AES had committed almost all of its resources to the Deepwater project. By then the contract, which required written agreement among thirteen players—AES, ARCO, Bechtel (which would build the plant), J. P. Morgan (the lead bank), eight supporting banks, and the General Electric Credit Corporation—had come unglued several times. Were the

contract not signed and soon, the deal would tumble and take
AES down with it. The temptation simply to forget the gypsum
scheme and get the deal closed was strong. But AES stuck to its
values. Gypsum stayed in the deal. After three months of mara-
thon negotiations by 4:31 P.M. on December 30, 1983 all parties
had signed the contract. (Had they waited another thirty minutes
the project would have died: A special provision of the Texas
tax-free pollution debt that made the deal work expired that
year; five o'clock, December 30, was the latest they could transfer the funds to seal the negotiations.)

AES people love to tell this and other harrowing stories about
their tenuous start. One reason, though they probably only recognize it implicitly, is that stories like these convey the boldness,
challenge, and sense of adventure capital on which this company
thrives. Raw challenge is an implicit value at AES (and not always a healthy one—because of it, family life can suffer, and they
can easily get themselves overcommitted.)

When the Deepwater plant was fired up in June 1986 it was
almost an immediate operating success. It remains so today,
maintaining sulfur-dioxide and nitrous-oxide emission levels that
beat regulatory standards by a factor of two, and yes, producing
very high-grade gypsum.*

LEADERS' VALUES ENABLE OTHER LEADERS

The power of an inspiring value not just stated, but enacted,
makes leadership possible at every level in the organization. To
see how that can happen, let's look at Sheryl Sturges and how
she was not only able to carry forward, but enrich, the emerging
tradition of social action at AES.

Though Sturges was one of the four who left the Mellon Insti-

---

*It turns out that the investment in gypsum production paid off and was not
the cash drain that they originally projected, but they could not have known
that at the time.

tute to join AES, she has never held a management position. This is partly because her preference has been to work on special projects with an AES consulting arm called "planning services," and partly because she had made special arrangements to work part-time at AES so she could devote more time to her family.

Her father is an ecologist, and, though she majored in psychology at Wesleyan University, she has always had a strong interest in ecology, energy, and the environment. She particularly remembers one physics course she took at Wesleyan in which the professor repeatedly expressed concern about global warming. That concern weighed on her mind as AES strategy headed toward coal-fired power plants. On the one hand, she could see the strategic necessity. AES could get long-term coal contracts, which meant it could secure non-recourse* project financing from lending institutions. This was the only way the then tiny AES could raise the capital to build big plants. Besides, though burning coal does produce more carbon dioxide (CO_2), than burning gas, many people argued then (and still do) that no compelling evidence exists that CO_2 contributes to global warming or that global warming is a real concern. "Then in the summer of 1987," she reports, "Roger Sant attended a conference at the Aspen Institute. That was at least a year or two before the global warming issue hit the popular press." But Sant had heard enough to be concerned. He and Bakke asked Sturges to start digging into the problem and thinking about possible solutions.

Everyone Sturges could round up—summer interns in the planning services group, even her sister—got involved. "We got our hands on everything we could read. The first avenue we pursued was technology. What could we do with the CO_2 our plants generated?" The trouble is that most uses of CO_2—freezing food or putting bubbles in bottled beverages—don't get rid of CO_2; eventually it gets back into the atmosphere. Another possibility was to inject it into the ground to enhance oil recov-

---

*A form of debt that relies on the viability of the project itself, not the company, for security. "Non-recourse" means that if somehow the project fails, the lenders can't look to the parent company for payment.

ery. (Pumping CO_2 or steam into old oil reservoirs washes up residual oil in processes called "secondary," "tertiary," or "enhanced" oil recovery.) The problem with that idea is that it produces another hydrocarbon that's going to be burned, producing more CO_2; besides, who knows whether the injected CO_2 will stay in the ground? And so on. Other ideas were proposed; all had drawbacks.

Then something dawned on Sturges: *trees*. Trees breathe CO_2 and produce oxygen, just as humans do the reverse, breathe oxygen and produce CO_2. Sturges says: "When I first presented the idea of planting trees as a way of using the CO_2 from our plants, I thought the operating committee would think I was crazy. I'm sure Roger was thinking I was going to propose fertilizer production or fuel cells, and here I was going to say 'trees.' But they were really open to it."

Soon the discussion shifted to how to do it. How many trees would be needed to offset the CO_2 generated by one plant? How could they possibly buy enough acres or grow enough trees near the plant to make any dent in the problem? Sturges talked to her father about her idea and her concerns. When he pointed out that global warming is truly a global issue, not a local issue, she suddenly realized that it didn't matter where you plant the trees. Trees anywhere on earth help solve the problem.

With that perspective and the full backing of the AES operating committee, Sturges began to contact groups that could help the company figure out how to make something happen. In this case the World Resources Institute, an independent research and policy foundation, was particularly helpful. The Institute was already deep into studying such problems as deforestation, reforestation, and global warming. Sturges says, "They helped us find our first project in Guatemala, figure out how many trees were needed to offset the emissions from one plant, and coached us on how to monitor a tree planting project and its progress." Soon and with the help from the World Resources Institute, Sturges and others at AES started negotiations with CARE and the government of Guatemala. Two million dollars were taken from AES funds to plant enough trees—52 million—to offset the CO_2 that the next plant would emit. That was in 1989. The $2 million AES invested in trees roughly equaled that year's profits.

These days tree planting (or preservation) is a routine part of all new AES projects. In fact, part and parcel of the project manager's responsibility is to make sure that a tree project is started somewhere in the world in tandem with the plans for a new plant. For example, AES has a 180 megawatt coal-fired plant in Hawaii on the island of Oahu in an industrial area called Barbers Point. In conjunction with this project, the company is donating $2 million to help purchase and conserve 225 square miles of the Mbaracayu forest in Paraguay. On this project, the partners and managers are The Nature Conservancy and the Fundación Moisés Bertoni of Paraguay.

It's hard for Sturges to contain her excitement over what she has fostered. It couldn't have been done without leadership's deep commitment to being socially responsible. But nobody in the top ranks of the company could have brought that value so much to life without Sturges's own leadership. In a company that thrives on values, leadership is everywhere.

EXPERIENCE COUNTS AND MAY EVEN BE FUN

Another characteristic of a noble and workable set of shared values is that it comes from leaders who are visionary—but visionary in a different sense than we usually mean. They are visionary not because of their ability to peer into the future, but because they are able to make sense out of a rich set of past experiences. This is true of all of the shared values at AES, but nowhere does it come through more clearly than in the importance they attach to fun.

The people at AES deeply believe that their work should be fun. They know full well that some days are more fun than others. Nonetheless, their goal is to maintain an atmosphere where people can flourish, using their talents and so enjoying the time they spend with AES. Founders Roger Sant and Dennis Bakke keep reminding everyone at AES: "We work because the work is fun, fulfilling, and exciting."

Commenting on the part fun plays in AES's values, Sant shows how heavily his own experience influenced his current outlook. "All my prior business experience proved to me that most people don't have much fun at work." He says this had been on his mind for a long time because he could always pinpoint times in his career when business had been enjoyable, not because times were good or bad, but because at these points he could combine understanding an issue deeply with feeling he had the freedom to do something about it.

He remembers: "The most fun I had before AES was when I was involved in a company called Wilkens Instruments. It was a little company when I joined. I thought it was really fun to help try to grow that thing and figure out what to do next. I had a wonderful time. It gave me a sense that the whole game of business could be fun."

For Sant, and perhaps many of us, contrived fun doesn't work. He comments on his experiences with Silicon Valley companies: "I am pretty skeptical when I see things like beer busts on Friday afternoon. It's certainly appropriate to have parties and celebrate achievements together, but it gets pretty superficial sometimes. That's not in my definition of fun; that's something else. Fun is when you are intellectually excited and you are interacting with each other—with one idea leading to another—and you're getting frustrated because there isn't an answer; you work and struggle and it's great when a plan comes together. It's the struggle, and even the failures that go with, that makes it fun." Sheryl Sturges, grappling with the CO_2 issue, is the first to admit that she was having fun. John Ruggirello, AES's manager at Beaver Valley, the firm's second plant, had fun negotiating a new labor contract.

On many occasions directors, outside shareholders, and even people inside AES have wanted to drop this value or change the word "fun" to something like "challenge." "Fun" somehow doesn't sound, well . . . businesslike. AES will not give up on the idea that work should be fun. But like all values there, the discussion is constantly open and the term is always subject to reinterpretation. That is healthy.

In his book *A Business and Its Beliefs,* IBM's Thomas Watson, Jr., says, "The beliefs that mold great organizations frequently grow out of the character, the experiences, and the convictions of a single person."[2] The AES experience fits closely. Here Sant was the main architect of values with strong support from Bakke. In the same book Watson also argues that any successful organization must have a sound set of beliefs on which it premises everything else—again, no argument from the AES experience. He then says, "I believe that if an organization is to meet the challenges of a changing world it must be prepared to change everything about itself except those beliefs as it moves through corporate life."[3]

This is where he may have been wrong. The AES experience, and probably IBM's, is that changing times and circumstances probably should challenge and maybe alter basic beliefs. Until recently, for example, the full text of the AES statement read, "We work because the work is fun, fulfilling, and exciting. *When it stops being that way, we'll change what we do*" (Italics added). That was fine when the company was smaller. Indeed, it gave them great negotiating flexibility and was a very attractive idea to new recruits. Today, however, AES is too large to make the latter part of that statement stick, as what happened in mid-1992 shows. The company got thoroughly beaten up in that period by a coalition of people who wanted to halt construction of a half-completed plant in Florida. Forget trees. Forget clean emissions. These people just plain didn't want a coal plant. For nearly three months Sant and other AES people were thoroughly vilified by the opposition and much of the media. When they finally won approval to go ahead, the banks got cold feet, reasoning that if Florida politics could halt the project once, it could happen again. Nobody at AES had fun during this period. At the same time there was no way they could responsibly *change what they do,* at least not in the short term. Because of the Florida experience, Sant and others at AES will devote time at strategy, board, and other meetings to rethinking what they mean by fun and how it plays against their other values.

My guess is that the answer to keeping fun compatible with responsibility lies in the way they use humor. A big part of the fun at AES has been the ability to laugh both at itself and the silliness that surrounds some ponderous process like contract signing. In the early days AES didn't have to take anything very seriously. There wasn't much to lose. Now that it's big, AES may be able to learn from Merck. One thing that impresses me about Merck is its sense of humor. In sharp contrast with other big companies, they take their business very seriously, but they don't take themselves too seriously. They have managed to find a nice balance. That may be the key to keeping AES and elsewhere fun.

MAKE YOUR FAMILY PROUD

Social responsibility and fun are two out of four parts of the written value statement at AES. The other two are:

Integrity: We seek to honor our commitments to both our own people and to customers, suppliers, and community. We try to be honest and reliable. We try to act with integrity, or "wholeness." We live with our agreements even if they might hurt us economically. Our people and our customers can rely on our word.

Fairness: We strive to treat fairly our people, our customers, our suppliers, our stockholders, and the governments and communities in which we operate. We do not try to get the most out of a negotiation or transaction at the expense of others.

Why bother to state these last two values in detail? Aren't they fairly obvious, even commonplace? Not really. At least not in the world of business. Many of us don't trust business, or organizations of any kind for that matter, to *strive* to be ethical and fair.

It's usually just the reverse. The bedrock belief on which most of today's businesses were built is that of Adam Smith's invisible hand. Smith's fundamental market law is the virtue of self-interest. He writes that it's not the benevolence of the butcher, the baker, or the candlestick maker that gives us dinner and light, but simply the pursuit of self-love and an intrinsic desire to accumulate wealth.

The question he then poses is, how will self-interest be held in check? What keeps profit-hungry individuals from holding society for ransom? His answer: competition. Any individual who permits his greed to carry him too far will, in Smith's view, be brought up short by a host of others pursuing their own self-interest, who slip in to take business from that greedy soul. As Smith's treatise unfolds, it's the market that turns out to be the natural regulator of the economy. Prices too high? Competitors will rush in. Too much production? The weak competitors will fold.

The appeal and magic of Smith's market model is that it regulates itself. Business people seeking their own interest are led "as if by an invisible hand" to promote the well-being of society. Directly from Smith flows the economist's dictum: caveat emptor, let the buyer beware. Directly from our unquestioning belief in the power of unfettered free markets and the strength of the invisible hand comes the scandalous behavior of business in the deregulated 1980s—insider trading, looting of thrifts, over-leveraged buyouts. The problem is that markets *aren't* perfect these days and perhaps never were. The invisible hand works only up to a point. Beyond that we do need something more than blind trust in the power of the competing, but unfettered, struggle for self-interest.

At AES a part of the answer is to stress what most of us would consider just plain and simple moral behavior: integrity, fairness, and the trust that results. People are proud to work at AES because the values they live at work are the values they like to tell their families about at home. As with the other values, integrity, fairness, and trust become real only when they are enacted.

They found this out at Beaver Valley, the firm's second plant.

It sits in the middle of an old World War II synthetic rubber
factory near Pittsburgh, Pennsylvania and is a retrofit of part of
that old plant, which AES bought from ARCO's chemical division. Physically, the plant contrasts sharply with Deepwater. For
starters, its walls are as thick as a medieval castle's. In the early
days of AES ownership, workforce attitudes were as impenetra-
ble as those walls and as rigid as the steel made in that area.
"AES values or not," the workforce would say, "as soon as profits go south, you'll treat us just as badly as every other company
has." It mattered little what Sant, Bakke, or other AES management *said* about fairness and integrity. *The folks at Beaver Valley
didn't believe them.*

But plant manager John Ruggirello began to change this attitude with the way he dealt with a contract negotiation. The
typical protocol for this type of negotiation is that the union
makes up its list of 150 or so demands. Management makes up its
equally lengthy list of demands. The parties meet at the negotiating table. Management presents its list of demands. Labor presents its list. They argue, and eventually they reach some sort of
settlement. Ruggirello decided to do things differently. The
negotiations started out according to the script. True to form,
labor and management sat down at the table. Union leadership
presented its long list and asked management for theirs. But then
Ruggirello broke the mold. "We don't have one," he said.
"What do you mean, 'you don't have one?,' " asked the astonished union boss. Ruggirello reiterated. "We don't have a list.
You figure out which of the items on the list are truly important
to you, which are in our mutual best interest, and which are fair.
Then get back to us and we'll probably go along."

The union leader turned to his lawyer. "Can they do that?" he
asked. They caucused. The labor lawyer couldn't see any reason
why Ruggirello couldn't do that. The union negotiators came up
with a list of perfectly reasonable requests. AES agreed to all of
them.

The story spread like wildfire through AES. Now it has
become part of the lore that reminds us what fairness, integrity,

trust, and open communication really mean. It's also another example of how sensible values inspire leadership down the line; Ruggirello did not have to ask anyone for approval to make such an unprecedented move.

OWNERSHIP AND AMBIGUITY

Another product of the founding group's background in government is its deep aversion to written policy, procedure, job descriptions, organization charts, and almost anything else that smacks of bureaucracy. The company abhors formal procedure (i.e., written documents that imply: "We don't trust you to do the right thing"). The value it puts on fairness and integrity is partly in response to this feeling. To the extent that trust, openness, respect for others, and individual dignity are prominently featured, the need for written policy is strongly curtailed.

Two other values AES stresses—ones that you don't typically encounter—are also a product of the leaders' backgrounds. The words they use to describe them are "ownership" and "ambiguity," two words that help define the kind of person who can, in fact, have fun in the AES environment.

By "ownership" they really mean a willingness to take responsibility. AES wants to attract the kind of person who, on discovering a problem or opportunity, will take a hand in seeing that something gets done—never mind whether the problem is litter in the parking lot or boiler maintenance, never mind your particular job or place in the organization. If you see the problem, it's yours. You take the initiative to solve it.

Take the technician who noticed that the computers kept failing because it was too hot in the control room in the summer. He pulled out a catalog and found $200 fans that would do the job, but soon realized he had seen practically the same fan at Kmart for $10. Before long he had bought out the supply at the local Kmart, charging the purchase to his own credit card, knowing full well the company would back his decision and reimburse him. The example is a small one and the savings weren't large, but multiply it by a whole company and the impact on efficiency and morale can be huge.

The idea of ownership is so pervasive at AES that the company seems routinely to achieve what may seem nearly impossible for others. Here's a company that started with no money, no experience in building big plants, and no experience in running them. Each project is monumentally complex: The financing always involves a dozen or so lending institutions, so that just closing each deal seems to take Herculean effort; and building a plant means close supervision of a host of contractors who are often working with new technology, so that when the switch is thrown, the plants never operate the way they are supposed to. Months, even years, of fine tuning may be required to get a plant operating at peak performance. In other words, when things go wrong, as they routinely do, there are a thousand possible (and reasonable) excuses. But at AES, the ownership idea means that placing blame elsewhere, however reasonable, is not acceptable. AES people take responsibility for living up to commitments. As things go wrong, everyone shoulders the burden to put the situation right. "Don't be an alibi Ike," was what my father and other World War II officers told each other (and what he later used to tell me with irritating regularity). In wartime everything can go wrong. But no excuse—no alibi—acquits officers of their basic responsibility to their troops; no alibi acquits troops of their basic responsibility to each other. AES has adopted this same attitude.

Tolerance for ambiguity is another characteristic that AES wants in its people. The world is a confusing place, and AES is in a changing, often confusing, business. Though the four AES values are reasonably clear, applying those values usually means making trade-offs, facing difficult decisions. What's fair if a contractor has missed critical deadlines for reasons entirely out of his control? Should AES forgive part of the penalty payment? Should AES hold its suppliers to its own standards of integrity? If, for example, a banker reneges at the last moment, should AES take the bank to court? If the fairness and ownership concepts are pushed to their limits, won't AES always end up holding the bag, collecting everyone else's mistakes? AES is caught up in these issues all the time. Sant calls them fun issues. Without some zest for ambiguity, it's hard to stay sane in the AES culture. It's not everyone's cup of tea.

THAT FAMILY FEELING

One of the toughest leadership challenges is satisfying the individual's dual—but often conflicting—needs to feel part of some larger purpose yet feel fulfilled, free, and in control as an individual. A value system, like that at AES, helps resolve the dilemma.

With Beaver Valley and Deepwater, AES started to become as much an operating company as a deal-making company. The board had seen this coming and had put pressure on management to bring in more people with operating skills and to learn more about operations themselves. One result was that all top executives at AES now spend at least one week every year in a plant, in work clothes, learning and doing every job. Guided by the workers, they load coal, tend boilers, fix machine parts in the maintenance shop, clean fouled equipment.

Another result was to hire Bill Arnold. Bakke says, "Arnold was an operating man, and he knew what to do. He set up the manuals, the procedures, hired people according to whether they were technically skilled, and generally did things right. Our first plant, Deepwater [just outside Houston, Texas] was running terrifically."

But something felt wrong. The early warning came from a companywide attitude survey. Things were hunky dory in corporate headquarters in Arlington, Virginia, but things were not fine at Deepwater. The employees there were definitely not having fun yet.

Bakke says that he was at Deepwater for his work week when the people there were working on the policy manual. "They were talking about how much time you should get off when your parents die. Would the policy be different if you were adopted or if you were raised by an uncle? What if the parent lived in London? Would you get an extra three days? I thought, boy, this isn't it. This isn't where we want to be. Why does this have to be written in a book? Why can't we trust each other to take whatever time is needed? This has nothing to do with the values we were talking about when we started this company."

Later that same month Dennis Bakke and other top officers were meeting at Roger Sant's vacation cabin at Donner Lake, California. Bakke told them about his experience. He said he believed that they had been treating the plant people differently from others in AES. It was partly something that had just happened, partly an implicit assumption held by top management and the board that you had to manage plants differently.

Bakke says: "Roger, Bob [Hemphill], and I had the most wonderful couple of days dreaming about turning [these assumptions] upside down. Why not go back to our same principles that we were using elsewhere?" Soon Bakke was back at Deepwater asking questions. What if we didn't have this book at all? What if we don't specify in writing the number of sick days? What if we didn't have supervisors? Dennis Bakke says that Bill Arnold called him into his office the very next day and shut the door. All his supervisors had been complaining. In their view Dennis's questions were causing chaos.

Bakke agreed. Maybe the questions were crazy. But he told Arnold and the supervisors that he didn't want the questions answered right away. All he wanted was to get them started thinking about questions like that over the next year or so. Bakke says: "That calmed them down enough to start talking about the principles involved. They immediately got very excited."

Within about a month the people at Deepwater were changing things faster than top management would have dreamed possible. The main change was to organize the plant into what they called "families"—a boiler family, a turbine family, a scrubber family, and so on. Members of the families would learn each other's jobs, rotate work from day to day, take care of routine maintenance, and—especially—take ownership of their own operation. The families would operate, in other words, much like

Procter & Gamble's self-directed teams (although the people in Deepwater weren't aware of the P&G system). For activities that crossed family boundaries, the Deepwater folks started playing around with other unconventional plant relationships. They talked about neighborhoods, communities, cells. In the end they designed a structure built on the family concept that they now call a "honeycomb," a neatly fitted structure linking a variety of families in a variety of ways. As the honeycomb idea went into effect at Deepwater, productivity and attitudes improved dramatically. Plant utilization at Deepwater, which had rarely been over 85 percent before the change, started routinely hitting 100 percent. This was partly due to the honeycomb's ability to knock out two layers of supervision.

Progress was slower at Beaver Valley. Like P&G, AES faced problems left over from a lifetime of contention between labor and the old management. Bob Hemphill noticed that there were problems at this retrofit plant during his week's work there. So to figure out what was wrong, whenever he was "trained" by the operators at Beaver Valley to perform an especially inefficient, unsafe, or dirty operation, he'd ask, "Why do we do it like this?" Invariably, the answer was: "They make us." "They," of course, was the past—old work practices, myths, and suppositions. "They" was an army of bureaucrats who'd probably vanished a long time ago, but at Beaver Valley their ghosts were still in charge.

A loose coalition, led by Hemphill, moved fast to rout the ephemeral enemy. Anyone connected with AES still remembers the day everyone in the company got a ceramic coffee cup in the mail with the words, "Who Is They Anyway?" baked into the glaze. Later, everyone was bombarded by a steady stream of patches, lapel buttons, Post-it notes, and sheriff's badges all with the word "They" covered by the international don't-do-it symbol, a circle with a line through it. Later, Bakke and Hemphill made and distributed large cardboard posters—a picture of Sant sitting behind his desk and a sign that read "NOT THEY"—to every AES facility. The poster said, "Send They a Letter." Tear-off sheets, one side for suggestions and complaints, were pro-

vided, postage paid. Not long after that, an orientation meeting
was disrupted by the sound of "gunfire." Four people stormed
the room, dressed in combat gear, carrying mock rifles, with
"anti-They" patches sewn all over their fatigues." The guerrilla
band turned out to be two of the company's senior officers and
their wives. What the officers had done, of course, was to take
the we-they problem, confront it head-on, and set "they" outside
the company. They relieved tension with humor as they knocked
down walls between functions and management layers.

In late 1991 a doctoral candidate in the business school at
George Washington University, who goes by the euphonious
name of John John, made a study of the AES Corporation. After
John spent several weeks at two plants he exclaimed, "I can't
believe what I've been seeing! First, they all tell me that they
really look forward to coming to work in the morning. Second,
they tell me they have the freedom to do anything they want. I
say: 'Really? There must be some controls.' They tell me: 'No.
We really can do anything we want.' " John John couldn't believe it and it isn't quite true. There are bounds, boundaries, and
controls. At AES they manifest themselves in measurement, peer
pressure and information, accounting, and auditing.

Measurement.   AES has a set of measures that are visible to
all and, where possible, are reported daily to everyone in each
plant. The measures, typically reported in the following order,
include:

- Safety: OSHA recordable injuries compared to industry average. The objective is an incident rate of zero. In 1992, AES
  operated at 40 percentage points below the industry average.
- Environment: Three measures here—Sulfur Dioxide (SO_2—
  the stuff that causes acid rain), Nitrogen Oxide (NOx—the
  stuff that causes smog), and other emissions. So far in 1993,
  SO_2 emissions were 60 percent of EPA permitted levels and
  dropping, NOx levels were 40 percent of EPA permitted levels
  and falling, and other emissions were at 20 percent of permitted levels and holding steady.

- Availability: The time a plant is available to produce electricity in relation to its rated capacity. Including the time a plant was shut down for maintenance, it averaged 93 percent in 1992.
- Heat Rate: A measure of the efficiency with which the plant converts fuel to energy.
- Income: Normally reported in two ways—the cost per kilowatt hour and the plant income statement.

Information and peer pressure. AES workers, for the most part, are as aware as management of plant and company performance. They get the same information that managers have. They are insiders. They are shareholders. And most important, they know what others in their own family—and probably in others too—are up to. Control comes from one of the most powerful, and most often overlooked, tools of management governance—simple peer pressure.

Auditing. Given the increasing complexity of the company caused simply by increasing numbers of plants, AES has instituted an internal audit function to supplement the routine outside audits. This was a tough decision. Given their backgrounds and beliefs, management recoils at the word "audit." Based on its own experience, the board felt that internal auditors, with the right attitude, could be very helpful. The board's view prevailed, and the function has been helpful not only in auditing financial controls but also in auditing compliance with the labyrinth of environmental regulation.

MANAGE THE VALUES

Culture, that is, the shared values of an institution, is supposed to be the soft side of management. Yet as anyone who has tried to change a culture will tell you, nothing could be harder. AES has it easier than most. It started with a reasonably coherent and noble set of values. Nonetheless, AES manages its values with the same care with which it manages plant emissions, safety, and daily power production. Training, hiring, measurement, and storytelling collaborate to keep the culture vibrant.

AES began to weave values into its fabric, first by talk among the executives, and then through training. In fact, the first time Sant remembers himself being explicit about AES values was at an orientation session for new employees. Today a video called "Introduction to AES" concentrates heavily on the values. Not just the four mentioned in the official values statement but the rest of them, right through ownership and ambiguity.

Most of the people watching the tape wouldn't be at the orientation session unless they seemed to fit with the AES culture in the first place. People who come into AES these days typically start at the plants in entry level jobs. Plant managers and potential co-workers interview them in depth, in part to find out the routine things, like whether they are qualified. But most of the lengthy interview is aimed at finding out something more important. Does the person understand the importance of shared values to AES, and will he or she enthusiastically subscribe to those values? If not, the candidate is out. AES builds and reinforces its value system by the way it hires.

Another way it institutionalizes its values is to measure them. The old phrase, "what gets measured gets done," applies to values just as surely as to anything else. If the leaders want something done, they pay attention to it. AES has been measuring values since they first wrote their statement of values. Each year AES surveys employees, customers, and suppliers to see how well these people think the company lives up to its stated values. The report on the annual values survey is the first item on the agenda of each year's strategy conference. These days the report, which includes all the write-in comments, runs to over one hundred pages. Summary results of the values survey appear in the initial pages of AES's annual and quarterly reports. What's more, evaluations of how each member of the company is doing in upholding the aspirations of AES determine roughly half of that individual's salary increase and bonus for the year. So people take notice.

Good old-fashioned storytelling is another one of the most powerful ways values become shared at AES. Though the company is young, the culture is replete with stories like gypsum at Deepwater, the we/they battles and frivolity at Beaver Valley, Ruggirello's singular approach to union negotiations, fans from Kmart, and the one that has captured most attention on the outside—investment in trees to curb global warming. Bakke and Hemphill, who have become master storytellers, hence keepers of the culture, leave little to chance. Take the orientation session for new employees and their spouses. Bakke roughs out the story of the negotiations to close the Beaver Valley deal, every bit as much a make-or-break-the-company cliffhanger as was the founding of Deepwater. Then everyone is given a role—some play the various teams of bankers, others are lawyers, others play the electricity and steam customers, while some play the role of AES executives and project managers—and the story is reenacted with great flourish. Through this role playing AES makes its points about integrity, fairness, trust, fun in seemingly impossible situations, ambiguity, ownership, and finally, the raw perseverance that built this company from nothing to the stature it has today. At AES they don't just tell the stories. They live them.

Last, and of critical importance, AES manages cultural expectations. Social responsibility, fun, fairness, integrity, trust, openness, ownership, ambiguity—that's quite a list. How can any group of humans live up to it? They don't. "AES values are not the way AES is," Sant and Bakke remind everyone, "but the way AES strives to be."

━ ━ ━

AES WENT PUBLIC in June 1991. It didn't really want to; the fear was that pressures from the outside would weaken the company's focus on values. But because all AES employees own stock, the number of shareholders was approaching 500, the point at which the Securities and Exchange Commission (SEC) considers a company public. So it had no choice. So far the values seem alive and well.

One incident just before the public offering conveys the mixed feelings we all have about being both businesslike and noble in purpose. AES had trumpeted its values in the section of the prospectus that describes its business. On reading that part as a final check, SEC lawyers made the company move a large chunk of the values section to the part of the prospectus entitled "Risk Factors." "Boy, that's pretty funny," said one of the underwriters' securities salesmen. "Our government's saying it's risky to try to do business in this country by relying on fairness and integrity." Go figure.

7.

SOMETHING TO BELIEVE IN

At Levi Strauss & Company
Managers Make Meanings
as well as Money

In the last chapter we looked at how AES grew up with a values-driven culture. For them it was relatively easy; they started that way. But can a company with over a century's worth of history and tradition, such as Levi Strauss & Company (or, as they call themselves, "Levi's"), change its culture? In particular, can it make life more meaningful and exciting for down-the-line people who have spent their whole lives stitching, sewing, packing, and selling jeans? Apparently so.

Blue Ridge, Georgia, a small dot on the map, nestles in the Blue Ridge Mountains, not far from the Tennessee border, but still a good bit short of Graceland. There, the biggest enterprise around is a medium-sized Levi's plant where 450 people turn out men's jeans. Although the Blue Ridge plant has been in operation for about thirty years, it has recently gone through a kind of industrial epiphany. Not long after the changes began to take hold, four Blue Ridge workers traveled to San Francisco to tell Levi's board of directors about their experiences. Brenda Burgess, who had sewn seams at the plant for seventeen years, reported: "A year ago I hated my job. I took night classes to improve myself, determined that when my children got through college I was leaving. But now I've changed my mind, and the

Lord willing I'll probably be here until I retire, or become a millionaire, whichever comes first." She explained that "a new pride in our job and commitment to our company makes it a better place to work."

The philosophy behind her change in attitude is captured in a document that proclaims Levi's mission and aspirations. (See Appendix 4.) This one page epistle is the result of chief executive Bob Haas's simple notion that there is no way he, his executive team, and his managers can be around enough, or effective enough, to tell Levi's workforce, now over 30,000 strong, what to do. Shared aspirations must guide them.

Among the lessons Levi's has to teach us are that:

- A noble purpose is just as important for people making jeans as for people starting a new company. Though managers sense this, they usually have trouble articulating a soul-stirring vision and take shelter in strategy. Levi's is solving this problem with a single word: Aspirations.
- Strategy and aspirations are closely linked. By itself strategy is dry, calculated, and unfulfilling for folks down the line who seek meaning in their work. On the other hand, people won't pay much attention to noble purpose if they think strategy is weak and their jobs are in jeopardy.
- As we saw at AES, aspirations do not arrive overnight graven on stone tablets. While the first version of the written statement was the product of a weekend retreat, what's in writing is just the visible tip of a very large and still incompletely fathomed values iceberg.
- Although top management must support a company's aspirations, the impetus to get moving can come from anywhere. In Levi's case, several women who had bounced off too many glass walls and ceilings kicked top management into action on the issue of diversity.
- As clear as Levi's written Aspiration Statement seems, people who are used to doing things differently probably won't get it. Not that they don't want to. It's just the power of old habits and tenacity of values previously shared. So at Levi's the first step toward understanding was a massive education program.

- What gets measured gets done. People won't really adapt, even to adopt something seemingly as exciting as Levi's Aspirations, if they still get measured and paid in the same old ways.
- Soft is hard. Culture, usually thought of as one of those soft, squishy sides of organization, probably is the hardest to change. That idea would seem obvious to an anthropologist, but is not a message get-it-done-yesterday executives choose to hear. But a vaporous concept like ethics can, with effort, be turned into a no-nonsense approach to making tough, gray-area decisions.

THE VISION THING

All over America folks sense the need for purpose. Thus, academics, planners, and consultants are busy turning perfectly respectable nouns into verbs as they urge activities like "visioning" and "purposing." Thus, also, a fair amount of confusion reigns. President Bush talked about "the vision thing" but didn't seem to have one. President Reagan, who had a very strong vision for the country, got hammered constantly for paying attention to his vision and nothing else.

The first thing leaders need to do is get through the semantic swamp. Both the literature in the field and the retreats I attend spend too much effort trying to define and then distinguish between words like mission, vision, strategy, values, purpose, aspirations, goals, and objectives. Folks are mired further when the verbal slough includes phrases such as long-range planning, strategic planning, game plan, business proposition, and the redundant forward planning. The words and phrases overlap, mean different things to different people, and will always be a little ambiguous no matter how hard we try to define them. The reason is that the underlying concepts—the ideas the words stand for—are difficult and ambiguous in themselves. The trick is to admit the difficulty and get on with the task.

AES, following something that Tom Peters and I put forward

in *In Search of Excellence,* tried to fit organizing ideas under a "7S" framework—strategy, structure, shared values, symbolic behavior, systems, staff, and skills. Eventually they found that too confusing and lumped the "S" categories they couldn't remember into something they call "stuff."

Vision or stuff, what AES strives for is to give their people a sense of worthwhile purpose. Levi's shares this goal and found that just two concepts were enough to articulate the sense of purpose that had Brenda Burgess, the Blue Ridge worker, so charged up. The first is what they do that sets them apart. They call it "mission"; others might call it "strategy." Most executives would settle for that—not Haas. The trouble with strategy, he says, "is that it's analytic, bloodless, and has no life in it." The truly successful enterprise of the future will have *soul,* he contends. "You can't energize people or earn their support unless the organization they are committing to has soul." So Haas argues for a second dimension to conveying a sense of purpose. At Levi's, they call it "Aspirations": not just what they do but how they want to be. Like the values at AES, this is the part of the vision thing that really speaks to the needs of people everywhere in the organization.

Levi's written Mission Statement is simple and straightforward: to sustain responsible commercial success as a global marketing company of branded casual apparel. As with AES's written statement, the words by themselves aren't too exciting. However, an assumption behind these words is that in products like 501 jeans and Dockers, Levi's makes a product that sets the standard for the world. Levi's people all understand this and are very proud of it. Further, the word "responsible" has crept in to modify "commercial success." Beneath that connection lies a ton of meaning. As Harvard's Kotter and Heskett would urge, Levi's wants to meet the needs of all its constituents, including the greater community in which they operate.

Levi's Mission Statement next talks to the strategic needs of the business: superior profitability and return on investment, market leadership, superior products and service. Then it begins to address values: "We will conduct our business ethically and demonstrate leadership in satisfying our responsibilities to our communities and to society. Our work environment will be safe and productive and characterized by fair treatment, teamwork, open communications, personal accountability, and opportunities for growth and development."

So far okay but still a little dull. It's the Aspiration Statement that really brings things to life and adds the grab-you-by-the-heart quality that we saw in AES's values:

> We all want a Company that our people are proud of and committed to, where all employees have an opportunity to contribute, learn, grow, and advance based on merit, not politics or background. We want our people to feel respected, treated fairly, listened to, and involved. Above all, we want satisfaction from accomplishments and friendships, balanced personal and professional lives, and to have fun in our endeavors.

The Aspiration Statement details the type of leadership that will turn this exciting dream into reality. In brief, it calls for leaders everywhere in the organization who will exemplify, model, and coach along several dimensions that, over time, will bring these aspirations closer to reality. Specifically, the Aspiration Statement calls for leaders at every level:

- who set, live, and teach very high ethical standards—refreshing these days when most news stories about business transfix us with scandal and outrage.
- who value and build on every aspect of diversity in the workplace—age, sex, race, sexual orientation, experience, perspectives . . . you name it.
- who will shove trust, recognition, and responsibility deeper into the organization, believing—as most top companies do these days—that this is the way both to release and benefit from the talents of all Levi's people.
- who heap recognition—both financial and psychological—on individuals and teams that perform well.

- who are committed to helping others learn, develop, and succeed. This is of signal import.

Finally, like AES and its "anti-they" campaign, Levi's wants to knock down all barriers to personal responsibility. In the Aspiration Statement, Levi's asks for leaders who don't dissemble but are direct—leaders who will acknowledge and be personally accountable for the problems they might (unwittingly or not) cause others—in short, leaders who build teamwork through trust. Through these aspirations Haas and others are trying to remind each other that the journey is just as important as the destination, that there's more to life than knocking down one milestone after another.

Chief executive Bob Haas is a thoughtful, articulate man who is the great-great-grandnephew of founder Levi Strauss. His charisma is that of a true gentleman, with an emphasis on "gentle." At work he dresses for his role as Levi's leader—typically jeans and a plaid shirt. Haas likes to stand back and ponder what really matters in life. Somewhat cryptically he keeps reminding Levi's people that, "You don't work *for* Levi's, you work for yourselves; you just happen to work *at* Levi's." The admonition is part of his struggle to put the needs of individuals on the same level as the needs of the organization—in other words, to help make life more meaningful for everyone who works there. Contrast that with what I was repeatedly told in my salad days with a former employer: "Your client comes first, then the company, and finally your family." If I'd really taken that advice to heart, I am reasonably sure that I'd have lost what I treasure most in life, my close relationship with my wife and children.

When talking with Haas, it's easy to forget that he's not a warm and furry idealist. He's also a battle-hardened leader who returned his company from the strategic blahs to success and profitable growth. He's the rare executive who not only survived a leveraged buyout (to take Levi's private) but paid off the massive debt incurred—early.

SIGNS OF SUCCESS

How compatible are Levi's lofty ambitions with business results? So far the case is compelling. Since the mid-1980s, when
Levi's took itself private in a $1.6 billion leveraged buyout, after-
tax profits increased almost sevenfold to $360 million in 1992.
Their average annual growth rate in shareholder value from
1982 to 1992 was 50 percent, which—if Levi's were a public
company—would have placed them second among the *Fortune*
500 in that magazine's annual survey. In 1992 and in 1993, the
company made the top ten in *Fortune*'s ranking of "most admired" companies. They are the first private company to have
appeared on that list.

But are Haas's ideas real or just talk in the comfortable executive offices at Levi's Plaza in San Francisco? They're for real.
Tom Kasten, the head of women's wear, remembers a recent
conversation with Sue Thompson, the firm's director of human
resource development. The two worked closely together on a
task force, and Kasten felt comfortable asking her for feedback
about his style. Tom smiles a little sheepishly as he talks about
the incident. "She told me, 'I used to think you were a real jerk.
These days, I really enjoy working with you and so do others.' "
Just in this one gutsy statement, we can sense something different
and exciting at Levi's. In how many companies would a mid-
level staffer feel free to say those words to a top exec?

Kasten's story highlights how dramatic, and how personally
trying, change can be. An ambitious man with a master's degree
in business administration, Kasten was raised to focus on success, and there was no place in his life for anything but the best.
He was right at home in the "old" Levi's, where his brains and
hard-driving style were what the culture valued and what gained
him quick and regular promotions. Impatient and dedicated to
hard work, Kasten remembers being known for pounding his
subordinates with "eighty-three questions"—give or take a
few—about every pending problem. Management by trust—the

idea of gaining control by giving it up—had no place in Kasten's style or at Levi's then. Kasten says that, before he began to understand what was really meant by the Aspiration Statement, "I never thought of my management style as a control issue."

But as others at Levi's sought to change, so did Kasten, and for him it has been a long journey that he suspects will never end. He not only participates in workshops on empowerment and leadership inside Levi's, but meets with an outside consultant as well. He regularly solicits feedback from co-workers and has learned more graciously to accept their praise as well as their criticisms.

Changing has been hard work, and Kasten occasionally encounters cynicism from people who have known him for years, but he believes the struggle is paying off handsomely.

Asked what words would best characterize what he'd like to be remembered for at Levi's, Kasten thought for a moment and then said: "respected," "trustworthy," "supportive," "great teacher," "fun." A few years ago, he said, he would have answered the same question with such words as: "successful," "smart," "knowledgeable," "good problem solver," "fast." The difference in the tone of those adjectives makes Haas's point about soul.

"I'm a lot more comfortable with letting go today than I was three years ago," he says. He admits that some of his colleagues "probably still say, 'he asks too many questions,' but at least the number is reduced" and the ones he asks are "critical." Kasten used to examine every single detail about Levi's new lines of women's clothing—for example, reviewing each style, color, and price. Now he gives the plan a once-over. And today he delegates many hiring decisions, something he couldn't have imagined relinquishing five years ago.

Not that Kasten has lost his competitive drive—it's still crucial to him that his division show steady gains in sales, profits, and return on investment, and he knows that the true test of his values—and the company's—will be whether they can stay the course during rough times. But is he a better manager today? Kasten's response is telling. "Better manager is the wrong word.

How about a better person?" Kasten's wife tells him he's calmer, putting less pressure on his children and being more patient with their foibles. He's also better able to help people in the nonprofit volunteer organizations he works with slice through politicking and find common ground for problem solving.

The sort of attitude change that Kasten's story conveys extends well beyond California. Blue Ridge workers, for instance, noted that they are more effective in church and P.T.A. groups as a result of recent training received at work. And R. C. Ledford, the Texas technical director, said, "I'm happier. It is much more pleasant to know I can be open and I won't be ridiculed." Ledford remembers being praised ten years ago for being "tough." Now he feels he's more effective by letting go of some of his authority.

And those who are gaining some authority seem to relish it. Before Levi's aspirations caught on, "I would see my brain turning into chewing gum," said Marji Meade, a sewing machine operator at Blue Ridge, who specialized in affixing waist bands to jeans. Levi's gave Meade and her colleagues training in communications, problem solving, and conflict resolution. These days she's part of a production team and participates in the plant's decision-making processes. "Now I understand what's going on and I can do something about it. I feel more respect for myself," she comments.

She and others at her plant not only now participate in decision making, they also get added recognition for their efforts. Besides the psychic payoffs, Blue Ridge employees are rewarded financially under a gain-sharing program. If they make a suggestion that saves the factory money—anything from recycling rubber bands to streamlining mail delivery—they take home half the profits added by the idea. (The only catch is that the plant must have met its production and quality targets before gain sharing kicks in.)

The program adds about $600 each year to a typical Blue Ridge employee's take-home pay. The money doesn't sound like much in these days of million-dollar executive salaries, but to Blue Ridge workers it means a lot. It enabled one family to buy a major appliance, another to beef up their insurance coverage; another individual to enjoy a getaway she otherwise might not have taken. And it's not just the money; it's the recognition.

RECOGNIZING RECOGNITION

Gain sharing is just one of many efforts under way at Levi's to applaud contributions from employees. At an old-line Levi's factory in Mountain City, Tennessee, pursuing the recognition part of the Aspiration Statement began with baby steps—a program that enabled people to nominate their colleagues for a free coffee mug or T-shirt for a job well done. "It's rather new that you're recognized for doing your job," says an obviously pleased Larry English, head mechanic, who also sports the title "Recognition Essential Manager."

At Levi's, as elsewhere, it's more difficult to measure and take note of the contributions made by white-collar office workers, a huge part of America's workforce. At the San Francisco headquarters, some departments have attacked that problem head-on with a creative peer-recognition program. Each year, every person gets a small number of "You Are Great" or "Aspiration" coupons. Individuals can then use these coupons to give on-the-spot recognition to any co-worker for a job well done. A recipient can trade the coupon in for $25 or a gift certificate. Cindy Paris, a merchandise coordinator in the youthwear department, was elated to receive two Aspiration coupons within a year, one of them after she helped out at a national sales meeting. "I really appreciated it," recalls Paris, who keeps the coupon on her desk. "I didn't think anything (of the work), but it obviously meant something to someone else." Paris thinks the coupons help build teamwork because "it makes you realize how people are dependent on one another in their jobs."

Another Levi's unit has actually turned recognition into something of a team sport. The womenswear division began with what it called a "Run for the Roses" built around a set of goals sketched on a colorful race track motif covering three walls.

Anyone who felt a co-worker went an extra mile toward over-coming a hurdle could award the person a rose. From the race track, the division graduated to a "Bank of Aspirations," a system under which employees had a "checkbook" of coupons they could give out, and then finally to an aspiration "Olympics" that was kicked off with an outdoor ceremony in a park.

The womenswear programs, all developed by people within the division, sound pretty rah-rah—and they are—but they also address an important nuance of giving recognition. It's simply tough to give out kudos. So often when we deliver a compliment, the recipient responds with "Oh, it was nothing," or "I could have done better." This typically leaves the grateful co-worker feeling, at best, awkward. The womens wear people dodged this problem by having neutral messengers, such as human resources specialists, available to deliver roses and coupons.

In the greater scheme of things, coffee mugs, roses, and coupons seem insignificant, almost not worth the bother. But Levi's has surprised itself with the power of these seemingly trivial rewards. Like most managers, those at Levi's were in the habit of taking people's contributions for granted, even when they had gone to extraordinary ends to get a job done. "It's what we pay people for," managers in companies all over America tell me, invoking the traditional tough-guy approach to managing in "these competitive times." "By contrast," says Donna Goya, Levi's senior vice-president of human resources, "it's amazing how hard people work for recognition." Echoing the truth of what researcher Frederick Herzberg proclaimed years ago, Goya notes that money is not motivational for very long. What she and Herzberg are both saying is not that most of us couldn't use more money. Rather, money only enters the motivational arena if we feel we're measured wrongly or underpaid. Then we're dissatisfied. For most people who believe they are paid fairly, more money is way down on the list of what turns them on. A much higher factor in motivating people is plain and simple recognition.

With a career invested in personnel, Goya already thought she knew the value of recognition but was brought up short

when she did an attitude survey in her own department shortly
after the Aspiration Statement with its emphasis on recognition
was published. Most people told her: "We don't feel recognized
at all." Taken aback and not quite sure what they meant, she
assembled a task force, half clerical and half professional, in
Levi's headquarters to help her come up with a recognition program. "They did a great job," she says. "Before, I had never
asked anybody. I just put in a recognition program that would
have worked for me maybe, but it sure didn't meet their needs."

The task force went at the problem on three levels. The first
need they identified was peer recognition. That was the source of
the "You Are Great" certificates and similar programs now in
other departments. People thrive not only on the cheers from
their peers, but also their freedom to give official kudos to others
without asking approval from any authority higher than their
own gut. The second need was for more meaningful but informal recognition by department heads. Now Sue Thompson, for
example, can give any of her people a spur-of-the-moment reward of up to $150. And it doesn't have to be cash. It might be a
dinner, a night on the town—whatever seems best to fit the
situation. The last need was to budget for recognition, now an
increasingly widespread practice in Levi's. Goya's first recognition budget was about $15,000. About a third of that went to-
ward "You Are Great" certificates, another third to department
heads for informal awards, and the last third to a formal event
where the whole division plus spouses and friends gather to hand
out "personnel hero" awards to a select few of the top contributors.

As the "recognition" part of the Aspiration Statement gains
momentum at Levi's, people all over the system report lessons
learned that are similar to Goya's. Even the little awards mean a
lot. Peer recognition is just as meaningful as an encomium from
the boss. Spontaneous awards enrich not only the recipient but
the giver as well. A number of small programs means more than
a single big one; that way all but the laggards can be made to feel
they are special in some way. In addition, a multiplicity of recog-

nition programs helps ferret out the quiet heroes whose deeds are so often unsung through normal channels.

THE JOURNEY BEGINS

Though it wasn't obvious at the time, Levi's search for soul began in the early 1980s. Through the 1970s Levi Strauss & Company had caught a wave and was riding it for everything it was worth. A combination of forces—the quality of the jeans, the age of the baby boomers, and the worldwide cachet of the Levi's name—made success seem easy. But by 1984, the year that Haas became president and chief executive, the wave had collapsed to a ripple.

The difficulties started in 1981. The economy was headed into recession. The baby boom generation began to lose interest in traditional jeans. And for the first time, stiff world competition threatened the cost competitiveness of many U.S. Levi's plants. Levi's management didn't know quite what to do. Years of continued success had distanced top management from its markets. Few senior executives saw the need to make regular calls on top retail accounts. The jeans had sold themselves, and unchallenged success had created a certain arrogance: Once the retailers bought the goods, said the prevailing philosophy, Levi's responsibility ended.

Management tried to attack the malaise in the market by broadening distribution. Levi's had never sold through chains like Sears and J. C. Penney; it started to in 1982. But what management didn't fully comprehend was that existing retail accounts were discounting the product to move it, so there was little room for them to cut their price further to compete with mass merchandisers. When Levi's made its move toward mass merchandisers, offering little explanation and seeking no guidance from heretofore loyal retailers, the apparel maker completely lost the support of its long-time accounts. By 1984 business had turned sour and the company was in the throes of its first large-scale layoffs. For everyone at Levi's, 1984 truly was a year of Orwellian shock.

Haas, who took over the reins in April of that dismal year, was confounded—and he admitted it. He didn't have a clear picture of either the right strategy or of the values Levi's needed, but his first priority was clear: He and his team had to move quickly to save the business. He told his managers, "I don't have the answers. But you folks are responsible for each of your businesses. Get back to me with your observations and a plan for what you will do."

Within a month, the group was back. Their general conclusion: Levi's was bloated with too many layers, too many plants, too many product lines, and too much administrative staff. The firm had to focus, and focus it did. By pulling out of the lines that were losing money or going nowhere, Levi's cut the number of different products it offered by almost two-thirds between 1984 and 1990. The payroll shrank dramatically, too, by 17,000 people between 1981 and 1986 as Levi's shuttered fifty-nine factories and service facilities.

COMMUNICATION AND TRUST

So much for strategic nuts and bolts, but Haas had to deal with a deeper problem—a culture inside the company that was authoritarian, bureaucratic, and rife with political backbiting despite the Haas family's outside works of kindness and generosity. The family was clearly involved in many community and social issues, but Haas knew he had to ensure that day in and day out, inside the plants and offices, Levi's was living up to its motto "Levi's Is People."

Haas wanted to do something about the Levi's culture from the moment he took over as chief executive. Tom Tusher, now Levi's president and chief operating officer, commented: "Although Bob had just stepped into his new role, he tried to explain the way the company would look and, even more importantly, how it would feel. At Bob's first meetings with the management group, he began to outline how he wanted people to relate to each other: more teamwork, more understanding behavior, better communication, commitment to each other's success, trust, respect—things like that." Employees reacted politely, but dubiously. The fuzzy stuff sounded swell, but sales were dropping, diversification into other lines wasn't working, and the stock was grievously depressed. Haas was learning another important lesson: If a company's very economic viability seems threatened, people don't want to talk about grander purpose. They don't want their leaders doing it either. It's like Maslow's hierarchy of human needs: First assure me of food and shelter, then we'll talk self-actualization.*

At Levi's, as at most companies, the first reaction to crisis was denial and suppression. Olin Dunn, now plant manager at Blue Ridge, reflects the feelings of managers throughout the organization. "Up until the early 1980s Blue Ridge didn't have to change. We had almost no automated equipment, and we thought we could sell everything we produced." When the Blue Ridge managers began to realize how tough things would be in the future, their first instinct was to hold back. Management worried that workers would react badly to the news that the firm had to automate and streamline. The underlying assumption is that most employees will not be able to deal with the bad news. Levi's in particular had a long history of paternalism, and the reluctance to be open was especially strong.

As tempting as it probably was to continue acting paternally, it would have been exactly the wrong approach. When the inevitable layoffs happened, they would have come quickly and without warning. Fierce loyalty would turn into feelings of betrayal, even hatred. Moreover, reticence to disclose discouraging news cuts off one of the most important sources of help. The very employees whom management is trying to "protect" could help tackle the problems, if they had enough information, that is.

Haas recognized this need for openness and during the 1984

*This may be why IBM's new chief executive, Louis V. Gerstner, Jr., doesn't want to talk about vision.

nadir he and other senior managers started laying waste to old barriers to communication. With the help of Donna Goya, who was subsequently promoted to senior vice-president, Haas and Tusher organized brown bag lunches for employees. Anyone could ask the top two officials anything. Executives were nervous. But so, apparently, were employees. "The times were so uncertain, and the venue so uncharacteristic of Levi's, that you had to be a real risk taker to stand up and ask a question," recalls Goya. So the protocol for questioning changed. People no longer asked questions directly, but put them on cards and sent them to Goya. Goya conducted the meetings and asked the unedited questions on behalf of employees. Not wanting the responses to sound canned, Haas refused to see questions ahead of time. The executives had few easy answers to the employees' tough questions, such as: "Will layoffs continue?" "Will we continue to shut down plants to take advantage of cheap offshore labor?" "Will my job be safe?" "Have we lost the magic in the brand name?"

Haas emphasized, in fact, that neither he nor his team had a clear view of where they were going when he became chief executive in 1984. "We were confused, and it took us a long time to muddle through and get clarity around things." Levi's management is "just the opposite of the traditional Dell-paperback image of the senior manager, always in control, always knowing everything, having a clear vision, heading for it like a beacon," Haas says. It doesn't work that way even for the chief executive. Haas adds, "Even today we fall off the wagon—with behaviors that we are not proud of or decisions that don't make sense." This message is important because it reflects the experience of Levi's people themselves. They are struggling amidst confusion. "If they see that it's okay to be confused and to admit to being confused," says Haas, "I think it really helps them relax and say, 'let's get through this change.' Nobody has to have the answer at the start."

Indeed, the whole process of developing corporate aspirations was one filled with setbacks. For example, in 1985, Goya and her co-workers arranged a lunch with Haas and told him that even though the statistics showed that Levi's exceeded federal equal opportunity employment standards, in reality a thick glass ceiling held back minorities and women. Half the professionals were female or minorities, but they weren't in senior positions. With Haas's encouragement, groups of senior managers, along with their minority or female subordinates, escaped to a resort in California's Napa Valley wine region for three days of professionally guided discussions.

The emotional sessions began when white males, women, and minorities were separately asked if the company had a problem with fairness. "White males invariably said, 'Well, we don't have very many [minorities and women] at the top yet, but we've all been here a lot longer and they don't have the experience,' " Goya recalls. They added, "The women want to have their cake and eat it too. They want families, and they want to work." "Well, the women just blew up at that," Goya remembers. "There was some shouting about, 'Who is going to have *your* babies?' Lots of issues surfaced. By the end of some of those sessions managers understood that their very narrow perspective contributed mightily to the problem."

More such meetings were held, and while they provided a forum for discussing the diversity issue, they served a more important function. They signaled just how dramatic and far-reaching the Aspiration manifesto might be. They put the notion of a beliefs-based culture in play at Levi's. If nothing else, they started people thinking and dreaming.

PUT IT IN WRITING

By early 1987, three years into the Haas presidency, the company's financial picture was starting to improve, and Haas felt the time was ripe to stitch together a greater purpose for Levi's. But crafting something eloquent and enduring was no easy task. So Haas and the executive management team headed for another week-long retreat to tackle two tough issues: What kind of company should Levi's be, and what legacy does this management team want to leave behind? At that seminal meeting, managers pledged that their legacy should be fuller and richer than merely producing jeans. Yet finding just the right words took nine grueling months of biweekly meetings. In the end, they produced the Aspiration Statement—476 words that fit on a single sheet of paper. By choosing the word "aspiration" instead of vision, the statement conveys a sense of constant striving.

In late 1987, tens of thousands of copies of the Aspiration Statement were printed in Levi's publications and on posters. Employees seemed to like it, but it was soon to become apparent that writing the words was only the beginning. The concepts were grand, but people had no idea how to implement them. Aspirations had had no part in their training or prior culture.

In late 1988, Sue Thompson was summoned to a meeting with Haas and Tusher. "People aren't getting it," they told her. "Help!" So it was that Levi's embarked on a massive, costly—and frequently frustrating—effort to turn words into reality. In a sense, Levi's management was trapped: It is practically a contradiction in terms to tell people to value diversity and then tell them what their aspirations should be. Nonetheless some telling *is* required. Not valuing diversity is not an option at Levi's. Still, employees had to learn by doing; they had to form their own aspirations in the very process of experiencing them.

The human-resources staff proposed, and management adopted, three educational programs: one on leadership, one on understanding and valuing diversity, and one on ethics. By the end of 1993, more than 1,500 of Levi's people had each spent a Leadership Week with co-workers of different races, genders, ages, and jobs, and from different geographic locations at a retreat in the peaceful hills near northern California's coast. There they struggled through exercises—admittedly somewhat contrived—intended to build enlightened leadership skills. Some of the exercises are deeply personal. For example, participants write an essay about what they're trying to create at Levi's and how they're going about it. They also draw a "lifeline": a diagram of the highs and lows of their career at Levi's. They analyze the patterns. What made the highs so exciting? What made the lows so blue? And after listening to Martin Luther King's inspirational, "I Have a Dream" speech, they write and then deliver their own stump speech to the group. Most focus their speech on their own values, dreams, and the legacy they want to leave.

One of the more challenging activities during Leadership Week is an outdoor exercise that is a metaphor for moving into the unknown. The exercise involves taking some risks, and successfully navigating through the endeavor requires relying on fellow participants for support. Effective support, it becomes apparent, includes practical safety considerations, as well as encouragement—some like to be cheered on, while others prefer quiet coaching. "The experience really provides an opportunity for people to be in a new situation that is fearful for some and to take a look at how they manage that fear, how they manage themselves in an unknown situation, and how they manage themselves as a coach," Thompson observes.

After this outdoor exercise, aided by video tapes of the exercise and led by the Leadership Week faculty (which always includes at least one member of Levi's top management), participants ponder their role as leaders. When a leader gives help, is the "help" really helpful? When a leader asks for aid, is he or she really open to influence and is it accepted in the spirit with which it was intended? Their skill at teamwork is also tested. One participant reported that while he yearned to complete the most challenging of several routines, his partner grew fearful. "I knew in my heart I wanted to say, 'Okay, see you later,' " said David Fernandez, who at the time managed a department that handled claims against Levi's. But Fernandez stayed with his companion, helping her to achieve more than she had expected. Then, when she felt secure, he went on to tackle the tougher challenges. Later his partner was overcome by emotion as she thanked Fernandez for staying with her and coaching her onward. That made an indelible impression on Fernandez. "I finally understood my natural tendency to compete and how that [often negatively] affects my colleagues," he said.

Getting the knack for "empowerment" is consistently one of

the toughest challenges for participants in Leadership Week. Some managers are inclined to abdicate responsibility in the name of empowerment, yet letting people sink isn't empowering. "What I see some of the managers doing is using [empowerment] as an excuse to not make decisions," said Fernandez. At the opposite extreme, some managers fear letting to. Finding the happy medium—between coaching, inspiring, and challenging, and between granting freedom and drawing firm guidelines—is a never-ending process.

PUTTING WORDS INTO ACTION

So Levi's people go off and get religion for a week, then what? How do they keep that inspiration? One way is through a program known as "We Need To's." During Leadership Week, participants each craft a list of the gaps they see between the ideal behavior espoused by the Aspiration Statement and everyday life at Levi's. The list is in three parts—what they as individuals can do to bridge the gap, what their departments can do, and what the company as a whole can do.

The lists aren't shoved into a drawer and forgotten. Three weeks after Leadership Week ends, each person's personal to-do list is sent to another Leadership-Week participant. That person then calls the list-writer and inquires into the progress being made toward making the needed changes; the two are supposed to work together to ensure that the ideas are put into practice. Also, while there's no official follow-up, participants are encouraged to share their stump speech with their departments, thereby disclosing their vision and intended actions to their colleagues.

On a corporate level, the human resources department compiles a short list each quarter of some of the companywide "We Need To's" that emerged from leadership training during the previous three months. The list is then forwarded to the executive management committee, which weighs the suggestions and decides whether, and how, to act on them. One of the biggest changes to result from this follow-up system was a massive over-haul of Levi's pay system, which Leadership Week participants consistently criticized as rewarding financial performance in-stead of aspirational behavior. In an attempt to serve as a model for teamwork, a task force of line managers from around the world worked on the new pay system after garnering comments from hundreds of employees. The new management pay system they devised is more closely aligned with the company's values, including a new emphasis on teamwork and a new procedure by which managers can be critiqued by their subordinates and peers as well as their bosses.

Another action that grew out of the heightened sensitivities at Leadership Week was Levi's decision in early 1992 to extend medical benefits to spousal "equivalents"—people who plan to spend a lifetime with a Levi's employee but who are not a legal spouse. After nearly every leadership retreat, participants would remark that Levi's policy not to discriminate on the basis of sex, sexual orientation, or marital status was not adhered to when it came to providing benefits. The decision to extend benefits to domestic partners has brought criticism from some of Levi's cus-tomers and employees. But Reese Smith, director of employee benefits, said the company's management has a consistent, firm response: "We are not going to have a discriminatory work-place."

ASPIRATIONAL CHALLENGES

Despite all efforts, Levi's is far from having a perfect record in achieving its ideals. To understand the struggle to live up to the ideals of the Aspiration Statement and ethical behavior, Levi's people have to look no further than their own experiences in San Antonio, Texas. The ordeal there began in January 1990 when Levi's management announced the closure of a large San An-tonio factory where 1,115 workers turned out Dockers, the im-mensely popular casual slacks for aging baby boomers. The plant, which had been purchased from another firm in the early

1980s, wasn't operating as efficiently as Levi's wanted, so the company had decided to move Dockers production to other U.S. facilities and to subcontract factories in Costa Rica, where labor costs were a fraction of those in San Antonio.

A senior vice-president from San Francisco delivered the news to the San Antonio workers on the morning of January 17, and set off a storm of protest that continued for years thereafter. Levi's management thought they were handling the closure in concert with their new aspirations. By almost any measure, Levi's severance pay and benefit packages were generous. The firm also went overboard to help the laid-off workers land other jobs. Like many firms that lay people off, Levi's staffed an out-placement office to help people find new work and obtain benefits. But because so many workers lacked the basic skills needed to qualify for other employment, Levi's also made English as a Second Language (ESL) and basic literacy classes available to all employees free of charge. Those who continued on to junior college became eligible to share in a new Levi's scholarship fund. Others who sought jobs after completing the training got help from outside job-placement consultants who were retained by Levi's from the autumn of 1991 to the spring of 1992. In addition, Levi's spent hundreds of thousands of dollars on community services, including day care, emergency assistance, transportation, and supplements to a federal job-training program, with the intention of helping out its former workers.

Still, loyal Levi's employees felt double-crossed. While rumors of plant closure had been swirling about for months, they say they had been reassured by an executive shortly before Christmas that their operation was expected to stay open. They also claim that Levi's pinched their severance packages by purposely pushing down their hourly pay in the final months of production, and they suggested that the firm's hidden motive was to avoid high medical claims from injuries caused by repetitive motions at the sewing machines—both assertions that Levi's management denies.

"They weren't big enough to face up to their responsibility," says Irene Reyna, who worked at the plant for seven years, even after contracting pain in her arm. After the plant closed, Reyna helped organize boycotts of Levi's products. As far as she and her colleagues were concerned, Levi's was not acting fairly and responsibly.*

How responsibly Levi's acted could be debated ad infinitum, but what really stung Levi's management was that the company was *perceived* in some circles as being unfair. Levi's honestly believed it was acting precisely in accord with its newly articulated value set, but many in San Antonio saw it otherwise. When either a Levi's or an AES wears such a bold heart on its sleeve, it sets up expectations that can't always be fulfilled.

The Aspiration Statement talks about empowerment and communication, but these seemed to plant workers to be in short supply in the San Antonio case, and with the benefit of hindsight, some Levi's executives can see their point. "Maybe we became a bit cavalier about plant closings," says Peter Jacobi, who oversees all Levi's manufacturing operations. "I suppose if I were in San Antonio and read this document called 'Aspirations,' it would be very easy to assume the company wasn't living up [to its beliefs]."

The San Antonio experience was one of those setbacks along the way that can build awareness and a resolve to improve. Conscious that future plant closures can't be ruled out, Levi's began literacy and skills training programs at some of its plants to help workers prepare for life after Levi's, should they lose their jobs, as well as to make them more effective in their current posts.

*Setting aside questions of fairness, the former workers were having a difficult time proving Levi's did anything wrong legally. They filed two suits against the company, one claiming the plant was closed for illegal reasons (such as to avoid paying disability) and the second claiming discrimination against a mostly Hispanic work force. By April 1993 the courts had dismissed both cases.

TYING THE KNOT

As the months and years go by, the spirit embodied in Levi's Aspiration Statement is woven deeper and deeper into the fabric of its daily business. While statements of vision merely sit on the shelf at many companies, Levi's is fast becoming a role model among firms that are discovering that good conduct and good business are one and the same. Consider the company's approach to the challenges it faced as the 1990s dawned—challenges much like those found in many American companies: Production was simply taking too long, causing customers to complain about missed schedules; manufacturing costs needed to be cut; medical claims were rising. Levi's managers found an answer to the problems not in a business textbook, but in the Aspiration Statement. One result is an ongoing effort to alter radically the nuts and bolts of its business—the way garments are made.

The frenetic Blue Ridge plant, where 400 sewing machine operators churn out thousands of men's jeans a day, was one of the first plants to begin to overhaul the work environment. Throughout its history, Levi's operators knew nothing but the piecework pay system. The more work you did, the more money you made above a base pay. It seemed to make sense, but psychologically and physically, operators grew weary. By the late 1980s, the frustration was being heard loud and clear at the top of the company, and Haas and other managers began to realize that "there may be better ways to organize the workplace that are much more in keeping with the aspirations of communication, teamwork, recognition and sharing the success of the enterprise with the people who create it."

A potential solution was found, almost by accident, at the Levi's plant in Fayetteville, Arkansas. There managers who were fed up with mistakes, high costs, and frequent turnover on one sewing line tried something different. They turned a few employees loose in a spare building and asked them to come up with a

new system for affixing borders to jackets. The experiment
worked. Before long, the newly empowered employees had designed a new approach. They liked it better—they designed it.
Levi's liked it better—the new approach saved money. So empowerment began to catch on.

One of the first plants to leap onto the bandwagon was Blue
Ridge. Beginning in late 1991, that plant started to reorganize
around teams, each with about three dozen people. The teams
are responsible for shepherding jeans from cutting through all
the sewing steps to shipping. Instead of being told by managers
exactly how to make jeans, they have a big say in arranging their
work flow. And instead of doing one task all day, operators are
trained to handle three different positions on the line. This not
only affords them more variety and challenge in their work, but
offers relief from the repetitious work that can cause injury.
Teams set their own production goals over a minimum set by the
plant management. They are headed toward the same form of
self-management we saw at P&G in Lima, Ohio.

"The team takes a lot of the stress off you," said operator
Jolene Bright, a Levi's employee for more than two decades.
Besides reducing stress, the system instills a cooperative spirit,
and operators help each other out in order to keep the work
flowing. Such collaboration increases efficiency by eliminating
bottlenecks that occur when one operator experiences mechanical problems or for some other reason slows the line down. And
because operators know several jobs, they can more easily com-
pensate for employee absences.

All of this shouldn't have been a surprise, but for Levi's it was
a true awakening. Early results of the team approach indicated
that jeans were ready to be shipped out of the plant only one day
after sewing began, compared to six days under the old system,
thereby enabling Levi's to react more quickly to retailers' requests and cut its inventory costs. The result: The company can
be more competitive. Its labor costs might not be as low as they
would be in Costa Rica or Indonesia, but its responsiveness to
customers is far better. Over time the team approach—a direct
result of Levi's value-laden culture—could well bring jobs back

to the United States. By mid-year 1993 nine of the company's twenty-seven production plants had fully converted to the team approach and the remainder were an estimated 70 percent of the way there. Since early 1990, when working in teams began to take hold, Levi's has added 2,500 jobs to its U.S. manufacturing base.

PRINCIPLED REASONING

One big win at Levi's is the way the company made real the exhortation toward ethical behavior. In the end, corporate ethics is really just the sum of the behavior of all people in a company, and Levi's is trying hard to raise individuals' standards and skills in dealing with moral dilemmas. While lots of firms talk about upholding ethical standards, Levi's is bold enough to wrestle with the real challenge—not just the plain cases of right and wrong, but the gray areas with truly difficult trade-offs.

For many years, Levi's had a lengthy list of dos and don'ts that covered such ethical issues as conflict of interest and apparent conflict of interest. But that list didn't go far enough. Neither did an effort to try to educate people in ethics—participants had no sense of the company's principles and no tool to apply to decision making. To remedy those shortcomings, the executive management committee, made up of Levi's top officers, wrestled for a year with trying to put ethical values into words. In 1991 they completed a one-page document called "Ethical Principles" that was based on the straightforward idea that people's consciences should be their guides in everything they do. Attempting to put a sharp point on an imprecise topic, the committee wrote that all employees should strive to live up to six principles: honesty, fairness, respect for others, compassion, promise keeping, and integrity. Integrity, the ethics statement says, means that employees should "live up to Levi's ethical principles even when confronted by personal, professional, and social risks, as well as economic pressures." That last phrase is noteworthy because so much in American companies, including Levi's, is typically driven by cost, not ethics. Remember, though, that Levi's mission statement declares that the firm strives for *responsible* commercial success.

Meanwhile, Beth Doolittle, a Levi's organizational development specialist whose background was with nonprofit organizations, took on the even tougher job of crafting a model for making decisions through an ethical lens. The idea was to recognize that any decision that affects other people—and that's just about every decision—has an ethical aspect to it. And when that's the case, it's important to take the time, if even just a few minutes, to weigh the impact any decision may have on others. The problem is not that people ignore questions of fairness or honesty when they make decisions, Doolittle said. Rather, such issues are often argued in black-and-white, moralistic tones, and in rushed meetings. "The time pressure is always there. The pressure to make a dollar is there," she says. "We're asking people to be more conscious in their decision making."

What Doolittle sought to do was create a framework for considering ethical questions in a disciplined way. "The challenge in all of our lives is, How do I make sure that my self-interest doesn't start to run me?" Doolittle notes. "The easy thing is to get lulled into thinking you have considered (everyone else)." The resulting model, called a "principled reasoning" approach to decision making, hardly seems earthshaking on the surface. It starts by asking people, first, to define the problem carefully and then take two more steps—to identify the various parties that will be affected by the decision and to identify the principles that should be applied. The affected parties, which Levi's calls the stakeholders, could be particular employees, suppliers, competitors, governmental entities, and so on. For all stakeholders, an analysis is made of how much they will be affected by a decision and how much influence they should have, if any, on the decision-making process. People involved in decision making also determine which principles should come into play—usually ethical principles as well as others. "The ethical principles trump business and profit considerations," says Robert Dunn, the vice-president for corporate affairs.

Then, through brainstorming and other techniques, solutions
are proposed. Each potential solution is tested by weighing it
against the ethical guidelines and the interests of the stakeholders. As the field is narrowed, potential solutions are also examined against the realities of implementation.

A GLOBAL TEST

Dolittle's ethical framework sounds all too abstract, lofty, and
complicated for many everyday business decisions. Indeed, the
principles aren't intended to be rigorously applied all the time.
But even a brief application to many decisions would be an
improvement over past practices.

Levi's did have a chance to put the model to a rigorous test in
1991 and early 1992. It was during that time that the company
undertook a massive evaluation of its policies for using overseas
subcontractors. The issue grew straight out of the "We Need
To's" from Leadership Week. Participants came away from the
course understanding the importance of trust and teamwork, but
they consistently asked a nagging question—how do these aspirations apply to the 600 subcontractors Levi's uses to sew clothes
in 35 foreign countries? For years, overseas contractors were
evaluated mainly on price and quality. Levi's people who selected contractors knew that working conditions, treatment of
employees, and other such factors were important, but they
weren't clear about how to factor them into a decision, or even if
they should consider them at all.

The question of how to apply the Aspiration Statement to
subcontractors led to a host of other issues, both subtle and profound. What is the responsibility of a multinational firm to help
bring up the living standards in developing nations by providing
jobs? Even if the working conditions don't match those in America, are some jobs better than none? Did Levi's have special
responsibilities to its domestic employees that might preclude
choosing certain overseas contractors? How can you set up

global standards—a fair, level playing field—and at the same time be sensitive to cultural diversity?

The exhaustive, six-month process of reevaluating the company's overseas sourcing policies is a fine but rare example of a company attempting to apply discipline and reason to such a subjective and emotional issue as ethics. Indeed, Levi's people have been unable to find any other firm that has implemented as comprehensive a set of guidelines to address the inevitable dilemmas of overseas contracting.

The process began with the formation of a sixteen-person task force, including people from merchandising, sourcing, marketing, manufacturing, human resources, and the legal departments. At times, their meetings lasted three to six days. After initial issues were addressed, each member of the task force was assigned a certain "stakeholder" group to interview. Among the stakeholders: sewing machine operators in the United States, merchandisers, overseas subcontractors, large holders of Levi's stock. The list of principles to be considered was also drawn up; in addition to the six ethical principles, the group added loyalty, corporate social responsibility, respect for cultural diversity, sustained, profitable commercial success, and longer-term global leadership. In other words, these eleven criteria were to be taken into account as the committee drew up guidelines for selecting overseas contractors. The idea was that whatever guidelines they ended up with, none should tarnish any of the eleven principles. (In addition, contractors would have to live up to a set of business standards, such as maintaining good quality and service.)

After several months, task-force members developed proposed guidelines and proceeded to share them with the stakeholders. The tough decisions involved weighing principles against one another. Is it more fair to allow a child of ten to work in a factory or more fair and compassionate not to? Is it more honest to disclose a problem or more fair to keep it under wraps? The committee also examined the impact of the proposed guidelines. What would happen if, as a result of the guidelines, Levi's had to pull out of some existing contracts? What if all production in

some countries were dropped? What impact would the guidelines have on Levi's bottom line? As for implementation, how
difficult would it be to ensure the criteria were met without forming a quasi–police force? How far up and down the supply chain
should they be applied?

The result of all the work was the publication in March 1992
of guidelines for picking business partners that go beyond the
basics of price and quality. These terms of engagement emphasize that contractors should minimize environmental impact,
provide safe workplaces (and, in some cases, residences) for employees, and abide by a set of fair employment practices. These
include:

- Paying wages and providing benefits that not only comply
  with local law but also match prevailing wages in comparable
  local industries.
- Not employing workers under age fourteen, or the compul-
  sory age to be attending school.
- Not exceeding the prevailing local working hours, preferably
  less than sixty hours a week.
- Not using forced labor or corporal punishment.

Going further, Levi's established a set of guidelines for selecting
countries in which it will contract out work, emphasizing that the
countries should respect human rights and be politically stable.

So much for the paperwork. Next, Levi's put the words into
practice. Teams fanned out in every direction to educate Levi's
own managers in each country and then to audit the subcontractors' facilities. The evaluations led to reforms, such as added
ventilation or fire escapes and cleaner restrooms. More significantly, Levi's terminated its contractor relationships in some
countries—including Myanmar (formerly Burma) and, very recently, China, because of human rights violations. The decision
to shut down sourcing, production, and sales in China was one
of the toughest Levi's management has had to make, given the
huge market potential in that country. "However," says Haas,
"never has an action by the company been met with such an

immediate, spontaneous, large, and mainly supportive reaction from people all over the world."

One of the more intriguing reforms occurred in Bangladesh, where Levi's personnel discovered that their contractors appeared to be employing children under fourteen years of age. (Determining their exact age is difficult; some people don't know their birth dates, others fudge their age in order to obtain work. In this case—in a less than totally satisfactory solution—contractors now use a stick to measure their height.) Levi's persuaded the contractors not to hire children in the future. As for those already working at the factory, whose income was likely essential to their families, Levi's negotiated an arrangement under which the children would return to school while the contractor continued to pay their salaries. Levi's paid for their school books and fees. An unusual arrangement, to say the least.

What's in such an arrangement for the contractor? Dunn suspects contractors are likely to want to please Levi's because of the high volume of business it can funnel to favored suppliers. Also, a contractor who can boast that he supplies Levi's is likely to attract more customers.

What's in it for Levi's? Dunn admits that requiring contractors to meet the guidelines might cost extra money in the short run—for example higher administrative costs and contractors raising prices to cover added expenses. Dunn figures, however, that there could be long-term savings as the ethics audits enable the company to slim down the number of contractors it employs. More importantly, though, Levi's people now have guidelines for doing what they know in their hearts is the right thing to do.

— — —

EVERYONE I TALKED WITH at Levi's is enthusiastically behind the ideas captured in their Aspiration Statement. But in the six years since the first statement was printed, Levi's people have learned how difficult the journey toward achieving those aspirations can be. The progress has been impressive but achievement is nowhere near where Levi's would like it to be. In an industry that virtually defined the word "sweatshop," following the path to "responsible commercial success" may be the toughest journey of all. But it's also the most rewarding. The reason is simple: A program such as Aspirations at Levi's brings people to life. It restores something all of us need desperately—pride in what we do, belief in the value of our work.

8.

SUSTAINABLE
COMPETITIVE EDGE

A New Product Every
Day at Rubbermaid

In the first seven chapters we examined various aspects of human motivation, their tight link to organization, and in turn the tight link between organization and strategy. Now let's turn it around, looking at how top firms build wealth-creating strategy and how tightly linked that is to the way they organize and motivate.

"Strategy" means different things to different people. The word itself—strategy—has a certain cerebral, yet macho, appeal. Intellectuals can pose as tough guys if they are strategists, and vice versa. Thus, much gets labeled strategic that is not. And, too, executives forget that great strategy, even in wartime, is the boring business of what Rubbermaid calls "sweating the details."

In business, strategy ought to mean just one thing: generating a sustainable competitive advantage. Perversely, competitive advantage seems to come not so much from direct attack on the competition, as the military connotations of the word "strategy" would imply. Looking at the actions of top companies, I conclude that the most successful strategists are those who best understand customers and markets. The key to strategic success is mainly this: building relationships with customers, suppliers, and employees that are exceptionally hard for competitors to duplicate.

Several approaches to strategic thinking seem to accomplish this end. Two shine most brightly in the companies I researched. First comes the raw ability to out-innovate the competition. In this chapter and the two that follow we'll look at three organizations that achieve this with distinction: Rubbermaid, Procter & Gamble (P&G), and Merck.

Second comes the mastery of the mundane, to be boringly reliable and consistent, to understand what customers expect and to deliver that, with awesome regularity. Much of the success that we already saw at Federal Express, in the service business, and will see in Motorola, in commercial electronics, can be explained by the will and skill of their people to serve (and often to delight) their customers.

Underlying both strategies is the need to keep costs in line— not necessarily to be the lowest cost producer, but to keep costs low relative to world competition. One major approach to this goes hand in glove with the way companies organize to innovate. They break themselves up into small, nearly stand-alone units. What? This would seem less efficient. How about economies of scale? How about the magic of coordination and vertical integration? Still, companies that *don't* break themselves up tend to be higher cost. Think about it. Big, centralized, monolithic companies tend toward decision-making and other processes that are nearly as sluggish as government in the old USSR was. Companies like Rubbermaid, with multiple, independent business units, introduce the market mechanism into their decision processes. To a traditionalist, their way of organizing seems less rational. Nevertheless, they are more efficient.

No one can prove this but I suspect that the durability of P&G has much to do with its historic practice of letting its own brands compete. By contrast, I suspect the downfall of IBM (and of GM, which ironically wrote the book on decentralization in its early history) grew out of its tendencies toward centralizing decisions.*

Another major approach to keeping cost low fits tightly with total-quality, total-service, and total-relationship strategies. We'll see this at Motorola. The reason is simple: Any company that hasn't taken a total-quality approach to life probably makes mistakes at the rate of 20 to 30 percent. Getting something fixed once the mistake is made, the quality gurus will tell you, costs four to six times as much as doing things right from the start. Huge savings accrue to those who've learned that screwing things up ought not to be business as usual.

Let's turn now to see how Rubbermaid organizes itself for its version of sustainable strategic advantage.

— — —

ON THE PASTORAL FRINGE of Wooster, Ohio, just a stone's throw from a community of Amish settlers who cling to age-old customs, sits the headquarters of one of the most innovative companies in America—Rubbermaid Inc. The contrast could not be more striking. As much as the environs of central Ohio's rolling countryside are bound by tradition, the only constant at Rubbermaid is change. Well, there is one other constant—Rubbermaid's reputation among retailers and consumers as a high quality, ever-reliable supplier of plastic household goods.

*As Dartmouth professor James Brian Quinn argues in his marvelous book, *Intelligent Enterprise,* companies should constantly be asking the question: Is this piece of the whole the best in the world? When a company breaks itself up—Rubbermaid divisions and operating units, P&G brands, Merck drug-development teams—the question gets answered regularly. The smaller unit must compete under relatively free-market conditions. Quinn would have us take the question several steps further. Do we have one of the best human-resources departments in the world? Best accounting department in the world? Purchasing? Research? If not, farm out the activity. The threat of farming out operations introduces the market mechanism into all areas of the company, including staff activities. This threat alone may bring a laggard function up to snuff. If not, better to look to an outside, more competitive resource.

Yes, this is the Rubbermaid that probably made the dish-drainer on your kitchen counter, the molded box that holds your knives and forks, and the sturdy can that hides your trash. It might well have supplied your garden furniture, a toy truck or doll house for your kids, the cooler you took to the ballpark, or the modular furniture at your office. From its inception in 1920 as a maker of toy balloons, the Ohio company has evolved from a rubber-goods firm into America's premier maker of plastic products for nearly every aspect of everyday life.

And the number of products it produces is growing daily—literally. In 1992, Rubbermaid introduced 365 new products, an average of one new product for every day of the year. What's the secret? Rick Margin, the preppy-looking marketing vice-president in the company's largest division—housewares—offers a paradoxical answer to that question: "If I start talking about a Rubbermaid business and the person I'm talking to starts yawning in five minutes, I know I have hit a hot opportunity. The [successful] products tend to be boring." What he means is that Rubbermaid finds opportunity where others might see only the tiny, uninteresting market niche.

Rubbermaid products all sound so pedestrian—and, frankly, they are. That's exactly what Rubbermaid can teach us. Mention the word "innovation" and we usually conjure up images of scientists fiddling with test tubes or computer nerds hunching over glowing terminals. We think of big gambles and billions of dollars, of stunning breakthroughs and Nobel Prizes. What we're thinking of, really, is *invention,* not *innovation.* Invention means discovery, yet often it has very little to do with the marketplace. Invention is what U.S. firms typically excel at. Where they often fall short, leaving the field open to overseas competitors, is in innovation, that often unglamorous process of incremental improvement. Typically, innovation is closely tied to the needs of the marketplace. It's both the new product that consumers didn't know they wanted and the small change that will give new life to an old item.

From Rubbermaid, we can learn that the exceedingly important ability to innovate is the result of very down-to-earth, no-frills business practices like discipline, focus, and attention to customers. More specifically we see:

- Love of what they do. Theirs is no cold study in financial success. The source of that success, Rubbermaid products, are on prominent display everywhere in the company.
- Delight in the mundane. Rubbermaid finds zest in products that might make competitors yawn.
- Focus. Extraordinary concentration on what others might dismiss as too small a market niche.
- Heavy customer involvement in innovation. Marketing people typically head the business teams. Customers participate in product development all the way from idea to national roll-out.
- An exquisite approach to being big but staying flexible. They organize into small, very autonomous business units and teams. The teams work cross-functionally.
- A set of systems and organizing ideas that all align to foster a favorable climate for innovation. Coupled with a pretty rigorous eight-step process that ensures bad ideas get shut down is deep understanding that you don't innovate without making mistakes. Rubbermaid expects and understands failure (at least, up to a point.)

Paying heed to the basics has paid off handsomely for Rubbermaid, where a continuous stream of new products (plus a few acquisitions) has helped boost sales for forty consecutive years, to $1.8 billion in 1992. By the end of that year, sales and profits had increased non-stop for forty-eight quarters. The success has hardly gone unnoticed—in 1992 the firm ranked number two on *Fortune* magazine's list of the most admired U.S. corporations, the eighth consecutive year Rubbermaid ranked in the top ten.

Most companies can only dream of the intense consumer loyalty Rubbermaid commands. It receives close to 100,000 letters a year from customers with praise, complaints, and suggestions, and sometimes even with complaints about a product that they think is Rubbermaid's but really is a competitor's. Rubbermaid employees answer every letter and more often than not include a replacement product, if the letter is a complaint. Its name recognition is so high that in a survey some years ago consumers ranked Rubbermaid as one of their favorite suppliers of rubber gloves. Rubbermaid wasn't even in the market at the time.

Some consumers are so attached to their Rubbermaid products that they can't imagine life without them, and they go out of their way to let the company know it. In 1991 the company received a letter from a woman who could no longer find a certain type of Rubbermaid sponge. She began her page-long poetic message like this:

> "I once was very happy, but now I'm very sad;
> I had a special dish device that made me very glad."

Appropriately, Rubbermaid's consumer service department replied in verse.

PRODUCT CULTURE

Much of Rubbermaid's current success springs from the vision of former Chief Executive Stanley Gault, a top GE official who returned to his home town of Wooster to head Rubbermaid in 1980. Gault "retired" in 1991. But two years later he was back as chairman.

Gault's and other executives' enthusiasm for Rubbermaid products is reflected all around their offices, where shelves are packed with Rubbermaid products, from toys to mailboxes. Grant most of these executives a second and they'll tick off the plusses of Rubbermaid's products over a competitor's. To them the possibilities for converting something else in the world to plastic seems virtually limitless, even if many of the products are, admittedly, "mundane." Likewise, they think scientists have only scratched the surface of exploring the properties of plastic;

not long ago Rubbermaid produced plastic dishes that closely resemble stoneware, to name one striking example.

Actually, a product-packed executive office is just a snapshot of the Rubbermaid product culture. Its corporate headquarters is understated in every respect except one—attention to products. Everywhere Rubbermaid goods are on display, in colorful hues and oddball shapes and sizes, stacked every which way, near entrances, in hallways, and in meeting rooms. It is the most visible sign of a company that infuses its employees with pride in what they produce.

There's no simple explanation, of course, for Rubbermaid's consistent success at churning out new products—more than a thousand of them in the past five years. But pressed to identify a key ingredient, Gault explains that it has much to do with a structure that allows people to focus on narrow product areas. The mindset is to segment, focus, concentrate, and plan at the lowest possible level. So Rubbermaid is structured into six operating units, defined primarily by product categories—home products, specialty products (seasonal goods such as ice chests and gardening aids), toys (sold under the Little Tikes brand name), commercial products (such as janitorial supplies), and office products, plus a European venture. With little corporate staff to support it, each operating unit has its own research, marketing, design, information systems, and manufacturing staffs. Although there's an informal system for comparing ideas and learning from each other's manufacturing techniques, the product lines and manufacturing systems are distinct enough that there is little overlap among the units. Responsibility for Rubbermaid's over 4,700 products is then subdivided further into close to twenty so-called business teams. In the home products division, for example, there are nine business teams, such as those for food storage containers, bath items, hardware accessories, cleaning products, and so on.

These cross-functional business teams are the heart and soul of Rubbermaid. They aren't what some companies would call product development teams, which conjure up new products, introduce them, and then pass responsibility on to the sales department. Instead, each team remains responsible for a category of products throughout its life cycle, from idea through sales and eventually through phase-out. Once a product is introduced, the team monitors sales trends in order to develop new merchandising, pricing, and advertising and to help identify ways to modify the item to spur sales.

Assigned to each team are several representatives from the key functions required to get a product from idea to consumer—marketing, research and development (which designs the products), manufacturing, sales, and finance. Within each of those categories are several sub-specialists, such as a packaging engineer from manufacturing and a consumer-research specialist from marketing. The core team calls on these specialized resources as needed. Altogether, a typical team has four to six members and meets formally every two to four weeks—but often daily on an informal basis—to churn through the status of products that are its responsibility.

One thing that makes the teams successful is that they operate as small, entrepreneurial entities. Although they have clear financial and product-related targets and a fairly structured, disciplined approach to researching and producing products, team members still have considerable freedom to achieve their goals however they please. They're almost like tiny companies unto themselves. Team participants live and breathe their products.

Another factor in team success is focus. For example, the Rubbermaid bath-products manager worries only about bath products and is responsible for determining everything that happens to that bath line: what gets introduced, what gets deleted, what gets changed, how it gets packaged and sold, and what bath customers might want or want changed. Focusing on a single category like bath products, Rubbermaid people explain, makes you more innovative. Suppose the person responsible for bath items also had to worry about trash containers and laundry baskets. If the bath-product line produces less revenue than other lines, bath products might begin to seem unimportant in the greater scheme of things. And if the bath line doesn't get attention and it, well . . . , goes down the drain, you lose a category of products that, given the right focus, could have been extremely successful.

CEO Wolfgang Schmitt, a twenty-five-year Rubbermaid veteran, reinforces the idea. For him one key to success is that the teams "sweat the details." In sweating the details Rubbermaid gives birth to the little ideas that make a big difference—the indentations in garbage cans so that they don't stick together when stacked in the store, the special compartments in tool boxes to keep nails from spilling out, the vents in storage chests that would prevent suffocation if a child were to be trapped inside.

Schmitt explains the success of the teams. "They have the advantage of being highly focused, but they have the competitive advantage of having a great resource base around them that they can draw upon on an as-needed basis." A side benefit of the business-team structure, he notes, is that "it's probably the best way that I know of to train your people. What you're doing is creating your next set of top managers. You're giving them the best kind of training: relevant, on-the-job, meaningful, cross-functional."

Another key to the achievements of the teams is the feeling of ownership and pride, the sense that each person can make a difference in a product that will satisfy consumers. "People have been empowered, so they're on the hook and they feel ownership," Schmitt says. Team leaders get some additional incentive to deliver on their promises because a portion of their compensation is tied to the success of their new and existing products.

The sense of pride and ownership in the products is pervasive at Rubbermaid. One manager looks at the spatula and spaghetti scoop on her desktop and calls them her "babies." An industrial designer points to a white plastic kitchen strainer, a product he designed, hanging from a hook on his wall, and explains, smiling, "What it's all about [is] I'm going to be somewhere and someone will say, 'Whoever did this did a great job.' "

And then there's Rob Cockfield, a senior product manager for cleaning products, who heads up a team that "owns" products like mops, vacuum bags, dust pans, and brooms. Cockfield came to Rubbermaid in 1990, having worked for ten years in the 1970s and 1980s in product management at GE. As difficult as it may be for an outsider to comprehend, these days Cockfield gets genuinely excited about brooms. In his office cubicle, which is stuffed with more cleaning supplies than you'd likely need in a lifetime, Cockfield reaches for one of his special favorites—an angle broom, a new product with bristles that are longer on one end than the other. The design may seem humdrum, but not to Cockfield, who explains that a special handle tilt that Rubbermaid was planning to introduce should make sweeping easier and make the broom a big seller. "How can you get excited about brooms?" he asks. "This isn't like *any* other broom."

What Cockfield goes on to explain reveals a key element that often is lost in media and Wall Street enthusiasm about innovation at Rubbermaid. Here we find a company that is not really innovation-driven or technology-driven; it is market-driven. What excites Cockfield is not that his new broom has a nifty new tilt, but rather that angled brooms are what he calls "drivers"— products that lead the line in sales volume and routinely deliver the expected financial return. As he puts it, "It'll put a lot of money into the cash register."

As we shall see, it is Cockfield's specialty—marketing—that drives product innovation at Rubbermaid. Marketing managers head each product team and product group. In a team of equals, marketing is slightly more equal, because marketing represents the consumer.

CLIMATE CONTROL

The team structure thrives at Rubbermaid in part because the company has created an ideal climate for innovation. That's something that builds up over the years and is passed on from generation to generation. Rather than fearing, as some companies might, that a new product would destroy the success of an old one, Rubbermaid people are always in search of the new, the improved, the different. Indeed, most of the new products Rubbermaid introduces are simply incremental improvements over existing products or extensions of existing product lines, like larger storage boxes or new varieties of trash cans. Or the company might upgrade a product line, as it did with its bathroom accessories. Rubbermaid added items that look different, such as plastic that is colored to resemble marble, so that bath products could be sold in "boutique" sections of mass merchandisers' stores, as well as in traditional housewares departments.

But the company also expands horizontally, continuously branching out into new product areas where something made of metal or wood might be refashioned, with a new twist or feature, into plastic. In 1989, for example, Rubbermaid plunged into insulated lunch boxes, toy trucks, infant products, and doll houses. The next year it introduced cleaning products, toolboxes, and lawn carts. In 1991 it added mailboxes, adhesive trims, and a composting container. The company actually had a goal for some time of entering a new market every eighteen to twenty-four months, but it was exceeding that so regularly that this goal has been lowered to every twelve to fifteen months.

Besides the all-important team structure, most other aspects of the way Rubbermaid organizes itself combine and conspire to make the climate neither too hot, nor too cold, but just right for innovation. For one thing, it has systems that constantly remind everyone that "new products are us." This means everything from dotting the corridors with your own products—*and those of competitors*—to sponsoring new product idea "fairs." In late 1991, Rubbermaid held a fair, dubbed "Ideas under Construction," in a partially completed building. After hearing presentations from product groups and brainstorming in groups, the 300 employee participants submitted 2,000 new product ideas on index cards.

Another of its systems forces close attention to market trends. Each year, for example, a number of demographic and lifestyle trends are made part of the corporate strategic plan, and each business team is expected to consider whether it can develop new products in those categories. Some trends of recent interest to

Rubbermaid include environmental awareness, elder care concerns, and the growth of the home improvement industry.

Yet another of its processes forces attention to specific customers (as opposed to markets in general). Rubbermaid's one hundred largest customers—including retail chains like Kmart and Wal-Mart—are brought in regularly to headquarters to share ideas for new products and for more effective distribution and merchandising practices. Managers also drop in on retail stores to get a feel for how Rubbermaid products stack up on the shelves against the competition.

Going beyond the immediate customers, the retailers, Rubbermaid people also really try to understand how consumers use or would use their products. They pay attention to myriad tiny details, such as how an item might be held by a consumer. Rubbermaid product designers have been known to work in restaurants or hospitals to see what problems users of Rubbermaid products encounter. While it rarely engages in test marketing, Rubbermaid routinely uses consumer panels and focus groups to brainstorm new product ideas in a new (or old) product category or to assist business development teams all the way through a product's development.

At Rubbermaid the reward system also stands squarely behind new products. For starters, managers' compensation is in part tied to new product introductions, but the reward system for ideas goes much deeper. Like many companies, Rubbermaid has a suggestion program to which employees can contribute ideas of how to make the company a better place. Many firms reward people with cash or a night on the town. Every year, Rubbermaid picks out a random collection of people who contributed ideas (not just those whose ideas were implemented) and treats them to a visit to a huge housewares trade show in Chicago. There they can see Rubbermaid and competitors' products side by side, and so gain a better sense of the competition and generate new ideas for Rubbermaid.

The company fully understands, however, the difference between good ideas and innovations. They put backbone into this distinction with a strict "return-on-assets employed" screen for each product. Among other things, this enables the firm to weed out likely losers before they reach the market. This ability to project winners and losers is a skill that can build up only over time, but Rubbermaid has been unveiling new products long enough to have a pretty good idea of what will sell at what price and how much profit it can reap from a product. If the expected return on the assets employed (in research, manufacturing tools, and so on) for a product line does not meet a specific target, usually about 13 percent, then it will likely be killed before it gets very far through the product development cycle. The number makes this discipline seem more scientific than it really is. One executive comments, "If this were all science, it would be dull." The reality is that they "swag"* their way into these decisions.

Finally, every employee is acutely aware of the set of tough goals handed down from the top levels of Rubbermaid. This creates something of a crisis atmosphere at the company, even while it maintains growth rates and profits that would satisfy most corporate executives. It's impossible to get complacent in a culture with targets that include:

- Achieving a 15 percent compounded annual growth in sales and earnings.
- Garnering 33 percent of each year's revenues from products introduced in the previous five years.
- Achieving in each division a 13 percent return on the assets employed to produce products.
- Realizing a 20 percent return on average shareholders' equity.

Such strict financial goals can have a detrimental effect at some companies, forcing people to strive for brass rings that are really out of reach. Clearly there are limits to any compound growth target. Rubbermaid recognizes this and says that when they start to feel the strains of that growth target, they'll adjust. But now, they believe, they are nowhere near the limit. They are

*From "swinging wild-assed guess," for those not already familiar with the technical terminology for this combination of hard numbers and experience.

doing what we saw David Swanson do in a different way at Procter & Gamble: creating a sense of urgency through a sense of crisis. (This sounds, and is, manipulative. On the other hand, most organizations don't seem to change without crisis. Leaders of renewing companies understand this and create a sense of crisis, they hope, before the real crisis hits.)

MAILBOX MANIA

The case of the rural mailbox offers a telling illustration of how Rubbermaid deftly mixes its rigorous product development system with a good dose of creativity and flexibility. Rick Margin, the manager who craves "boring" products, counts it among his jobs to identify trends, and year after year one unmistakable trend emerged from the consumer mail that crossed his desk. Leading the list of what customers wanted from Rubbermaid was, of all things, a mailbox. The letters arrived in particularly great volume each year after Halloween when Americans with mailboxes at the end of the driveway found them mutilated by pranksters. Couldn't Rubbermaid make one that was vandal-proof?

Mailboxes weren't exactly in the mainstream of Rubbermaid's product offerings, but starting in the mid-1980s the idea began to make some sense. It was then that Rubbermaid, having captured nearly all the shelf space it was likely to get in retailers' housewares departments, began to expand into hardware. And there mailboxes would fit right in. Still, for years the idea of making mailboxes would crop up on potential new products lists at Rubbermaid, only to be dropped like a hot potato. It wasn't clear to the company how it could bring value to the consumer—how it could make its mailboxes clearly superior to the next vendor's. And if Rubbermaid people don't think they can add value to a product line, they won't pursue it.

Finally, in 1989, mailboxes began a long grind through the housewares division's semi-official eight-step product development process, with a few unexpected detours along the way. The eight-step process includes precise phases of evaluation, development, design, capitalization, and introduction, which teams adapt to the product at hand. A brand new product might pass through all eight official stages, while the process would be less strictly applied to a line extension, since Rubbermaid would already have considerable data about buying patterns and costs. At various points, division management reviews the plan so that by the time substantial money and effort have been invested, the new product is almost a certain "go."

Although the product development system is fairly straightforward and not much different from what one might find at other companies, how rigorously it is executed is different. So is how Rubbermaid has managed to do what so many firms just talk about: getting input early on from the many parts of the organization that will eventually have to handle the new product; working up front with customers; enforcing rigorous financial targets and keeping costs under control. The cycle from idea to commercialization, which typically takes about twelve to eighteen months, is structured to protect financial and personnel resources—to involve as few people and dollars as possible at first. As the idea passes various hurdles, more resources are added until the product is finally introduced.

The process starts with identification of the product, in this case mailboxes, followed by a brief research phase that involves assessing market potential and financial viability. If, after those steps, a product receives the nod from managers in the division, a product manager from the marketing department is assigned to it. The next step is what Rubbermaid calls concept development, when employees in marketing, manufacturing, and research work together to consider options for the product's design, to look at what challenges the factory would face, and so on. That's followed quickly by screening, the process by which the product proposal is subjected to financial analysis and in some cases discussed with retailers.

Ideas for the Rubbermaid mailbox design came from all sorts of channels. For one thing, the company turned to its favorite method of testing consumer tastes—focus groups. In Boston,

San Diego, St. Louis, and Atlanta, consumers were called together in small groups and shown both the mailboxes already on
the market and Rubbermaid's mock-ups. In a novel twist, Rubbermaid held focus groups for this product with postal carriers,
who turned out to be far more outspoken and opinionated than
the average mailbox buyer. The company also conducted mail
and telephone surveys with the aim of finding out why people
buy new mailboxes. (The answer: a third said theirs were worn
out, a third said they had fallen victim to vandalism, and a third
said they were for new houses.)

From this research a number of requirements emerged. Carriers complained that they were always getting blamed for ripped
catalogues and magazines that had to be jammed into too-small
mailboxes. So the boxes should be larger than most on the market. Consumers also complained about damp mail after rain
storms. So they had to be water-tight. Consumers complained
about installation—anchoring a post in the ground and bolting
the mailbox to the post was usually considered far too much
work. So they had to be easy to assemble. And consumers were
frustrated that they'd sometimes walk out to their box, only to
find the mail hadn't yet arrived. So they had to have some way of
signaling that the mail carrier had been by. Finally, more than
anything, consumers complained about mailboxes being
knocked down by overzealous kids, usually armed with a baseball bat and a mean swing. So they had to be sturdy. "I wanted it
baseball bat–proof," Margin remembers.

Because of input from manufacturing experts at Rubbermaid,
the designers faced several tough engineering requirements, too.
For example, Rubbermaid wanted the mailbox to be made from
one solid mold, thereby eliminating seams in the plastic to make
the box more durable.

Although its own designers were involved, Rubbermaid
turned first to an independent design firm in Columbus, Ohio, to
come up with mailbox concepts that would meet the requirements that the market research had uncovered. The partnership
was kicked off with a meeting between several people from the
design firm and the nascent Rubbermaid mailbox team. It was

held in a room packed with thirty different mailboxes from other vendors, which helped the participants brainstorm ideas for their new design. Some ideas flew; others got shot down. For example, a few of the developers wanted to supply numbers so that people could put their address on the box, but that proved uneconomical. There also was talk of having a mailbox with two doors so that people could retrieve their mail without stepping into a busy street. That idea died also; too expensive.

After just a few weeks, the outside designers presented a number of potential designs, which the Rubbermaid team narrowed to three. Those were fine-tuned and finally reduced to one, which was brought in-house for more detailed work. Then the engineering stage kicked in, during which the final details of the product plan were drafted. Cost estimates were honed, and a final budget was drawn up that took into account manufacturing and merchandising needs. In November 1990, the team again turned to consumers, this time to find out what colors would be best. It sponsored mall intercepts* in Cleveland, Tulsa, and Albany during which shoppers were asked to review several Rubbermaid mock-ups. From these interviews, the team decided on producing black and deep blue. Then, when the Rubbermaid team toted the prototype around the country to give key retailers their first glimpse, they learned that in Florida, buyers insist on white mailboxes.

The next step was to get final approval from the managers of the housewares division. Once that was granted, the mailbox progressed into the capitalization phase. The process really picked up steam during this phase, when sizable expenditures were made for designing and building molds for the plastic, for creating advertising and merchandising displays, and for finalizing pricing. Manufacturing faced a special challenge with the mailbox. Because of the requirement that the box be sturdy and made of one piece of plastic, manufacturing had to invent a new type of tooling.

Things are supposed to go smoothly after the capitalization

*A sampling of consumers interviewed while they are shopping at malls.

phase, but in the case of the mailbox, there were several hitches. Mailbox specifications are set by the government, and Rubbermaid got caught several times in the grip of Uncle Sam. For one thing, the interior of the mailbox turned out to be a tad shorter than required, so the inside of the door had to be shaved to make the interior longer. The handle had to be redesigned, too, for easier operation by someone wearing a glove. All this required a costly redesign of some of the manufacturing tooling that had already been completed. Then, Rubbermaid was forced to delay introduction because the government was late in issuing new regulations, and it couldn't certify the box until the new regulations had been approved.

Finally, the Rubbermaid mailbox was ready for commercialization. It made its debut in February 1992, four months behind the hoped-for introduction date around Halloween 1991. The mailbox emerged in three colors (black, blue, and white), and in three sizes, with a leak-proof door, a design that made it easy-to-install, and a little yellow flag that pops up after mail has been deposited in the box. Rubbermaid people feel certain it's baseball bat–proof, too, but they don't dare advertise that in case there's a budding Babe Ruth on the block. One added bonus in the eyes of Rubbermaid's environmentally conscious top management: The post is made of recycled resin.

All the mailbox's key features, the pricing, the packaging, and the manufacturing details, had been decided by the business team. Says Jim Dehner, who was group product manager for hardware during the mailbox development: "The teams have a tremendous amount of freedom and latitude."

TEAMWORK AT WORK

It is a Friday morning and Rob Cockfield is sitting in a windowless conference room, at the corner of an oblong table, leaning forward in his chair and ticking through agenda items at a rapid pace. It's the monthly meeting of his cleaning-products, rubber-gloves, and vacuum-bags team, and a glimpse of how they spend their two hours offers a brief picture of the Rubbermaid innovation process at work.

Gathered around the table are specialists from manufacturing, packaging, purchasing, finance, consumer research, product design, engineering, and Cockfield's department, marketing. Together they're responsible for several dozen different products, some made under contract to Rubbermaid by outside firms and others made by Rubbermaid itself. There's a good bit of joking and needling of one another, and people jump in freely whenever they have something to add. This process offers some checks and balances. Someone from marketing really wants a new product; manufacturing poses the financial or technical constraints. One person wants to forge ahead with a new item, another points out the logistical problems with meeting a proposed deadline. Through an ongoing exchange of ideas, a process that continues long after the meetings officially end, compromises always seem to emerge.

Cockfield keeps the meeting moving swiftly by working line by line through the four-page minutes of the last meeting, which constitute this meeting's agenda. For instance, one item is the question of new blue rubber gloves, which are coming from an outside supplier whose claims about their features contradict those found in Rubbermaid's laboratory tests. One participant notes that consumers have complained about fingers on existing gloves sticking together. There's also the item regarding what pattern to have in the material that will make up a new mop head. Several are laid out on the table. Should the pattern include the Rubbermaid logo? "Somebody will get upset putting the Rubbermaid name on the floor. It's like putting the flag on the floor," Cockfield suggests. Including the logo is nixed.

The team runs through other items—packaging that's falling off one type of scrub brush; a planned barbecue brush that might not be ready for the summer season. But the heftiest topic for the day involves a new line of modular cleaning equipment that Rubbermaid hopes to introduce. Instead of buying a mop or broom all in one piece, a consumer could pick up the head and the pole handle separately. Rubbermaid figures that should make for a neater display in the retail store as well as save costs in packaging and shipping. It's one piece of a strategy to boost Rubbermaid's cleaning products line, which wasn't performing up to the company's financial standards. The line is somewhat unusual because of its reliance on outside vendors. Cockfield hopes eventually to make the items in this line in-house.

A sense of urgency takes hold in the room as team members review the myriad details that have to get done in order to make a deadline, two months away, to begin testing the modular concept in certain Target discount stores. (Test-marketing is rare for Rubbermaid products, but this is an exception.) Components are coming from all over, including Italy, Canada, and Rubbermaid's own factory in Statesville, N.C., where the products will be assembled, and no one is quite certain how they'll all fit together yet. One problem of the morning: the white heads from one supplier don't match the white poles from another. The group resolved the issue of which white they should shoot for by making a trip downstairs to Rubbermaid's color lab, where store light and day light can be simulated, so that they could compare the components under different light.

That's how decisions are made: a group of people, experts not in color but in common sense, trading ideas and thoughts and reaching a consensus. Within a few minutes, everyone involved agreed which white should prevail. Cockfield believes the group decision-making process is far more successful than relying solely on individual judgment. "With ten people sitting around the table, if there's something missing, someone will catch it," he says.

One key to the product teams' success is that they represent a blend of group and individual dynamics. Each person brings a particular expertise to the table yet must be knowledgeable enough to challenge the others' assumptions. And that person must be able to do so without fearing a backlash. In the same sense, each person has certain tasks, but in order to accomplish them he or she may well need to depend upon others on the team. Finding the formula for successful teamwork is tough for many companies, which often swing too wildly toward either "groupthink" or individual accountability. Rubbermaid has found the right balance. While there is a certain camaraderie at Rubbermaid that makes working together fun, each member is motivated by his or her own specialized task and by a personal sense of responsibility to the group. Few people miss deadlines in their assignments, because they know their colleagues are counting on them. "If you miss a date you feel real [guilty]," one team member said.

And because each person has a specialized task, each one can also come away with that always-important sense of ownership. Everyone can feel they made a difference, an important factor in keeping people motivated. "It always impresses me how much of an influence each of us has," says Bob Miller, a twenty-seven-year veteran in the purchasing department. Miller could scarcely contain his enthusiasm over his contribution to a soon-to-be-released Rubbermaid broom. He had found the European vendor that could supply the broom and reviewed that idea with his team members, who quickly saw the merit in the concept. "I worked out the whole deal," he says. "I feel good about that personally."

Of course, some more mundane factors also keep the team members' batteries charged. For one thing, they're individually evaluated for compensation. For another, financial return on asset and agreed upon sales growth goals are always hanging over their heads. "It is our job to make sure we're meeting our financial objectives. It's our personal challenge to make this thing work," says Dave Sudzina, a manufacturing specialist. "What drives a person is a sense of urgency and challenge."

Another motivator is simply that deadlines are always looming. There's little time to kick back at Rubbermaid, because the list of things to do keeps growing. A division might have an active list of hundreds of potential new products and revisions that need to be made to existing product lines. That forces people to set and reset priorities constantly, a healthy process and another way of keeping focused in the midst of complexity. To be sure, this creates a certain amount of pressure. One employee said top managers always want "more, more, more," while another said he faced "a lot of demands." Yet both said the stress was manageable.

There's also a certain amount of "creative tension" built into the process at Rubbermaid, to quote a favorite expression of CEO Schmitt's. He defines "creative tension" as "competition between great ideas," and by that he means that everyone walks into a meeting touting his or her own solution to a problem and walks out united with everyone else behind a group decision. Employees say it's not always quite that smooth. One manager describes the process this way: "It's like a sled with five horses going in different directions." He adds that somehow the sled keeps advancing, however.

Finally, Rubbermaid people stay motivated to innovate because they know they can fail without reprisal. About 90 percent of the new products Rubbermaid introduces each year are successful. That is partly because the firm is often just making incremental changes to a product or extending a product line, so it has built up enough of a track record to know what is likely to succeed. Indeed, Rubbermaid is far more successful in introducing incrementally improved products than in introducing brand new items, where Schmitt estimates the failure rate could be as high as 50 percent. But when such products do fail, there isn't much remorse because no products are ever expected to be out-of-the-park home runs. With so many mundane but reliable moneymakers scoring every day, a few outright losers barely impact company results.

And back at headquarters, top management tries to emphasize that it's okay to take risks, whatever the result. A favorite story of Schmitt's is to reminisce about his early days at Rubbermaid, when he was in charge of a line of winter and summer recreational products. The line included plastic boats and plastic sleds, but some strategic mistakes and a couple warm winters caused the line to flop. Schmitt remembers: "The important thing is we sank the business and the then-chairman came down and said, 'We just wanted you to know that even though this business is being liquidated, we don't in any way hold you or your team accountable for its demise. You have great futures here.' "

— — —

NORMALLY when you think innovation, you think high-tech. Rubbermaid is not that, at least not in the scientific sense. But its systems for inventing products that meet or anticipate market needs are as sophisticated, and in that sense high-tech, as any you will find. And normally when you think strategy, you think of the brilliant general who makes great decisions. Certainly the executives at Rubbermaid do some of that. More than anything else, however, their strategy anticipates the needs of customers and innovates to keep them more than pleased. What makes their strategy, well . . . strategic, is how well they have organized themselves to innovate.

9.

HIGH-TECH SOAP
Great Products Make
for Great Marketing

Until I started interviewing in Cincinnati, I thought
of Procter & Gamble as a fine consumer-products company. I
still do. But now, first and foremost, I think of P&G as a technology powerhouse. Of course its people are great marketers. But
for them, marketing would be an empty discipline if they didn't
have something outstanding to sell. When they go to market with
a new product, P&G employees firmly believe that it's far better
than anything else out there.

As we'll see, Procter & Gamble sells better mousetraps. No
wonder it has committed, turned-on people. When the company
slaps the words "new and improved" on a product label, the stuff
inside really is. At P&G we find:

- Highly visible top management interest in—and commitment
  to—research and development (R&D).
- Hefty spending to maintain technological leadership
- The formation of global R&D teams, which may be why
  P&G's investment in technology has paid off so handsomely in
  recent years.
- Seemingly mundane products that are technically quite so-

phisticated. If P&G says "new and improved," it really is. (Their marketing secret: something better to sell.)

- A combination of information, organizational flexibility, and commercial purpose that brings order out of seeming chaos.
- An ingenious way of linking R&D to market need.

It's not hard to pick up on P&G's commitment to technology. The trail takes you straight to the company's famous eleventh-floor headquarters. My first meeting with Chairman and Chief Executive Ed Artzt had to be rescheduled; he was attending an important research and development meeting. When I did see Artzt, my first question was about the four or five main challenges facing American business—and P&G—as we move toward the third millennium. His immediate response: "Technology is really what drives our business. For our company the main challenge is to maintain an edge in technology."

Artzt's biggest concern is protecting the company's investment in R&D. And he asserts that this is an issue for all Americans. Foreign governments and companies have detailed information on some of our most sensitive technology. It's not that their spies are so great. It's that we have to reveal so much to get U.S. patent protection.

Artzt's predecessor, John Smale, agrees that American firms must bank on technology. Like Artzt he deeply believes that the company's commitment to research and development is central to its 150-year history of success. As Smale said, "I have the rock-solid conviction that anything we achieve in the way of volume and profit growth has got to be based on superior product.

"If you look at the basic products that make the company profitable today, the vast majority were discontinuities when they were put on the market—real innovations at the time: Tide, Always, Crisco, Crest, Pampers, Head & Shoulders. Always is a relatively new product that's taken the leadership position in the sanitary napkin business. Why? Not because we're better mar-

keters or better packagers or even better manufacturers. Always
is a superior product."

The best indication of the importance P&G attaches to technology is not its words but its actions. Gordon Brunner is P&G's
senior vice-president in charge of R&D. His office isn't cloistered
in some research center. He sits on the eleventh floor with all the
other top brass and reports directly to the chief executive. "As
you look back over the years," he says, "our CEOs have been
the leaders of innovation. They have to be. Any innovative company has to be led by innovation from the top."

Brunner's relationship with the CEO not only signals the importance of R&D; it also keeps him and the other top operational executives on the same wavelength. He's in constant touch
with what their divisions need. In turn, the operating companies
are in constant touch with what's possible through technology.

In 1992 P&G spent approximately $900 million on R&D. It's
a big number: 3 percent of sales. Motorola spends 10 percent of
its sales dollar on R&D. You'd expect that: Motorola is a high-
tech company. But when you figure the relative size of the two
companies—P&G with $30 billion in total revenues, and
Motorola with $13 billion—the raw dollar amount spent on
R&D is about the same. On average, P&G spends one-and-a-
half to two times as much as other consumer-products companies spend for R&D.

P&G is in a wide variety of businesses, from beverages to
pharmaceuticals. And its people are the first to point out that the
percent of sales is only a rough indication of the importance they
attach to technology. Obviously the money put into beverage
research will be proportionately less than what's devoted to
pharmaceuticals. The kicker is that whether it's soap, sanitary
napkins, or any other apparently ordinary item, Procter & Gamble applies leading edge research to make better products. They
want to surprise and please consumers with superior performance.

GLOBAL REACH

Employees of P&G still like to tell the story of a soap shipment that was delayed for a day, solely because it was not up to P&G's quality standards. The customer was the army. It was wartime and the troops badly needed the soap. They're talking about the Civil War. P&G's 150-year history is one of product leadership and a belief in marketing nothing less than the best product its people know how to make.

Despite its long commitment to product leadership and technology, the company may have only recently hit full stride in learning to manage R&D. As Brunner reflects, "We were very decentralized in the seventies. Each of the operating divisions had its own R&D operation, and then we had a corporate R&D unit in our Miami laboratories. But people were pretty much doing their own thing. Corporate would come in and throw something over the fence every once in awhile, and that's the way it was."

P&G's structure in Europe cast harsh light on the situation. "I first went to Europe in 1976," Brunner explains. "We were in nine countries and were doing nine different things on every product. We had nine different Camays, Dashes, and so on. We were working our tails off doing very little. Every time we found something that was good—a technical advance or a new marketing idea—we couldn't apply it elsewhere because every country had a different system. So we were going nowhere fast."

P&G decided that it ought to look at research on a pan-European basis. Instead of focusing on national differences, it concentrated on similarities. P&G looked across country boundaries at competition, product needs, and consumer needs, and then set research priorities based on Europewide understanding. The assumption behind this was that a true product breakthrough would be as appealing to the French as it would be to the Germans. Furthermore, by linking research across Europe, P&G reasoned that the flow of ideas and information would improve dramatically. The best ideas would match the main product priorities whether the ideas came from Sweden, England, or Luxembourg.

Brunner says that the idea was not readily accepted at the time. The European units were used to operating independently. Would this new organization be as responsive to local market needs, they wondered? But the scheme worked and became the model for what P&G is now trying to do globally. "We now know that if you can hit the toughest needs anywhere in the world, you are liable to have a product which will better meet consumer needs everywhere in the world. It's that simple."

Liquid Tide was P&G's first effort at worldwide product development. Market research showed that many consumers prefer suds in liquid form. At the time, however, the granular form simply worked better: In the granular product you could get a higher concentration of water-softening chemicals. Another problem was that in concentrated liquid form, some of the enzymes necessary to the cleaning process reacted in the bottle, before they got into the washing machine. One other issue: Consumers found liquid detergents messy; they dripped down the side of the bottle. In the early 1980s P&G put together a global team to invent a liquid that performed at least as well as any granular product on the market. By 1984 they'd solved the chemistry problems. They'd also developed a bottle cap to seal in, measure, and permit drain-back into the bottle after measuring, which solved the gooey bottle issue. Today, liquid Tide is the number one liquid brand in America.

The company's ability to pull together a world team on liquid Tide is directly related to a major reorganization that took place in 1983. A vice-president was given responsibility for R&D for each business sector, including laundry and cleaning, beverages, paper, and so on. Those people reported straight to Brunner's predecessor in Cincinnati, who in turn reported directly to the CEO. At that time, Brunner managed R&D for laundry and cleaning. Reporting to him were a group of the discipline's best and brightest scientists. He also had direct access to the key research folks in P&G laundry and cleaning operations around the world. The company looked to Brunner and his counterparts in other sectors to set worldwide research priorities. Their job was to say to general management: "Here are the three to six key things we have to get done to capture or maintain product leadership around the world." Working with top management and operating managers, their job was to pull together global teams around those priorities and make sure the teams were well staffed and well led.

BETTER MOUSETRAPS

Consumer-product science isn't rocket science, but in some cases it is nearly as complex. Just look at the list of product breakthroughs that P&G made in the 1980s.

Liquid Tide   The first big win and, as we saw, a huge breakthrough both technically and commercially.

Pert Plus   The question was how can you deliver a shampoo and conditioner in one package. When you take shampoo, which is negatively charged, and mix it with conditioner that's positively charged, the two interact. "You end up with this goo that doesn't clean or condition," says Brunner. "Other than that, it's okay." The team's goal this time was to develop a hybrid product that cleaned and conditioned as well as the best shampoos and conditioners on the market.

The chemistry of Pert Plus is complex, but the breakthrough came when P&G invented a special polymer, a matrix of long-chain molecules. While the mixture is in the bottle, this polymer keeps the chemicals that do the shampooing away from the ones that do the conditioning. When Pert Plus comes out of the bottle, goes on your hair, and gets a little wet, the shampoo comes out of suspension and does its thing. Then, as you lather up and further dilute the mixture, the conditioner comes out of suspension and goes to work. "It's an outstanding technology," boasts Brunner. "I think we will look back on it as one of our great innovations. It got us back into the leading position in hair-care products around the world, a position where we were weak." Indeed, these days Pert Plus and its international brand counterparts are top brands in the United States, Japan, the Far East, Europe, and Latin America.

Tartar Control Crest   In the early 1950s, P&G came up with a toothpaste called Crest. Although the fluoride in the product did reduce cavities, consumer awareness of (or perhaps, belief in) Crest's advantage stayed mystifyingly low. In 1954, John Smale, then brand manager for Crest, had a bright idea. He talked with the American Dental Association about endorsing the product. Six years later they did. The ADA has since endorsed lots of toothpaste brands, but Crest won a leadership position that it has never lost.

It might have lost, however, were it not for another 1980s worldwide research effort. Now you can buy Crest with both flouride and an antitartar ingredient. The research story behind this one is another example of how P&G uses its global resources. Because of its experience in the laundry business, P&G knows calcium chemistry. Calcium compounds make water hard and have to be taken out to get clothes really clean. Calcium carbonate is the tartar that builds up on your teeth, causes stains, and gives you pain when the dentist scrapes it away. At P&G the chemistry used to soften water inspired the research leading to tartar control.

With this product P&G has taken over about 40 percent of the dentifrice market in the United States and has strengthened its position in Latin America and Europe. For example, when P&G merged with Richardson Vicks in 1985, it acquired a brand in Italy known as AZ toothpaste. By putting their tartar-control technology into that brand they tripled their market share in fairly short order.

Didronel   "As we were learning how to control calcium in both toothpaste and detergents," Brunner recalls, "we were also learning a lot about how calcium builds bone." This understanding led to a new prescription drug called Didronel. Brunner and others at P&G talk about several studies recently published in the prestigious *New England Journal of Medicine.* One study was conducted in Denmark by a group of Danish scientists. The others were carried out in the United States. The researchers focused on postmenopausal women and others who are susceptible to osteoporosis. Each study reports a reversal in bone loss as a direct effect of taking Didronel. Brunner says that, Didronel is the only drug known to have that effect.

P&G is now applying for FDA approval. They already have approval in the Netherlands, Great Britain, and France. Didronel could be the product that kicks the company's fledgling pharmaceuticals business out of the nest.

Tide with bleach   Chlorine bleach has been around a long time, but it has three problems: it fades colors, it's not stable when mixed in the same package with detergent, and it has questionable environmental effects. There are certain forms of oxygen that can also be used as bleach, but they don't work well in short-cycle washing machines, such as most of those in use in the United States and Japan. They also don't work when a washing machine's water temperature is set on its warm or cool cycle.

To overcome these problems P&G came up with something they call "activated bleach." It involves two chemicals, perborate and an activator, that are stable in a detergent granule. But when a consumer adds them to the wash, they interact to form a new bleaching compound called "peracid." Says Brunner, "It does a marvelous job of cleaning, and we own all the patents on it. Nobody had made it previously, so we had to develop it from scratch, prove its safety, and put it in the marketplace. Today we can't fill the demand."

Downy   Fabric softeners have been around for at least twenty years. Though P&G held the lead in this business, there had been no real innovations in this product category for about fifteen years. Then Lever Brothers came out with a product similar to what P&G was offering but at a lower price. Since there wasn't much difference between the two, the Lever product cut away at P&G's margins.

Once again P&G put together a global team. People from Europe, the United States, Canada, and Japan joined forces to develop a fabric softener that consumers everywhere in the world would recognize and accept as a superior product. The team created a cationic, or positively charged, material that has a 50 micron particle size and a soft feel. Fabrics have a negative charge. When the new Downy goes into solution in the wash, it's immediately attracted to the fabric surface. Its tiny particle size allows it to penetrate deep into fibers of cotton and other fabrics, causing them to feel soft. By 1990, Downy's success had restored P&G's share of this business to levels not seen since 1970.

Always   Built on a dryness strategy, Always is a sanitary napkin with a top sheet made of an unwoven polypropylene. If you put it under a magnifying glass it looks like a host of tiny volcanoes arrayed in a serpentine Z-shaped pattern. The purpose of this strange looking construction is to allow fluid to flow only one way and to hold a lot of that fluid in a fairly thin sheet. For the consumer, this combination of a dry feel and non-bulky construction has been extremely appealing.

Ultra Pampers   In the 1960s and 1970s, P&G's megahit was Pampers, a brand name almost synonymous with disposable diapers. In the same category, the big innovation in the 1980s was Ultra Pampers. Interspersed in this diaper is an absorbent gelling material that has the capacity to hold about two hundred times more water than the cellulose used in disposable diapers of the past. Urine passes through the diaper and is locked in. It can't be squeezed out by the squirmiest baby, whose bottom thus stays dry (and the baby may be less likely to cry.)

Along with soothing parental nerves, Ultra Pampers technology also slightly eases their troubled environmental consciences. Ultra Pampers use about 40 percent less material than regular Pampers, so that much less goes into landfills. P&G folks believe that Ultra Pampers have revolutionized the diaper category worldwide.

— — —

THEY HAVE A RIGHT to tout their products. P&G's saga of invention in the 1980s is exciting. Not only does their leadership in technology make for great strategy, it also keeps people everywhere in the organization charged up. P&G is not in the mundane business of peddling soap: P&G makes and sells high-tech soap. Looking at it from inside, one can make a case that P&G's business is every bit as exciting as the computer business—maybe more so these days when there are so many computer manufacturers selling such similar products.

MANAGING CHAOS

"It's much more difficult to manage really good R&D," says John Smale, "than to manage anything else, be it advertising, sales, or manufacturing, because there's much more of the unknown about it." The history of innovation not only supports him; it makes you wonder if you *can* manage R&D. Consider the following:

- Green mold grew accidentally in a petri dish in 1928, and Sir Alexander Fleming discovered penicillin.
- Working at IBM, Benoit Mandelbrot tried to simulate price movements on the cotton exchange. Noticing that the pattern of movement, whether the data were hourly, daily, or yearly, looked roughly the same, he discovered a new field of mathematics called fractals—a field that could become as important as Newtonian calculus.
- In the winter of 1961, M.I.T. researcher Edward Lorenz, trying to simulate weather patterns, turned off his computer midrun. When he turned it back on and entered the same data, the result started to come out differently. A new and important field of science—chaos theory—was discovered.[1]

- Singing in church, Art Fry, a 3M employee, grew irritated that
  the pieces of paper he used to keep his place in the hymnal
  kept falling out between services. Spence Silver, another 3M
  employee, was working on bonding material. He invented
  something sticky but not sticky enough, so he sent a memo
  around the company asking if anyone needed something like
  that. Nobody did, except for Art Fry, and the ubiquitous Post-
  it was born.

What do these stories have in common? On the surface nothing. From green mold to chaos theory to Post-its, the history of
innovation is itself a history of apparent chaos. But just as chaos
in nature seems to have general, and usually quite beautiful,
patterns, so does innovation. The pattern that seems most common is a kaleidoscope of information, direction, determination,
and flexibility. From Fleming to Fry, innovators are deeply informed about the relevant technology in their fields and those
closely related. From Silver to Mandelbrot, innovators work
under institutional arrangements that are goal-driven but ex-
traordinarily flexible. Neither side of this teeter-totter of information and flexibility, however, works by itself. If would-be innovators are merely well informed, they will study things but
rarely actually *do* any innovating. If they're not goal-driven and
are working under conditions that are too flexible, they may
invent nifty stuff, but stuff that is often not useful in any commercial sense.

Organizations continue to err on both sides of the balance.
The big ones frequently over-manage, making institutional arrangements so inflexible that people are not permitted to make
mistakes. But how do you innovate if you can't experiment?
How can you experiment without making mistakes? The discovery of penicillin was a "mistake." Many other researchers had
thrown out petri dishes contaminated by green mold. Thus the
keys to innovation that we talked about in *In Search of Excellence*
and that I reported on in *The Renewal Factor:* skunk works, boot-
legging, product champions, small divisions. That's why the
higher proportion of innovation per research dollar seems to

come from small companies. These places aren't hog-tied by all the "normal channels" and structures; they give innovators some space to make mistakes.

But the "small is beautiful" mentality is only half the story. Small companies repeatedly get themselves into big-time trouble by being too flexible. It happens in my back yard, Silicon Valley, all the time. Companies get started and prosper on the strength of one innovation, usually the idea of someone who has left an information-rich corporate environment. That was the case of Steve Wozniak, who left Hewlett-Packard to join Steve Jobs and start Apple Computer. Unlike Wozniak and Jobs, others often founder. They get rich and lose the sense of mission that got them started. They lose the ability to keep up with the science in their field. Or they simply get bored with what to them might seem like the grubby business of commercialization. They'd rather work on the next whiz-bang thing. So, the commercialization of new technology gets done by others, often the Japanese.

P&G's management of R&D seems to pull all the right elements together nicely. Through the use of teams, they stay flexible. Because they direct their technology only toward consumer products, and spend big on it, they stay abreast of the latest relevant science. Notice, for example, how many of their breakthroughs relate to the calcium chemistry needed originally for better soaps and detergents. Keeping up with that area bled over into other areas of product development. Now that teams are global, sharing their insights, they stay even better informed. Finally, because management stays closely involved, R&D goals are clear: don't just invent; innovate and commercialize.

MARKET UNDERSTANDING

For years P&G has charged its R&D people with the responsibility for understanding the consumer. This means that the very same people who need to be great technical researchers are also very competent market researchers. P&G researchers explain that much of their progress depends on how well they can measure what they are trying to achieve. Take hair for example. The consumer says, "I want my hair to be conditioned." What does that mean? Do consumers look at that in terms of softness? Do they judge it by how hair combs when it's wet? How it feels when it's dry? How it combs when it's dry? What about shine? How do you measure all these facets?

The trick is to take the consumers' very subjective answers, find out what they mean by a term like "softness," and then turn that into something that the labs can measure physically. Turning subjective consumer preferences into hard science is so important to P&G that almost all technical people spend time in what the company calls its products-research function. There they work with market-research people to design tests, learn how to measure consumer response, and become expert on consumer research.

Brunner and others commented that they had no idea how unusual this approach was until they started acquiring other companies. Then they realized the real power and uniqueness of their approach.

One of the things P&G researchers learn sounds just like Rubbermaid's admonishment to sweat the details. Brunner calls it "being a little bit obnoxious about detail." He says that you have to get exercised about how high a cake rises or how much foam a shampoo generates. "Sometimes we get all excited about what seems to be a very trivial thing. Yet it's that combination of trivial things that makes a truly better product," he comments, getting very excited about that idea himself.

— — —

IN PROCTER & GAMBLE WE HAVE another company that maintains strategic edge by simply out innovating competition. And like Rubbermaid they achieve this edge through the way they organize to innovate. In both companies something else happens that we shall see strongly in evidence at Merck. Once momentum starts, each part of the system reinforces the others. Exciting results attract top people (the challenge factor again), and top people produce exciting results.

10.

DESIGNER MOLECULES

**Merck Invests and
Invents . . . Big Time**

In the fall of 1975, Dr. Julianne Imperato-McGinley of New York's Cornell Medical College published an arcane monograph on the people who inhabit a remote village in the Caribbean—not the usual reading material for the top brass of billion dollar companies. But Merck, the $9.6 billion pharmaceutical company headquartered in Rahway, New Jersey, is different. Dr. P. Roy Vagelos, now Merck chairman, but then Merck's chief of basic research, says that he came across that paper and said to himself, "Gee, that's got to be [something] we should follow." He walked down the hall to find Glen Arth, a senior biochemist. "Glen," he recalls, "was walking toward my office holding the same article."

The article described people deficient in the enzyme 5-alpha-reductase (5AR). Because of this deficiency, while the fetus is still in the womb normal production of a principal male hormone—dihydrotestosterone—doesn't occur. As a result, many normal male characteristics don't develop until male hormones really start to rage during puberty, or they never develop at all. People with this deficiency are what the scientific community calls "pseudohermaphrodites." Hermaphrodites have the sexual organs of both genders; pseudohermaphrodites appear to have the sexual organs of both genders, but in fact are primarily one sex or the other.

The people in the Caribbean village affected by the 5AR deficiency look female at birth. In fact, their families raise them as girls. But as they mature their voices deepen, they grow external genitalia, and they develop a masculine muscle structure. All those afflicted, it turns out, had a common ancestor. She passed the mutant gene on to one of her great-grandchildren. Seven of her great-great-grandchildren inherited it, as did fourteen of her great-great-great-grandchildren and seventeen of her great-great-great-great-grandchildren.[1] (Inbreeding among the people increased the odds that parents would pass the defect on to their children.)

The research was fascinating, but what really caught Arth's and Vagelos's attention was Imperato-McGinley's description of one particular aspect of the physical condition of the adults: "The prostate . . . remains small [throughout the person's life]."[2]

The prostate is a walnut-sized organ positioned near the urinary tract, the bladder, and the penis. It provides the lubricating fluid that transports semen during sex. As men age, the prostate enlarges, interfering with urine flow and reducing the capacity of the bladder. By the time they reach their sixties, more than half of all men experience prostate enlargement, and the proportion increases with age. Unfortunately, the common surgical treatment of advanced enlargement is almost as bad as the disease: It is painful and can result in impotence. It is also expensive: American men spend an estimated $3 billion annually on the procedure.

Perhaps the condition of the Caribbean villagers might yield a clue for a nonsurgical way to combat prostate enlargement. Apparently, the absence of 5AR prevents the conversion of testosterone to dihydrotestosterone, which seems to be related to development of male organs in children and teenagers but also enlarges the prostate.

Seventeen years later—count them, *seventeen*—on June 22, 1992, Merck won FDA approval to market Proscar. This drug promises to be the world's first effective nonsurgical treatment for prostate enlargement. Like Rubbermaid and P&G, Merck wins in the marketplace by out-innovating the competition. Many analysts predict that Proscar may eventually be the company's third billion-dollar drug.* The others are Mevacor, which lowers serum cholesterol and Vasotec, a drug introduced in 1986 to combat high-blood pressure and now an effective drug in treating congestive heart failure.

From its role in 1942 as one of the pioneering firms producing penicillin, Merck has sustained the development of new drugs at a truly astonishing rate. Profits have followed, and executives from near and far applaud the company's success: In 1993, and for its seventh straight year, Merck topped *Fortune* magazine's most admired company list. Merck is not only the world's biggest pharmaceutical company; it also invents more new drugs each year than any of its competitors.

We argued in *In Search of Excellence* that companies succeed in innovation, as Rubbermaid does, through lots of small wins. Hit lots of singles and doubles, we urged, and the home runs will follow. Well, there must be more to it than that. For drugs like Proscar, the time from initial idea to the hoped-for commercial success averages twelve years, with costs averaging $230 million and increasing every year. So with that kind of investment, Merck can't settle for singles and doubles; it needs to hit home runs. How do the folks at Merck do it?

Of course, there is no simple answer. But there are some patterns that should become clear over the remainder of the chapter:

- They are absolutely committed to great science. Merck invests with a long-term, science-driven perspective. The company wants to be either at or creating the leading edge of the sciences relevant to its business. Few fields today are under-

---

*As with any new drug, it's hard to make predictions about its success, both in terms of treatment and sales, but in its first year on the market Proscar has been introduced in thirty-six countries and has given hundreds of thousands of patients worldwide an alternative to surgery.

going the revolution that is now turning medical research upside down. Merck leads the charge as that revolution gains
momentum.

- Merck directs its research and its development in two very
  different ways. Research is relatively cheap and needs nourish-
  ing, not managing. Development is hugely expensive and
  needs tight, disciplined, tough-minded managing.
- Though the company commits to basic science, research is
  different here than in universities in two ways. First, Merck
  scientists *typically* work in cross-functional, interdisciplinary
  teams. Second, the research, though often arcane, must not be
  completely abstract, but rather connected in some way to drug
  development.
- They invest heavily in people. This has a kind of snowballing
  effect in organizations like Merck. Top talent attracts other
  top talent. As Dartmouth professor James Brian Quinn points
  out, a small core of the very best in a field finds—or generates—the most interesting problems. That attracts more top
  people, and so it goes.
- Like P&G and Rubbermaid, Merck closely couples its research with market needs. In Merck's case, however, the market targets are obvious. Pick the big diseases: cardiovascular,
  AIDS, cancer, Alzheimer's, arthritis, osteoporosis. There you
  will find Merck scientists more focused. There you will find
  Merck committing the bulk of its development money if it's on
  the trail of a breakthrough.
- The company offers top scientists a proposition that few can
  resist—the encouragement to pursue their basic scientific interests actively and the chance to put science directly in service
  not just to their customers but to humanity in general. Rich,
  liberally-disbursed awards rain down on those who bring a
  project to fruition.
- Merck stays closely coupled with the world around it. Merck
  people publish, teach, hire top-of-field consultants, and stay in
  very close touch with the leading academics all over the world.
- Lastly Merck stays innovative by being big but acting small.
  We saw the same quality in Rubbermaid, which breaks itself
  into highly autonomous divisions and business teams. P&G

accomplishes the same thing with separate, often competing brands and brand managers. Merck does it by breaking itself into separate teams, each responsible for most aspects of a drug from development through marketing. Moreover, primary dependence on teams—what in my last book I labeled adhocracy—spoils the inclination toward bureaucracy that occurs in any company this large.

DESIGNING A DRUG

For the nonscientist, parts of this chapter might be a little heavy going. I try to treat the scientific aspects of the chapter as engagingly as possible. Feel free to skip them. However, part of the excitement at Merck is the revolution taking place in the biological sciences. To understand Merck fully you need some feel for the nature of that revolution.

One change in new drug research and development is especially important. It's called "rational drug design." Current advances in such fields as chemistry, biology, microbiology, and genetics make rational drug design possible. At Merck it's a powerful way to bring focus to drug research—like the focus we saw at Rubbermaid but different.

Rational drug design means understanding the fundamental biochemistry of disease and scientifically targeting research efforts to find the chemical cause of the problem. Sir James Black, a British-born pharmacologist, pioneered the approach and, with Gertrude Elion and George Hitchings, won a Nobel Prize for his efforts. His first success was with a class of drugs called beta blockers that control adrenaline and hence reduce high blood pressure and elevated heart rates. His second success was with a drug that blocked the formation of acid in the stomach and therefore is particularly effective in treating ulcers. Smith-Kline Beecham markets this drug under the brand name Tagamet; in terms of sheer sales dollars, it's one of the most successful drugs ever.

Rational drug design starts with the fact that a certain kind of protein, called an enzyme, is at the heart of most chemical changes in the body. These include good changes, like turning food into energy, and the bad changes that we call disease. With prostate enlargement, the bad change is the conversion of too much testosterone into dihydrotestosterone. The enzyme culprit is 5AR.

Enzymes can be thought of as rather large molecules with a keyhole. They are biological catalysts. They speed up a chemical reaction, even though they don't change as the reaction takes place. Thus in the prostate example, the testosterone molecule fits for awhile in the keyhole of the 5AR molecule much like a key in a lock. As it does so, other chemicals interact and, *viola*, testosterone becomes dihydrotestosterone.

The idea, then, is to block that keyhole by creating a molecule that also fits and will get there first—the biological equivalent of filling a keyhole with chewing gum. Now we can see what Proscar really does: It gets to the 5AR enzyme and the lock. In doing so it gums up the works for testosterone and thus inhibits prostate enlargement.

But rational drug design would not have been possible without recent advances in the biological and molecular sciences. For example, modern x-ray crystallography, combined with state-of-the-art computing power, makes it possible to model the transition state between testosterone and dihydrotestosterone in all its complexity and in 3D. Now scientists can see the exact shape and nature of the molecule and its keyhole.

So the problem, and it's a big one, is to invent a molecule that will get to that keyhole, fool the enzyme into accepting it, and not have any toxic or other distressing side effects. Says Roy Vagelos, "Making a molecule that fits into a pocket in three dimensions ain't easy."

Vagelos came to Merck as senior vice-president of research in 1975 from Washington University Medical School, where he was chairman of the department of biological chemistry. At Washington, Vagelos and a colleague, Alfred W. Alberts, had developed a formidable expertise in lipids—fatty substances like cholesterol that block arteries and cause heart attacks. One of his first contributions to Merck was to bring Alberts with him to head and champion a small team to look for a cholesterol fighting drug. In 1978 the team discovered that a microorganism in a soil sample produced a substance that would help block an enzyme called HMG-CoA reductase, which is the catalyst for the formation of mevalonic acid, a critical chemical in a chain of reactions that leads to the formation of cholesterol.

Research slowed a little in 1980 when the team learned that Japan's Sankyo Company found that a substance similar to Merck's caused cancerous tumors in laboratory animals. The pace resumed, however, as Merck scientists tested their own compound and learned that it had no similar side effect. By 1984 the would-be cholesterol fighting drug was in large-scale clinical trials in humans with a high risk of coronary disease. The results were spectacular. As Vagelos reported in an article in *Science,* "Total cholesterol levels of 300 mg/dl and above dropped to around 200, to the initial astonishment of the physicians conducting the trials."[3]

In late 1986 Merck submitted incredibly detailed documentation to the FDA—over 41,000 pages of it. (This in itself is interesting. It's one outcropping of the company's careful management of the expensive development process: When a drug is this far along, Merck wants to make sure no potential FDA question or concern goes unanswered.) On August 31, 1987, the drug Mevacor gained FDA approval. By 1991 Mevacor sales slightly exceeded $1 billion annually. It was truly a research and commercial *tour de force.*

But even more important than the expertise that helped develop Mevacor, what Vagelos brought to Merck was the commitment to rational drug design with special emphasis on finding, understanding, and blocking enzymes that cause various maladies. Vagelos says that when he joined Merck some work like that was going on in other companies but not much. These days, Merck's approach has infected most companies in the industry, though there seems little doubt that Merck remains on the cutting edge.

It's hard to overstate the importance of the approach. Merck's other billion-dollar drug, Vasotec, was developed in much the same way as Mevacor and Proscar. In this case the suspect enzyme was one part of a system that helps guarantee that the body maintains the right blood pressure level. Scientists at Merck and elsewhere knew that high blood pressure correlates closely with the conversion of something called angiotensin I to angiotensin II. A team of Merck researchers led by Dr. Arthur Patchett began searching for a drug that would block the enzyme (called ACE) that catalyzes this conversion. The result was Vasotec. Launched in 1986, Vasotec was selling at the annual rate of $1.75 billion by the end of 1991. Not only was the drug a spectacular success in reducing high blood pressure, but later research showed it to be effective in treating congestive heart failure as well.

The designer-molecule approach to drug research promises to be far more effective in treating human (and animal) afflictions than anything we have known in the past. It used to be that to discover, say, an effective anti-inflammatory, researchers would have to inject animals with something that caused inflammation. Then they would try various substances, almost on a hunch, to see whether any of them reduced the inflammation. The cynical industry term for this "scientific" method was "screen and pray." Writes Vagelos, "Early antidepressants, antianxiety drugs, drugs for infectious diseases, peptic ulcers, [and] pain relief . . . were based on these kinds of experiments. . . ."[4]

With rational drug design, the next half-century should be filled with medical breakthroughs on a scale and frequency that humanity has never seen before. In a 1991 study, the Battelle Memorial Institute predicted that pharmaceutical advances over the next twenty-five years will reduce annual leukemia deaths in the United States by over 80,000, lung cancer deaths by 400,000, and cardiovascular deaths by 4.4 million. The Pharmaceutical Manufacturers Association (PMA) boldly predicts that "in many diseases, such as AIDS, Alzheimer's, and arthritis, pharmaceutical R&D is likely to generate nearly all the future medical progress."[5] The PMA reckons that heart disease—the leading cause of death in the United States—and related deaths will be cut by two-thirds over the next twenty-five years. Almost half of that reduction will come from pharmaceutical treatment (the rest from better health, better surgical techniques, enhanced ability to identify high-risk individuals).[6]

Even with rational drug design, however, developing a drug to fight cancer, which now accounts for 22 percent of all deaths in the United States, will be enormously difficult. The problem is that cancer is not one disease but more than a hundred, each characterized by uncontrolled growth of renegade cells. Fighting cancer has usually involved a combination of chemotherapy, radiation, and surgery. Still, pharmaceutical approaches now offer promise. While progress will be slower than any of us would like, drug research is starting to make breakthroughs. For example, injections of a genetically engineered drug called interferon-alpha causes tumors to shrink 15 to 20 percent in kidney-cancer and melanoma patients. The same treatment is effective in 90 percent of patients with certain kinds of leukemia. Ben Shapiro, Merck's executive vice-president for worldwide basic research, gets very excited at the prospect of drug treatment of various forms of cancer. "If we could only slow the growth of breast cancer by 50 percent," he enthuses, "we will have made major progress." He explains that cancer of the breast is a relatively slow growing form anyway. Further reduction in its rate of growth would allow less radical treatment and reduce the odds of its frequent and often fatal spread to the rest of the body.

RESEARCH IS CHEAP

People see Merck as a gigantic company with a highly disciplined approach to getting new drugs to market. They assume these factors must make the culture bureaucratic and then wonder how Merck can be so creative. Part of the answer is that Merck's guidelines for managing basic research are broad. While the choices of what they will work on are not quite as open-ended as scientists might find in the academic world, within Merck's loose guidelines, scientists can pretty much do as

they please. In fact that's the first guideline: Merck expects them
to take the initiative in deciding what they will work on. The
other consideration is that their efforts must all be directed toward relieving or curing disease. Therefore, according to Merck
Research Laboratories president Ed Scolnick, they tend to focus
basic research efforts where four criteria meet. First, is there a
significant medical need? Second, might the need be met with
drug therapy? Third, is enough biology of the problem known to
be able to hypothesize a target that would inhibit the biochemistry of the disease? Last, considering what is known, is it reasonable to expect that Merck scientists can do the chemistry required to attack the target?

Given a rough—sometimes very rough—fit with those criteria, a project can get started at Merck in dozens of ways. For
example, it can start because an entry-level researcher in a lab
has an idea and pulls together one or two others on a part- or
full-time basis. Presto—a project is underway. Scolnick comments, "They can do that with very little bureaucratic approval." He and others elaborate that getting projects going is
basically their job description when they come to work at Merck.
For Merck scientists, standard operating procedure means running off in some new direction. They need little by way of formal
approval. "A lot of those things I may never hear about," Scolnick remarks, taking obvious pleasure in the freedom that the
Merck system gives its scientists.

Other projects might get going, or gain impetus, because a
department head, the director of research, or even the chief
executive believes the company should be doing more. Scolnick
says that often something pops up in a meeting or in the literature that looks promising. If Merck isn't already active in the
field, management will try to marshal a team of interested champions. Says Scolnick, "We will do it with a few or a lot of people,
depending on how important we think the project is."

Proscar's history reflects a little bit of both. The project was
born in the late 1960s, when Dr. Gary Rasmusson, fresh from a
postdoc program at Stanford, joined Merck. "I spent a year and
a half or so working on antibiotics and antibacterials. Then I was

moved over to work for this Dr. Glen Arth, who became my mentor." Arth was one of the few scientists in Merck at the time who was still actively pursuing steroid research. Most others had given up on the field because steroids, though potent, invariably produced strong and unwanted side effects.

At Stanford, and earlier at MIT, Rasmusson had specialized in steroid chemistry. Arth and Rasmusson felt they might be able to develop a compound that would be effective in treating male hormone related conditions. For example, early studies focused on acne. Despite their enthusiasm, the project was not making much progress up to and through the mid-1970s. Top management didn't see much promise in their work, and wouldn't devote more resources to it. On the other hand—and this is something that distinguishes all innovative companies—top management did not kill the fledgling effort.*

Then Arth, Rasmusson, and Vagelos all saw Imperato-McGinley's paper on 5-alpha-reductase. They immediately recognized some parallels between their work and prostate therapy. Now, with not only the support but the enthusiasm of top management, they shifted their focus from acne to prostate treatment and began to build a bigger team to attack the problem.

Here is another example of the informed opportunism I talked about in the last chapter. Scolnick reinforces the idea: "That's why we invest in basic research. It doesn't take a big effort in a field to stay up on it." If someone isn't working in the area you might not see the opportunity for what it is—or seize the moment as quickly as Merck did. When you do see the possibilities, "you can always marshal lab resources, put a bigger team together, and go after the project aggressively," Scolnick observes.

MANAGING THE BIG BANG

Though Merck considers research cheap, people at the company fully comprehend that development is expensive. As a pro-

---

*They do kill big projects that are going nowhere as we will see later.

ject like Proscar gains momentum, costs start to rise fast. A part of Merck's innovative genius is the way it manages cross-disciplinary teams and controls the bets it places on big projects.

Dr. Elizabeth Stoner joined Merck in 1985, leaving behind her job on the faculty at Cornell University Medical Center and bringing with her a specialty in disorders of sexual differentiation. Though she had joined the company specifically to work on Proscar, she didn't spend much time on that project until her second year. Merck was in the final throes of pulling together the FDA application for Mevacor, and the team developing that product needed all the help it could muster. In retrospect she says that apparent diversion was a blessing. Seeing another project in full crescendo would prove invaluable to the leadership role she was about to get.

Things happen fast at Merck. After that first year, Stoner found herself not just on, but in charge of, the Proscar team, which then numbered twelve people and would eventually grow to over two hundred. At the time she took over the project it was about midway through development: Finasteride—the active molecule in Proscar—had proved effective in test-tube trials and in early animal studies. Clinical studies with humans had not started.

Stoner likes the way Merck organizes teams. In addition to the inventing chemist (in this case Gary Rasmusson, with help from Glen Arth), a team of the kind Stoner joined might include other organic chemists, microbiologists, drug metabolism specialists, virologists, biophysicists, veterinarians, and even marketing people. Stoner says, "One of the really exciting things for me when I first came here was seeing how these groups of people, with very diverse interests, came together." She adds, "Even before we really knew whether the project was going to be successful, these people could sit together, resolve issues, and if one department needed something to be done by another department it just got done. It was amazing."

Stoner, Shapiro, and others found the cross-disciplinary team, as obvious as the concept sounds, to be one of the most remarkable differences in the way Merck does research. Stoner comments, "It's different from what happens in academia where people are very much into their empires [and seldom work cross-functionally]. I was very suspicious at the beginning." She says she thought it must be some political game in the business world that she hadn't caught onto yet. Soon she concluded there was no game. "It really is people all working together to reach a common goal."

My own experience is that the difference is not just between business and academe. In my distant past I used to work in exploration geophysics, where, silly as it sounds, geologists and geophysicists often would not collaborate. During my career I've also consulted with a number of high-tech companies or departments. One of the biggest problems all seem to have is in putting this seemingly simple concept—adhocracy (teams that cut across bureaucratic lines)—to work.

Vagelos says it's just part of the Merck research tradition. "The best of our scientists are almost uncontrollable in the way they go between departments. There are no walls for these people. They walk from one laboratory to another, from one department into another. Because they're so driven by what they want to do, they cannot be stopped. I love that." Gary Rasmusson, the chemist who pioneered and championed Proscar, finds the cross-functional team an absolute must. As a chemist trying to develop a drug, "you have to learn what the biologist is doing, what it means when he or she gets a result, and then how you can respond to it. It really keeps you going. There's a certain drive that comes out of the team effort and learning from each other."

Teams form early at Merck and begin to grow when the project shows promise. Rasmusson explains that in early stages, before Stoner joined the group, the team was fairly small—"two or three chemists and two or three biologists"—but that the project required pretty tight coordination between the two disciplines. "I learned a lot of biology, and the biologists were learning chemistry. It's a synergistic type thing. The biologists would let me know their problems, and I would let them know whether we could do the chemistry they needed."

This was especially important in the development of Proscar. Some of Merck's (and other pharmaceutical companies') drugs come from fermentation broths of various natural microorganisms. Mevacor is one example. The drug is a highly purified version of a molecule that occurs in nature. Proscar is different. The necessary molecule had to be created from scratch in the labs. Scolnick called it "a real *tour de force* for medicinal chemistry."

And that takes time. The paper that headed them in the right direction was published in 1975. It was not until the early 1980s that some promising compounds started coming out of the labs. Even at this point nobody at Merck could be sure they were on the right track. They knew they had something that would block 5AR in a test tube. They knew men with 5AR deficiency had small prostate glands. What they didn't know was whether their chemical wizardry would arrest—or better, yet reverse—prostate growth in older men.

Fortunately, there is a fairly close animal model for the disorder: Aging dogs have the same problem. The project really began to pick up momentum when Merck tested finasteride on these animals and found that it both caused prostate shrinkage in aging dogs and did not have any disastrous side effects.

This was a little after the time that Stoner entered the program and when Merck people started to get really excited. The year was 1987, and limited testing with human volunteers was just beginning. Those results showed that finasteride not only blocked prostate growth in humans but shrunk prostates already enlarged. It had no apparent side effects, and it relieved the most unpleasant symptom that accompanies an enlarged prostate: the inability to urinate normally.

Merck now began to bet really big bucks on a very large clinical testing program. "That's where you really hold your breath," says Scolnick. "Lots of resources have been committed and the expectations are very high." As a project like Proscar moves into clinical trials the investment starts to grow at a near exponential rate. Scolnick says that's when their project management style shifts from fairly loose to rigorous. "We have a very formal process for reviewing and scrutinizing projects when they get to this stage," he says.

First, the teams have regular monthly meetings. On the Proscar project Stoner said, "Typically we'd meet once a month for a long half day. She used those meetings as a kind of issues forum. "We try to bring up all the positive things *and* all the negative things in the team, and try to come to some resolution as a team." And most issues do get resolved in these team meetings.

In addition to the regular meetings, the teams also set up milestones. "We work on very tight target dates," Stoner says. Everyone who has to make something happen by the target date is expected to keep his or her commitment. "I think that's part of the unwritten culture here. We're all part of this pyramid, and if someone's piece is missing we can't go on."

As the pace of the project really picks up, so does the frequency of meetings. As momentum grew, Stoner said, "we tried to meet all day. Various members of the team were in two different facilities, ninety miles away from each other so we all spent a lot of time on the New Jersey Turnpike—not very productive. Now we have video conferencing, which has really revolutionized our lives (though we still need to meet face-to-face occasionally)."

Scolnick amplifies: "If an important project [like Proscar], which has immense economic consequences for Merck, runs into an unexpected problem, we meet as often as it takes to solve the problem—every two weeks, maybe every day."

In addition one of the great strengths of Merck is its ability to shift resources to the priority projects. Scolnick says, "If we need twice the number of people, we will just take them from somewhere else." He adds that the company has no trouble with quickly resetting priorities and focus.

Part of that focus, as we have seen in other chapters, comes from the way top management spends time. Says Scolnick, "From the autumn of 1991 to early winter 1992, I was spending 90 percent of my professional time on that one project." He says it's not so much that he could contribute some breakthrough technical thinking. Rather, when the head of research is seen to be saying, "This project is so important to us that I am going to meet with you weekly and spend all my time on it," it really gets attention. "So everybody concentrates. They always have fifty other things impinging on their time, but if the head of the organization is saying 'It doesn't matter, forget all the other things you are doing. Do this one thing really well,' then they follow your lead and they do it too. Everybody goes home every night and thinks about Proscar, they come in the next day and think about Proscar." He says that what you can achieve with that kind of focus is phenomenal. "Everybody then understands the problem and all the aspects of the problem." Problems fall like cardboard. It's like a nuclear reaction that has hit critical mass.

After all the intensive meetings and reviews, Proscar still looked like a winning bet and went forward. Later we will see how Merck reacts when a big bang project starts to fizzle.

THE RIGHT STUFF

One message that rings loud and clear at Merck is *invest in intellectual capital.* Vagelos says: "A low-value product can be made by anyone, anywhere. When you have knowledge no one else has access to—that's dynamite."[7] But most managers have little idea of how to assign value to the human capital in their employ. It's much easier to assign a value to a fractionation column than it is to the playful mind of a scientist who may or may not make an important discovery in the future. But, reports *Fortune,* Merck tries to put hard numbers on its investment in knowledge.

Merck's chief financial officer, Judy Lewent, has managed to pull together two fields that seem at war in other companies: the long-range thinking this investment in intellectual capital represents and corporate financial analysis. She's done it by creating a financial planning model that supports the company's research-driven culture.

It uses a discounted cash-flow (DCF) technique to calculate

the net present value of its patents. In doing so it factors in product life cycles, which are getting shorter these days. DCF is usually the enemy of investment in things like research spending. Time horizons generally aren't long enough, and the conservative financial profession typically underestimates the upside potential. Consequently, big spending on R&D looks dubious through the typical DCF lens. Merck, as usual, looks at it differently. The company uses its DCF approach to help decide proactively whether the company is putting enough into R&D to keep its investment in intellectual capital alive and flourishing.

Merck puts extraordinary emphasis on getting, keeping, and developing the best people the company can find. Dr. Ben Shapiro, a recent addition to the Merck team, says that he believes Merck's success stems from its commitment to excellent people practicing excellent science. Gary Rasmusson, the inventor of Proscar, sees it the same way. He says that innovation is in the very atmosphere at Merck. "That comes from companywide attention to recruiting," he explains.

The company's reputation also helps in its recruiting efforts. What attracted Rasmusson to Merck twenty years ago? "They seemed to be on the cutting edge of science." It was a phrase I heard repeatedly. Shapiro calls Merck's approach to developing drugs a "spellbinding thing to see." That, and the chance to be part of it, brought him to Merck. "People want to have pride in what they're doing," says Rasmusson. Merck's luster is something they want to be associated with.

What gives Merck its luster? It's the company's track record in discovery. It has a history of firsts, going all the way back to the 1930s when it pioneered the synthesis of a string of essential vitamins and stretching down to the present with Vasatec, Mevacor and Proscar. Rasmusson notes that many young scientists in the health-care field believe they can have more impact at Merck than "going off, say, into academics or something like that." And though new recruits have a lot to learn about developing drugs, they start contributing almost immediately. Says Rasmusson, "Just having bright people coming out of graduate

school keeps you up with your chemistry. You'll make suggestions to them, and they'll come back to you and say, 'That's
being done this way now.' " Rasmusson smiles as he comments,
"That keeps you humble and keeps you learning."

Shapiro's story gives us a feel for the magnetism of Merck's
commitment to investing in brainpower. By almost any standard
Shapiro had it made before he joined Merck in 1990. He was
head of the biochemistry department at the University of Washington in Seattle. He had been at the university for twenty years
and had been head of the department for five. "I was very happy
in Seattle. In fact, I still have a home on Puget Sound. We had
an excellent department of biochemistry; we all got along well;
the research was going terrifically well; and we were well funded.
I was having a great time."

Then he gave a seminar at Merck and was offered a job to
work for Scolnick directing worldwide research. His initial reaction was negative. Why leave a great lifestyle and job? But he
realized, "If I didn't say yes, I couldn't look at myself in the
mirror." Here was a singular chance, he thought, to be quite
literally an important part of changing the future of medicine.
(Shapiro is a physician by training, though most of his work has
been in basic science.) He explains that the whole field of biology
is in revolution right now. Breakthroughs on almost every major
disease seem possible, and Merck knows how to discover new
drugs. "No one learns about drug discovery in an academic
environment," Shapiro told me.

For many of the scientists I talked with, Merck is *more* intellectually stimulating than the academic world. Many find less bureaucracy and politics at Merck than in academic settings. Others comment that they like Merck because they can concentrate
on research instead of splitting their time between research and
teaching. Many like the fact that they can do some teaching or
guest lecturing. All seem to relish the combined freedom and
responsibility that Merck gives them to live at the state of their
art. They are actively encouraged to publish, read, and stay in
touch with their counterparts in the scientific community.

I asked Vagelos the obvious question: "How do you keep

people creative, especially in such a big organizational setting?" His answer went straight to the heart of it: "You start with very creative people. We really recruit very carefully, very hard." During his ten-year reign as head of research, Vagelos personally interviewed every scientist and physician they hired. So does Scolnick today. Vagelos points out that there are two kinds of people in research: Some work best alone and occasionally will make a breakthrough; others want to do something that Vagelos calls "harder than that." Merck looks for those people, the ones who want to use today's cutting-edge science to stem or cure disease.

Vagelos also made it his business to stay close to the source. "I would lecture widely at universities." He still does whenever his schedule permits, visiting both medical and business schools and lecturing on either biochemistry or business, depending on "what flavor is right for the audience." It's one of his ways of staying in touch with students and faculty. "I recognize most people on the faculty and most faculty people know me. It's easy for us to find very, very high quality people."

Merck also rewards creativity. One way they do it is by granting special cash awards to scientists who have been instrumental in developing a new drug. Art Strohmer, Merck's executive director of strategy and policies in human resources, told me, "I just signed sixty-nine special awards today for people who had a recognizable and visible impact on the development and bringing to market of Proscar."

Of even more significance is a program that grants very substantial stock options to the key members of a drug development team. The options don't vest annually as management options typically do. Rather, they vest as the drug passes various milestones. For example, a certain amount might vest on completion of successful test tube trials. More vests as the drug passes various stages in clinical trial. Then there is a big vesting when the drug wins FDA approval. According to Steve Darien, vice-president of human resources, the rewards program creates even more excitement around successful drug development. "It's our attempt to mimic what the little biotech companies do," he says.

Merck tries to be fairly liberal in the way it rewards scientists.
The members on a project team who did not discover the drug
but did make important scientific contributions also get special
bonuses or options, for example. One of the main reasons for
being generous and expansive with the reward system gets right
back to the matter of keeping the best people. The issue is ego:
Many of the best and the brightest that Merck wants to attract
and keep come packaged with big egos. In one sense that's good;
they venture where angels fear. And big egos usually aren't a
problem when the project outcome is still uncertain. The sheer
challenge binds people together who otherwise might not get
along. The problem is success, which, to paraphrase the famous
saying, has hundreds of fathers and mothers. Nobody can really
pin down who contributed what. The only sure bet is that many
people will feel their bit was the critical part. That's when petti-
ness sets in and egos defeat wisdom.

This is one disease for which the people at Merck see no cure.
The best they can do is to be lavish in rewarding all contributors.
Scolnick says, "I feel personally that the best way to deal with the
problem is to try to give the rewards out as broadly as possible,
but not so broadly that you then denigrate the really unique
contributions made by a few." For despite the generosity and
variety in its pay systems, Merck is resolutely committed to paying for performance. Strohmer says that they try to drive programs like options and bonuses, that are, in many companies,
reserved for management, right down to the lowest levels in the
organization. "But," he says, "we are very much against a give-
something-to everybody philosophy. We put a heavy emphasis
in all of our programs on the fact that they are performance-
based." The only exception was a special grant of one hundred
shares of stock to all Merck employees in 1991. The occasion was
Merck's one hundredth anniversary. Scolnick admits that he's
never dealt with the ego problem as well as he'd like. There are
always a few unhappy campers.

But, recognition—pure and simple—counts for a lot. When I
talked with her, Stoner said, "May I show you something I'm
very proud of? We have this little newspaper," she said showing

me a copy of *The Daily,* a two-page internal newsletter. This one featured Rasmusson and Stoner on the cover as the key people who brought Proscar to life. "For me, it's one of the nicest things that has come out about Proscar. I like it better than the *New York Times* article." She was referring to a front-page business-section story that appeared in a Sunday *New York Times* in February 1992.

WHEN A BIG BANG FIZZLES

Everyone I talked with at Merck agreed that the toughest and most important management decision in R&D is knowing when to put a stop to a big project that is going nowhere. The problem, as noted earlier, is that big projects use up big resources. Unless unsuccessful projects are shut down or redirected quickly, huge amounts of money and talent are wasted. The trouble is that by the time a project has gotten big, a lot of human beings have a lot of years, ego, and career invested in it.

Merck's experience with one experimental AIDS drug presents a bittersweet example of how to deal with such issues but also of how agonizing these decisions can be. "We came up with a drug for which the virus was too smart," Vagelos comments. Merck was sure it was on the right track. The team had invented two closely related compounds called reverse transcriptase inhibitors (RTIs). These compounds interfere with the activity of an enzyme called reverse transcriptase, which is produced by the AIDS virus and is necessary for its growth.

Unfortunately, this virus mutates with alarming alacrity. Trial showed that use of the drug did attack the virus but in doing so just encouraged the rapid formation of mutant forms. The drug, which had seemed so promising, was making things worse. "We were very down," Scolnick told me. "Everyone thought we were really going to be able to do something for AIDS with this effort. We didn't [and had to quickly shut down that project]. It was emotionally very tough for everyone"—tough but necessary to keep development costs from chewing up the company.

Though the initial RTI approach was abandoned, Merck's AIDS research program is still their most ambitious ever. Instead of an approach they call "monotherapy" (using only RTIs), Merck is now conducting clinical studies using RTIs in combination with two other drugs, AZT and DDI. In addition, in February 1993 the company began human testing of another approach using another kind of inhibitor.

Scolnick reckons their discipline in bringing the RTI monotherapy project to a quick and dead halt got them a year's jump on better approaches. Vagelos agrees. "The number of people working on [the new approach] is now enormous. So is the sense of urgency." The urgency stems both from the epidemic nature of the disease and the simple, competitive truth that Merck would like to be first. "We have essentially committed to stay with it until we make it or fail."

Vagelos smiles broadly, "We don't like to fail."

— — —

WITH MOUNTING PRESSURE on drug prices, will Merck continue to perform as well in the future? Who knows. On the one hand, pharmaceutical costs are only an estimated 7 percent of total health-care costs, therefore not the first place one would look to save money. On the other hand, notoriously profitable drug companies make juicy targets, and neither the public nor the politicians seem willing to grasp the joint truths that we already have a natural cost regulator in this part of the health-care system—it's called free market competition—and that medicines are a very cost-effective form of health-care spending.

And that, for me, is the most persuasive argument for not over-controlling a company like Merck. Drugs such as Proscar, Mevacor, or Vasotec save millions of dollars each year in surgery and hospitalization that would otherwise be needed.

Besides, Merck sets a wonderful example as a corporate citizen. Several years ago the company saw the need to control health-care costs and voluntarily limited its drug price increases to within the rate of inflation. Today it is taking steps to increase its marketing of generic drugs. In certain instances Merck gives

away medicines when people cannot afford to pay—for instance, a pill that prevents river blindness in sub-Saharan Africa—or makes special efforts to get important medicines to those in need—vaccines in the inner cities and hepatitis-B vaccine in China.

Merck has been profitable because Merck has been innovative. However desperately we need to control health-care costs, the last thing we should do is to go about it in a way that kills the innovative spirit in a company like Merck.

11.

"OUR QUALITY STINKS"

Muddling, Anticipating, and Committing at Motorola

$\mathbf{A}$s Levi's Bob Haas comments, strategy can be something cold, analytical, and bloodless, but that's not always the case. Listen to Motorola's Patty Barten talk about this commercial electronic company's strategy to satisfy the customer completely. "Thing is, I've never worked so hard in my life. It's absolutely worth it though. I go home at night feeling I've made a difference. And it's not just a difference to cellular, it's not just a difference to Motorola, it's a difference to the country itself."

Barten is a mid-level supervisor in a Motorola factory not far from corporate headquarters in Schaumburg, Illinois, that makes the infrastructure for cellular phones. What has her and thousands of other Motorolans so enthusiastic? A set of programs launched in 1981, two years after a sales manager told an astonished chief executive, Bob Galvin, that in his opinion, "Our quality stinks."

From Motorola's all-out drive to combat malodorous quality we can learn just how strategic an effort to boost quality can be. Of the lessons Motorola has to teach, these seem most important:

- Total quality and total service are one and the same. They add up to one very strategic advantage: what Motorola now calls "total customer satisfaction."
- Dramatic quality improvement takes more time and effort than you would think. That's what makes it good strategy—most competitors don't have the patience or, as CEO George Fisher says, "the will" to copy you.
- Total quality, which sometimes sounds like a fad or buzzword, should be the bedrock of corporate strategy. Motorola shows us the way—it takes time, effort, unflagging attention from top management. Of utmost importance, Motorola directs its effort outward (toward customers and suppliers), not inward (toward pleasing the boss).
- Despite the jumble of tools and gurus that surround the American movement toward total quality and service, the underlying concepts are fairly simple and straightforward. However, the adaptation of the concepts is anything but simple. Motorola, like other successful total-quality companies, developed its own distinctive approach.
- The old assumption about quality, and one still held by many managers, is that putting more quality into what you do must cost money. Philip Crosby dispelled that notion with his wonderful book *Quality Is Free*. Actually, Crosby was understating the case. The total-quality investments at Motorola added a welcome $3.2 billion to Motorola's bottom line between 1987 and 1992: Total quality is a money-maker.
- Most great total-quality programs start with outrageously ambitious objectives. These work, and savings of the kind just mentioned are possible, because companies make mistakes at much higher rates than most of us would ever imagine. And fixing something once it's done wrong is enormously expensive.
- Processes to improve quality and to shorten cycle time (for example, the time between customer order and product delivery) are inextricably linked.
- Virtually all a company's stakeholders benefit from total-quality efforts.

- Motorola's shareholders benefit from both the cost savings and the enormous strategic advantage that a total-quality program can yield.
- Motorola employees benefit because total quality plays to so many basic human needs. It puts pride, challenge, learning, and craftsmanship back into the job. It shoves control way down the organizational ladder.
- Customers benefit because the program forces Motorola to define quality as doing what makes the customer happy.
- Managers at all levels benefit through a process called benchmarking that encourages them to learn from the best in the world, not just from their own mistakes.
- Suppliers benefit because the ones most able to supply quality products to the company start working in partnership with Motorola, which affords them a certain long-term security. They don't get diverted in continuous battles with less able competitors who undercut on price.
- Communities around Motorola benefit because total quality demands an investment in better education, so companies like Motorola invest more and more heavily in education.
- Thus total quality as strategy is not just about quality or service. It's about developing relationships—relationships that are very hard for competitors to displace.

IT TAKES TIME

When asked to pick a single event that triggered Motorola's passionate drive for quality, most insiders would point to a now legendary meeting held in early 1979. "In 1978 we had a batch of problems," former chief executive Bob Galvin told me. "The nature of them was such that I proposed a companywide officers' meeting." Nothing revolutionary about that—Motorola, like most firms, had a long history of officers' meetings. But this would be the first time that all the company's officers (numbering eighty at that time) would spend three full days together in a downtown Chicago hotel.

"If you had sat through it," says Galvin, "you would say you'd been to a thousand meetings just like it. A good agenda, lots of good presentations, plenty of time for discussions, lots of issues that were unique to us—but not significant in any grand sense." At least not on the surface. But consider the reason for the meeting: Galvin, picking up on something his father, Motorola founder Paul Galvin, had taught him, said the real purpose of the meeting was "to stay in motion for motion's sake." This sounds like a trivial idea; it's not. It's a fundamental strategic precept. If we've learned one point about strategy in the last two decades, it is the futility of prediction. So what do you do when you need strategy but can't rely on forecasts? You try something, and if that doesn't work you try something else. In other words, being in motion for its own sake is a form of planning.

In the case of Motorola's 1979 officers' meeting, motion for motion's sake changed the course of the company. Near the end of the meeting a sales manager named Art Sundry, who had been sitting quietly through most of the three days, stood up and said: "Good agenda. We're making progress. But we're not on the right subject. Our quality stinks. My customers tell me that they don't like our quality." That simple-sounding statement hit the assembly like a concussion grenade.

Neither Galvin nor anyone I've talked with in Motorola seems entirely sure why Sundry's comment had such a profound impact. Most of us have seen people like Sundry make an impassioned plea for change, only to be ignored, or lost in the momentum of the agenda. Sundry *was* a heavy hitter, the sales manager for the fastest growing, most profitable piece of Motorola's business and the one with the biggest world market share. But I believe the reason Sundry's remark had such an impact—it marked a watershed moment in the company's fortunes—had much to do with timing: Motorola's officers were ready to listen.

To understand why, consider this snapshot of how service and quality have played a key role throughout Motorola's history. Motorola took shape in September 1928, when Paul Galvin and his brother Joe began assembling battery eliminators (a device to eliminate the need for batteries in early radios) in a rented loft on Chicago's West Side. Soon thereafter Paul, the visionary, sensed a relationship between the radio and America's love affair with the car. In 1930 they decided to build car radios, and with that Galvin Manufacturing changed its name to Motorola—a name that was intended to connote sound in motion. Music on wheels was a fine concept, but in its execution Motorola had its first encounter with what we would now label a massive quality problem. Auto dealers and distributors were ill-equipped either to install or to repair car radios. Paul Galvin saw the problem almost immediately; he personally built a service organization that would train dealers. The concept worked, and Motorola's business went into high gear.

What made what he did so important then is the same thing that makes total-quality programs so important today. He recognized that customers don't buy a product alone. They buy a package of features that includes the product itself, the producer's reputation for quality and service, and of course, price. In fact, most customers will pay a bit more for quality: a product that works or one that they know can be easily repaired when it doesn't.

From the car radio it was not a long step to the product that launched the company into the big time. While traveling in Europe in the 1930s, Paul Galvin strongly sensed the immediacy of war. He anticipated a huge need for a product Motorola was making for police departments—portable, two-way radios. First launched as the Handie-Talkie in 1940 and then sold as the more familiar Walkie-Talkie in 1943, this product took Motorola sales from just under $10 million in 1940 to well over $80 million in 1944. (The end of the war caused just as sharp a drop. By 1946, Motorola sales dropped to $23 million. By 1949, with the success of their television business, Motorola was back to $80 million.)

ANTICIPATE AND COMMIT

"Anticipate and commit" were the ideas guiding Motorola's strategy. Today Bob Galvin still laces his business conversation with the phrase. These concepts had, after all, characterized the firm's success: Motorola anticipated the need for music on wheels and committed resources to solving the service problem. It anticipated the need for the Handie-Talkie. It also anticipated the fast-growing television market, and in 1947 introduced the first TV set that consumers could buy for less than $200. And after the transistor was invented late that year, Motorola started committing in a big way: Over a ten-year period, it poured millions into semiconductors. In 1992 Motorola was the second largest semiconductor manufacturer in North America and fourth largest in the world.

While Motorola's succession of products had for years flowed logically from one to the next, semiconductors were a technical discontinuity. Most companies never bridge such discontinuity; they have too much invested in their old ways. RCA, Westinghouse, and General Electric—all heavy hitters in the vacuum tube business—tried but never could make the transition to transistors.

The reluctance to make such a shift is common and is extensively documented in Richard Foster's book *Innovation: The Attacker's Advantage*. To a company that's already successful in one technology, continued investment in that technology always looks more profitable and less risky than trying something new. That's because our usual measures for evaluating investment alternatives, though they're not supposed to, tend to stress the short term.

Motorola almost got sucked into the tube vacuum along with the rest. Neither Paul Galvin nor his son Bob was especially enthusiastic about investing in solid state. But one of their key scientists, Dan Noble, was. Noble had read about AT&T's invention of the transistor and could see its importance. He pushed hard and Galvin had the good sense to listen. Bob Galvin still likes to tell that story: In doing so, he lets everyone know that bosses are not always the smartest, that people down the line ought to be heard and taken seriously, and that even the founder and chairman ought to be challenged.

Still and all, Art Sundry might never have been listened to at that fateful managers' meeting had Motorola not previously *failed* to anticipate something. It was the Japanese success in consumer electronics. Paralleling what it learned in the car radio days, Motorola introduced its Quasar television in 1967. At that time it was not uncommon to buy a new television, plug it in, turn it on, and have it fail within the first few hours of operation. Early failure in the field was so common to all electronic products that it was thought to be just part of doing business. Hence the rise of the expensive, often inept, but seemingly ubiquitous TV repair man.

True to its view of quality and service, Motorola set out to do something about this. Steve Allen and his wife, Jayne Meadows, explained it to the public in commercials that introduced the Quasar. The tubeless set contained solid state modules, or plug-in "works in a drawer." If one part of a unit failed, a technician could simply snap it out and replace it—no more fiddling or hauling the set to the shop. Just as in the early radio days, Motorola had seen and solved one major customer problem. But it didn't anticipate the real problem—that customers didn't want their TVs to break down in the first place. Japan did.

Tired of their image as producers of cheap, copy-cat products, Japanese electronics firms became followers of W. Edwards Deming and Joe Juran, quality gurus then and now. A part of the Deming message has always been to get it right the first time. There was no room in Deming's gospel for accepting field failure as normal. Thus, while Motorola touted the virtues of easy repair, the Japanese designed sets that rarely broke. Eventually Motorola abandoned consumer electronics.

Motorola vice-president Paul Noakes reflects: "My own view is that if we had not considered early-life failure as normal and had done more on design and process quality to eliminate latent defects, we'd still be in the television business in the United States today." Not everyone agrees with him. Others in Motorola make a very reasonable case that Japan's trade practices would have doomed consumer electronics anyway. Perhaps the fact that Motorola, along with other U.S. companies, had been creamed in consumer electronics is the reason Sundry's remark about smelly quality had such an impact. They knew that inadequate quality had doomed them in television manufacturing. They were not about to let the same thing happen to their core business—commercial electronics.

MANAGEMENT BY MUDDLING AROUND

Galvin says he can't recount exactly what happened during the first months after the watershed meeting. Lots went on; none of it proceeded in a tight, highly organized way. Motorola's senior management did decide to make quality their top priority, albeit as an informal goal. But as Galvin says: "People tried a few things; we muddled around with various ideas and approaches. We mainly decided to keep working on it." Once again—motion for motion's sake: management by muddling around.

The idea is not as crazy as it sounds. Jim Adams, a Stanford University professor who studies the process of creativity in individuals and organizations, concludes that muddling is part of the process of doing anything new. He makes the point in lectures when he rhetorically asks students to compare how long it took them to write a paper compared with how long it *should* take. Most of the students agree that it takes too long by a factor of five or ten times. "Dead time!" exclaims Adams. The creative process, which he explains encompasses everything from inventing new products to writing a thesis to redirecting an organization, almost always involves a lot of dead time and consequently takes longer than it "should." Research, he explains, shows that dead time is the inescapable partner of any sort of creative change.

Dead time, however, does not mean time spent brain-dead.

Motorola people didn't simply kick back and turn on an old Quasar waiting for lightning to strike. They fired off a host of initiatives, all aimed in the general direction of the problem. One initiative was to bring in numerous consultants and advisors who presented a whole batch of ideas, most of which Motorola management seemed to like.

Another was to appoint a "corporate facilitator" of quality, someone highly credible. In their minds that, most emphatically, did not mean a quality expert. Instead, they chose Jack Germain, a line manager who didn't know much about quality programs, but who was highly credible as assistant general manager of Motorola's very successful communications group. Shortly after Germain took the new assignment, key people from Motorola's operating units started meeting with him regularly in what became formalized as a corporate quality council. By late 1981 most of the operating divisions had Germain equivalents reporting directly to the division head.

"It was like putting ornaments on the tree," says Galvin of all the ideas and initiatives, "with each one, the tree started to look a little prettier." Motorola people muddled, tried a lot of paths that turned out to be dead ends and, in retrospect, had lots of what they now would consider dead time. These days, armed with tools like benchmarking, good examples set by companies like Motorola, and now the Baldrige Award guidelines, companies don't have to do quite as much muddling. But some is inevitable and ought to be expected.

Muddling, in fact, may be the necessary step to tailor total quality to each company's unique culture. Not doing so may lead to the place where most quality programs go awry. Uttering the words "it's no panacea," companies then go on to treat total quality as if it were one. Managers rush to join the parade and beat the drums, knowing little more than the fact that *it*—whatever "it" is—seems to be working for somebody else. They slavishly follow what they take to be someone else's road to success.

But every company I know that has been successful with total-quality programs—companies such as Motorola, Federal Express, Procter & Gamble—has developed its own highly idiosyncratic approach. Every organization must find its own path, which means that a certain amount of dead time is inevitable. Those who try to wait until the path is clear—or can't tolerate the ambiguity that goes with muddling—will be those who get left behind.

WHAT IS TOTAL QUALITY?

Our current obsession with quality is understandable. Poor quality relative to the highest quality possible left open the legendary hole you could drive a truck through in most American companies. And Japanese, German, and other foreign competitors hopped in that truck and drove all over us, in consumer electronics, in the auto industry—we all know the list.

So now we are desperately trying to plug that hole. Total-quality programs give us the right tools. Few realize the magnitude of the job. What is this thing known as total quality or total service? Describing it is simple. Achieving it is hard.

Total quality or total service is a dizzying array of boring processes that, put to work in every nook and cranny of an organization, ensure that you do right by the customer, that customers can count on you to deliver a product that works, that they can count on billing and other administrative procedures that are error-free, that they can depend on you for extraordinary service, if service is part of what they are buying.

I used the word "boring" following the lead of LTV Steel's general manager of integrated process control, Roger Slater. In his nifty book, *Integrated Process Management: A Quality Model*, he says:

> There are few things in life more boring, more lacking in distinguishing features, than a process running the way it should. . . . [By contrast] what is more electrifying than a disastrous breakout of a blast furnace, especially at night? Or the fireworks of a defective running stopper on a steel ladle dumping more molten steel on the floor than in the molds? Or

a mishap known to manufacturing people as a rolling mill 'cobble,' where red-hot ribbons of metal leap violently and unpredictably up and over roll stands and into aisleways, and perhaps even tangle themselves high above the mill floor in the roof purlins?

But even more exciting than these undesirable events themselves is the usual response to them. Talented people swing rapidly and decisively into action, knowing exactly what to do. Why shouldn't they? These things are routine. Exhibiting all the right skills, mechanics, electricians, and other specialists quickly rid the operation of its problem, often leaving behind strange and wonderful twisted shapes of destroyed product and equipment. . . . Meanwhile [Japanese competition] plugs along its boring way. Eating our lunch.[1]

As Slater, the people at Motorola, and others testify, exciting, out-of-control operations and heroic technicians and managers saving the day are not confined to manufacturing. "Consider the poorly run office," says Slater. "Here may be found something better described as entertaining than exciting—a comedy, perhaps, if it weren't such a tragedy. But the organized office—now there is a place where there really is nothing to see. Boring."[2]

I quote Slater extensively because it's in the contrast he presents so starkly that we can best see what's meant by total quality. Total quality is a process wherein things work routinely. Where's the news in that? In American industry something that works routinely is the exception, not the norm. What routinely happens in most organizations is the equivalent of the steel industry's cobble and the military's snafu (situation normal, all f----d up). Motorola and others have proved that snews (situation normal, everything works) soon may not be news. Our expectation, and in turn that of our customers, ought to be that cobbles and snafus are on the endangered species list. Motorola embarked on its quest for total quality in 1981; by 1992 the company was close to achieving its total-quality objectives.

MORE THAN ITS OWN REWARD

It doesn't take a Sherlock Holmes to deduce that taking a company from snafus to snews takes a heroic investment of time and money. Does it pay off for the shareholders? Motorola's experience says that the returns are big and almost immediate. Paul Noakes reports that company people have been tracking the payback on its quality investment since 1983. They figure that in that time, they've reduced total costs—measured as a percent of total sales—by a little more than 5 percentage points, roughly the same number as their after-tax profit margin. That means that the savings in 1991 from the total-quality program would be about $600 million. Between 1987 and 1992, when Motorola really poured its all into the quality initiative it calls "six sigma," Noakes estimates that the total savings were nearly $3.2 billion! He concludes that it's just plain good business sense to work on quality.

Return on investment in quality comes from several sources. For one, there's just simple cost savings of the kind Noakes talks about. Estimates vary, but most of the cognoscenti on total quality seem to agree that any operation that hasn't been scrutinized through the total-quality microscope is probably kicking out errors at the rate of 20 to 30 percent. Whether the operation be shipping, order processing, billing, manufacturing a product, or processing x-rays in a hospital, the odds of something going wrong are much higher than any of us want to believe.

A simple personal example: Not long ago my wife was in an accident. The ambulance took her to a well-respected hospital. X-rays were taken, but she was then told they would have to be done over. They had botched the first batch, she was told, because she had small bones. (It doesn't take an expert to observe that.) Then the hospital lost the second batch and wanted to repeat the procedure yet a third time.

About a year later, her parents were in a serious auto accident. The x-rays showed that her mother had fractured her hip and that her father had broken his leg. Somehow the hospital got the films mixed up and was going to release her mother the day following the injury while getting set to treat her father's "broken hip." Fortunately, my wife caught the mistake (just as I had forced the other hospital to find the missing x-rays).

Mistakes at steel mills and hospitals make good stories because the potential damage is huge. But the tendency to screw up routinely is all around us. Recently, I sat in on a management meeting of a company that most of us would rank among America's most successful. The good news: errors in orders processed were down sharply from last year. The bad news: 37 percent of orders processed still have errors somewhere—incomplete shipments, billing mistakes, wrong goods delivered, and so on.

From well-regarded hospitals to prestigious companies, the only safe assumption is that the rate at which things are done wrong is a lot higher than most of us would ever guess. And that's costly. Estimates vary, but quality experts seem to agree that fixing a quality glitch costs you five to six times more than doing something right the first time. Richard Buetow, Motorola vice-president and director of quality, believes that the average American company's processes are probably kicking out defects at 500 to 2,000 times the rate of the top competitor in the industry, *even if the average company uses the same equipment, technology, and suppliers as the top company.*

The cost savings from doing something right the first time help explain Motorola's competitive edge. Motorola is first or second in most of the markets it serves around the world. Noakes and others don't believe they would even be in the game were it not for their quality program. Their cost base would be too high. His studies show that companies that are truly world leaders in quality spend less than 1 percent of their sales dollar fixing defects, while the average company spends 10 to 15 percent fixing things that go wrong. A study released by the management consulting firm of A. T. Kearney strongly supports what Noakes and others at Motorola have learned. Kearney finds that for the average U.S. company, the cost of poor quality in the late 1980s hovered between 10 and 20 percent of sales. Since the net profit margin for the typical American company is 5 percent, the cost of our snafu approach to life runs two to four times our profit margins.[3]

But quality hits the bottom line in a way that's much more important than cost savings. A very large segment of most markets—not the whole, but a large segment—has a strong preference for dealing with those who offer better quality and service. So the biggest cost of poor quality, whether you're a company selling widgets or a hotel chain selling hospitality, is the loss of customers. A. T. Kearney says 68 percent of all people who stop doing business with a company do so because of poor service— they just aren't satisfied with the way they've been treated. And, Kearney says that a disgruntled customer goes on to tell, on average, nine other people about his or her unhappiness.[4] People at Motorola think the number is even higher.

For years the Strategic Management Institute in Cambridge, Massachusetts, has been studying the profit impact of various market strategies. Its sample includes over 2,000 business units. Analysts there try to correlate business success with every imaginable dimension of business. One of the strongest correlations they find (by a lot) is quality and service relative to the competition. Companies that offer outstanding quality and service typically earn twice as much on investment as their competitors at the low end of the quality/service spectrum. Institute founder Bradley Gale argues that the main reason for this difference is the simple fact that customers are willing to pay more for quality, service, and reliability.

At a very personal level the experience of Motorola's Scott Higgins, an operations manager who works closely with suppliers, verifies the finding. In an effort to reduce cost in his unit, Higgins found a supplier who claimed he could sell Motorola an electronic part for power amplifiers of the same quality, but at a lower cost, than the existing source. "Well, when the parts came in and we put them on the [production] line, all of a sudden our yields started to go down." Yield in the factory, or the number of salable items out of all these produced, was the only definition of quality that the customer, in this case Motorola itself, cared about. Motorola went back to the higher-priced supplier. Higgins reports, "It's not always best to go to the lowest-cost supplier; in this case he was costing us [more] because of the yields."

The Kearney study strongly supports this idea. Kearney reports that a straight commodity product—one that is in no way physically different than what the competition sells—can command a price premium of up to 10 percent when "accompanied by outstanding service."[5] Clearly, our concept of total quality ought also to include total service.

Of course, better quality and service don't always mean customers will pay more. My former colleague, Don Potter, now head of the consulting firm of Windermere Associates, has spent the last fifteen years studying winning and losing strategies in a variety of industries. Potter notes that in industries or at times when supply exceeds demand, as for the airline or paper businesses in the early 1990s, it's rarely possible for any vendor to charge more, even if that vendor's quality and service *are* superior to all others. Nonetheless, he argues that quality and service strategies are essential: "They keep you alive."

They keep you alive because a true quality strategy is all about building relationships with customers that are very hard for others to attack. Potter finds that competitors have to knock at least 10 percent off prices to buy business away from a competitor that has a very strong relationship with its customer. Motorola seems to understand this fully. Almost everyone at Motorola these days carries around little wallet sized plastic cards that say on one side:

OUR FUNDAMENTAL OBJECTIVE
(Everyone's Overriding Responsibility)

Total Customer Satisfaction

On the other side of the card Motorola lists a host of beliefs, goals, and initiatives to yield total customer satisfaction. (Central to its idea of total customer satisfaction is the total-quality initiative sparked by Sundry in 1979. Curiously, the word "quality" almost gets in the way. It implies relevance only to widgets and manufacturing, and it has the potential to divert our attention from the real essence of total quality—serving the customer.)

PRIDE, CONTROL, CHALLENGE, AND LEARNING

An effective total-quality program doesn't just benefit customers. Run right, total quality is one of those rare management ideas that, like self-direction, can really benefit most middle managers and employees as well. One reason: Such a program is typically organized in a way that shoves challenge, control, and learning way down the line in organizations. Another: It quite naturally fosters pride in work. People are craftsmen at heart. They want to produce products and give service they can be proud of. They also like being part of a team that strives to be the best at what it does.

Most firms organize total-quality programs in a broadly similar way. First, the whole organization divides itself into small, say, two- to seven-person teams. Armed with a big goal for improvement and trained both in quality techniques and team skills, each team identifies the main products it produces or services it provides. There may be only one or several.

Second, teams identify the customer or customers for their products and services. They talk to them. They find out what customers consider important. Significantly, this way of approaching quality forces people to define quality in the way that the customer sees quality. This is crucial and explains why total quality and total customer satisfaction are so closely linked at Motorola. In the old days of quality control, quality was usually defined by the engineers or manufacturing people. That's when quality gets expensive. Companies add all sorts of bells and whistles that the customer doesn't care about, while entirely overlooking what the customer does want. (Note that for many activi-

ties performed by a unit, the customer will be internal—one
department of an organization serving another. Thus, quality
buffs talk about both *internal customers* and *external customers*.)

Third, the team members analyze the way work currently gets
done. They figure out how it might be dramatically improved.
They start by analyzing the major sources of customer complaints. Then they move on to the smaller ones. Often they
uncover work that's completely unnecessary, a common source
of almost immediate cost savings.

To see this process at work, look at Rick Chandler, who runs
something called the "cellular infrastructure group" at
Motorola. This group produces equipment that picks up your
call on a cellular phone and connects you with whomever you're
calling. Chandler says, "We are changing the way we look at
quality. Now the issue always comes down to how what we are
doing affects the customer. Will what we are doing make the
customer happier with us? Can we make it easier for him to do
what he is doing?"

Chandler contrasts the old way of thinking about quality with
the new. He told me that Motorola people had always known
that their customers expected products within four weeks. "I had
internally generated charts that showed that we were regularly
hitting that four-week goal. But when we started talking to customers, they told us we were doing a lousy job." As Chandler
and others talked with customers, they learned that it was taking
the Motorola system four weeks just to get the order from the
customer to the cellular infrastructure group. They were then
taking another four weeks to build and ship the product to the
customer. So, while it looked like four weeks to Chandler, "the
customer's perception, which is the only thing that counts, is
eight weeks." Chandler says they went to work on the front-end
part of the process, the part they didn't have direct control over,
and got a little better. "We got it down to 3.6 weeks. . . . So then
I took our four-week build cycle [the part of the process he had
direct control of] and got it down to two days. Now I can deliver
in four weeks. Now the customer says: 'Thank you very much.'
That's exactly what I wanted."

The general problem with quality in America today, Chandler laments, is that people have all sorts of charts and graphs "proving" that they are meeting targets. But the data are internal. "You've got to get out and find out what the customer wants." It sounds obvious but, in Chandler's view, we as a nation are far from making the practice routine. Chandler wants everyone to understand that their job is no longer to please the boss. That's internal. Their job is to please the customer. That's total quality.

Perhaps nobody I talked with better personifies what Chandler has in mind than Hossain Rasoli, a technician who works in Chandler's group. Rasoli says that before he was swept into Motorola's total-quality drive, "I was always interested in knowing how my product was doing in the field, but I never really knew. Going back about five years, I didn't have the slightest idea. I didn't have graphs or any solid information on how the product performed." Several years ago Rasoli was given the responsibility for improving the quality of a power amplifier that's used in cellular base stations. "I call it my baby," he says, pointing to the power amplifier, or PA. "I take pride in this product. If it fails in the field, I feel hurt, or I get depressed. Sometimes, when I see a rack of them coming back from the customer, I'll tell our team, 'Listen, this is our problem, and we've got to work on it right away.''

Rasoli points to his baby and compares it with the old product. "This is the PA they started building about four years ago. This is our new PA. We've changed everything that's inside these PAs except the cable—actually we changed a couple of cables too." Rasoli is not an engineer. Under the old school of managing, even at the old Motorola, he would never be given this kind of responsibility. But under the total-quality system, management gave him basic data on the PA failures in the field and lots of training and told him to do whatever he needed to get the problem fixed.

"I started going to the field to gather information from customers," says Rasoli, "and then I went to work with component engineering to analyze the failures." Using his training on problem solving and statistical process control, Rasoli found the parts responsible for the greatest number of failures. These included capacitors prone to blowing out, silicon that cracked under thermal expansion, and solder problems. So he went to development engineering, discussed the failures, and asked them to redesign the parts. Rasoli now has a data base. He analyzes every PA that comes back from the field, "And," he says, "we make graphs—weekly graphs [that show] this is what our main problem is, and this is the second main problem, and this is the third. Then we just attack these problems one by one."

When Patty Barten explains how the total-quality program helps people develop, Rasoli is obviously one person she has in mind. Talking about him and his efforts she says, "He is now recognized in this organization as Mr. PA. He knows more about this product than any designer, any vendor, any manager, anyone else." In just two years, she reports: "We've made over a 400 percent improvement in our PA field quality." Almost all of it, she says, is based on what Rasoli and his team have done.

These days, Rasoli is clearly working for the customer and not the system. He talks openly about his problems with the bureaucracy that come with any big company, even one the caliber of Motorola. "In some cases I had to go against the procedures because of red tape around here," he says. "You're not supposed to take parts from one department to another without getting authorization. But [once] I needed some parts in a hurry and couldn't let the management know where or how I was getting them." The resourceful Rasoli engineered a deal with a technician in another department, a man who faced a similar problem. Rasoli would slip the devices his counterpart needed into his pocket, stroll over, and casually make a trade. He admits that he probably could have gotten the same things through normal procedures. "But I knew that if I went through the right people it would take time. And if it takes time, it hurts our customers. We wanted to get the better quality parts into the field as soon as possible. I had to go through different routes to get under the red tape."

Barten relates another example of Rasoli's drive to make the system work for the customer. Purchasing had decided to bring in a different vendor on a component that goes into the PA. "This mild, very gentle, soft spoken gentleman absolutely exploded. He was taking on vice-presidents saying: 'You are not going to put this in my product.' " Rasoli's dedication, persistence, and commitment to his customers is a fine example of total quality working the way it should.

In Rasoli we find an excellent case of how a total-quality effort, at its most basic level, is inextricably linked with treating people right. Rasoli was given responsibility and support, which enabled him to succeed. That success, in turn, motivated him to strive for and achieve even more. Rasoli has broadened his skills and deepened his self-esteem, and in the process, Motorola has gained a better product, happier customers, and higher profits.

OUTRAGEOUS OBJECTIVES

Chandler and Rasoli make clear the vital role of down-line people in making total quality work. But the top has to work hard at it too. At Motorola, a combination of unflagging management support, outrageously ambitious goals for improvement, and continuous benchmarking combine to keep the program moving swiftly forward.

Bob Galvin says that Motorola would never have become focused on quality if the trio in the chief-executive office (at that time, Galvin, Bill Weisz, and John Mitchell) didn't consistently and unequivocally show they were serious about it. "When we went out to visit the operations we forced ourselves never to ask about productivity," recalls Weisz. "We asked about quality. What can you do to improve quality here? How do you fix quality problems there?" They learned to ask the question, "Why?" at least six times. "If something fails, you ask why," says Weisz. "You get the first generalization and you ask why again. Finally you get down to the root cause." One must come across as being vitally interested in quality. "This is the first point I make to other top executives. If you are not going to live this thing personally every day and in every way, it [total quality] is going to fail," Weisz says.

Early on Galvin got quality on the agenda of Motorola's operating committee, which, next to the board, is the top policy-making body in the company. Everyone agreed with the wisdom of the idea. But the problem was that sometimes quality got talked about, sometimes it didn't. Operating committee meetings started at 8 A.M. with what Galvin calls nuts and bolts matters—budgets, performance against forecast, and the like. If they got around to it, quality discussions would begin about noon. On January 1, 1988 Galvin turned the chief-executive role over to George Fisher. However, he still wanted to remain involved with quality, and the operating committee wanted his input. Knowing that quality was far more fundamental to Motorola's future than the budget item of the moment, he convinced the committee to put quality as the first item on the agenda. That way he could leave the meeting at noon, if he wanted, knowing that he would have been involved in those discussions. More important, that way quality never would get bumped off the agenda.

Before the not-so-simple act of demonstrating the importance of quality through constant attention, the operating committee sent its first strong signal on quality when, in 1981, it adopted the beginning of what would prove to be a set of seemingly *outrageous* goals for improvement. The committee asked every unit in the company to improve quality tenfold in the coming five years. True to the spirit of customer-defined quality, the specific measures would be left to operating units and teams. But whatever measure was chosen, the goal was tenfold improvement by 1986. Noakes probably speaks for most at Motorola when he says: "I was a nonbeliever when that goal was announced." He explains that the old culture had found that improving anything by only 10 to 15 percent per year was hard enough.

Mathematically a tenfold improvement in five years means almost *sixty percent improvement each year*. It's no wonder that to Noakes and others the goal sounded crazy. But remember the figures presented earlier on the sorry state of American quality even today. By 1981, Motorola's operating committee had seen similar statistics, talked to the experts, and heard about the Japanese experience. The goal for tenfold improvement was arbitrary but, to the operating committee, seemed essential. In retrospect, Noakes says, the goal was a great thing for the company. "It forced us to change the way we run our business."

One of Motorola's early discoveries was that customers mostly measured quality by the frequency with which the product failed in the field. That made sense, but for Motorola, keeping track of what caused failure in the field was a problem. The real breakthrough came in 1982, when Motorola won a big contract for a communications system with the Pennsylvania state police. With that contract came excellent access to field failure data, and one Motorola quality pro was able to track failures by serial number right back to the factory. He discovered a fascinating and very important correlation: Field failure was directly related to manufacturing glitches. "The more we had to fix something in the factory," says Noakes, "the more likely [the product would] eventually fail in the field."

The truth of what the quality experts had been saying all along hit home. There is no way you can control quality through inspection. It's not just that it's more costly to fix something once an error is made; it's that the item doesn't really get fixed at all. You have to catch quality problems at the source, and this means finding, measuring, and fixing defects in the manufacturing process itself. That was news.

And this news also led to another breakthrough. By 1984 management and the field were experiencing serious—and in retrospect quite understandable—communication difficulties. Says Noakes: "We spent the first forty-five minutes of any conversation explaining our various metrics [measures of quality] and had no way of understanding how we were progressing as a whole." So the following year, frustrated by this confusion and armed with the knowledge that defects in manufacturing correlated directly with defects in the field, senior management put

out a directive that from then on the key quality measure would be defects per unit of work.* This meant that the whole company could rally around one measure that, more than any other, stood for customer satisfaction—process defects.

Then came the blow.

Motorola was starting to benchmark, which means that, as a new challenge arises, whether in manufacturing, design, distribution, or accounting, the team charged with the job of improving things sets out to identify what organizations handle that function best. The organization may be in the same industry. It may be in another. If there are no competitive conflicts and the other organization is willing, they arrange a visit to learn what the best organization in its class has accomplished—and how.

By 1986, Motorola had declared victory on its tenfold improvement goal. At that point Motorola was incurring only 1.5 glitches during the production of a typical product, down from 15 five years earlier. Not bad, Motorolans thought, when you consider the number of parts and steps that go into fabricating a complex piece of electronic equipment.

Meanwhile, Richard Buetow, who eventually took over from Germain as vice-president and director of quality, was leading a benchmarking team in the Far East. As much as Motorola thought it had improved, Buetow and his colleagues found that there were many electronic goods manufacturers who used similar manufacturing processes and virtually the same components as Motorola, but that had to repair only a mistake in every 1,000

---

*On the surface of it this measure seems in conflict with the idea that each unit defines quality goals in the way their customer looks at quality. In practice, both kinds of measure seem necessary. One is an overall measure that gives the company a common language and rallying phrase. This is what SQI (Service Quality Indicator) does at Federal Express and what, as we will see, six sigma does at Motorola. Within that, then, plenty of room exists for more tailored measures. Moreover, as Rick Chandler explains, there is great latitude in the simple definition of a defect. "What's a defect?" he asks rhetorically. In which part of the process do you locate the defect? Is it shipping a bad unit, an operator putting the wrong part in and then having to fix it, or—more subtly—an operator merely reaching for the wrong part?

items produced. "It was earth shattering," reports Noakes. "Here we are. We have just improved ten times only to discover companies operating 1,500 to 2,000 times better."

That's when top executives really got serious. In January 1987 they announced some truly outrageous goals:

- Another tenfold improvement by the start of 1989.
- A 100-fold improvement by the start of 1991.
- "Six Sigma" quality in everything they do by January 1, 1992.

Six Sigma? The term refers to the number of standard deviations from the center of a normal distribution of errors. For nonstatisticians, it means no more than 3.4 defects per million tasks. To get a feel for it, suppose you held yourself to that standard in school. Your average test score would be 99.999667 percent!

How is the company doing? By early 1992, Motorola had exceeded Six Sigma capability in some products and processes, but its average in manufacturing operations was 40 defects per million opportunities—a 99 percent drop from its error rate of 1986 but still not the Six Sigma goal of 3.4 mistakes per million opportunities. In 1992, Motorola's top officers reaffirmed the goal of reaching Six Sigma as soon as possible, with a continuing goal of reducing defects by a factor of ten every two years.

Meanwhile, consider these strategic results:

- In April 1989, Motorola took the lead in the world cellular phone business with the MicroTAC, a tiny phone that slips into a coat pocket. When introduced it was more reliable and a third lighter than the next best product on the market, a unit produced by Japan's Matsushita. Each year the *Nihon Keizai Shimbun*, a prestigious Japanese newspaper, gives out Nikkei awards for excellence in new products. Motorola's phone was one of the winners for 1989. (The 1992 model MicroTAC Ultra Lite weighs in at only 5.9 oz., 4.8 oz. lighter than the original.) MITI—Japan's Ministry of International Trade and Industry and the integrating force behind much of Japan's

success—gave Motorola the Foreign Product Design Award
for the MicroTAC.

- In 1990, the company introduced a wristwatch-sized pager,
the kind of product that Chester Gould, Dick Tracy's creator,
envisioned decades ago. Industry expert John J. Egidio says
that with this product, Motorola seems to have "scooped the
world by a year or two."[6]

- A microprocessor made by Motorola's semiconductor group
is the brains that drives the enormously successful home video
cameras made by Sony. Sony's Handycam was another 1990
Nikkei award winner. Yet another Motorola microprocessor
lies at the heart of Canon's enormously successful EOS II
35 mm camera.

Motorola takes particular pride in its successes in Japan. Arnie
Brenner, executive vice-president and general manager for the
Japanese group, says that people often ask him why the Japanese
are so successful in world competition. "To me it boils down to
one thing," he says. "The Japanese are the most demanding
customers in the world. If you can satisfy the Japanese, you can
satisfy [anyone]." People at Motorola know full well that the
company never could have been successful in Japan, or as successful elsewhere in the world, without the push for Six Sigma
quality.

Motorola's program, as we've seen, has seemingly simple
components—small, empowered teams that analyze and re-
structure processes; a fixation on the customer; wildly ambitious
goals for improvement; continuous benchmarking; commitment
to quality from the top; and a never-ending desire to improve.
The payoffs in cost savings, better products, and long-term relationships with customers are impressive.

SURPRISE REWARDS

Overall, their total-quality program has given Motorola a
hard-to-duplicate strategic edge. Striving for Six Sigma also gave
Motorola some surprise rewards—rewards that weren't foreseen

back in 1979. One is improved cycle time. Noakes defines cycle time as the period between identifying a need and filling it. In the case of a customer order, it is the time from when a salesperson makes the sale until the customer gets the product. In the case of new product development, it's the time from when the new product is defined until Motorola has designed, manufactured, and shipped the item to a customer.

We saw that Rick Chandler's team was able to reduce the cycle time for his group from eight weeks to four. Another cellular product used to take twelve weeks to make, which upset customers. After the company put an emphasis on improving cycle time in 1987, teams from purchasing, engineering, production, and elsewhere put their heads together. Now they can make the product in four or five days, and quality has been greatly improved. The whole process of rethinking, called "design for manufacturability"—that is redesigning a product to make it easier to manufacture—takes out many sources of recurring defects *and* reduces cycle time.

The linkage is critical. Designing for manufacturability typically means fewer parts and easier assembly. Fewer parts and easier assembly both mean less chance for error. Also rethinking (the pop word these days is "reengineering") the whole process from start to finish can yield big ideas for doing things better. Noakes says that if they'd realized the tight link between cycle time, quality, and customer satisfaction they would have almost surely started cycle-time reduction efforts when they started their total-quality program.

Perhaps Motorola's most impressive demonstration of the connection between benchmarking, short cycle times, and customer satisfaction is in Boynton Beach, Florida. There Motorola runs what is likely one of the most advanced factories in the world. It mass produces pagers, but in lot sizes as small as one. Orders from the field are given a bar code that reflects the widely varying individual requirements of each customer. In the factory the bar code is read by a sophisticated system of computers and robotic equipment. In two hours, the product is produced and sent on its way to the customer.

The plans for Boynton Beach never saw paper until a group from Motorola known as "Team Bandit" had spent a year and a half benchmarking. Their travels took them as far afield as Italy's Benetton, the sweater company that stays tightly linked with its customers through a computerized system that almost instantly apprises the factories of what colors and styles are moving in Benetton's worldwide marketplace. Boynton Beach now uses a very similar system to track and respond quickly to the apparently style-conscious customer for pagers.[7]

A second unexpected benefit from the six-sigma drive was an improved relationship with suppliers. Bruce Bendhoff heads up Craftsman Custom Metal Fabricators, Inc. His company is a "supplier-at-large" to Motorola, providing them with fabricated metal parts and metal stamp parts. Bendhoff reports being with other suppliers in 1989 in a Motorola seminar on quality when Bob Galvin walked into the room and told the audience that the operating committee had just made a revolutionary decision. In the future, every supplier who wanted to do business with Motorola would have to apply for the Baldrige Award. "Everybody went into total shock," says Bendhoff. When Galvin finished his remarks, the group took an unscheduled coffee break. According to Bendhoff, it was "an oxygen break for some of us."

Did Galvin really mean it? He absolutely did. Galvin says that he concluded that the company could not keep improving unless the suppliers themselves were improving. He's convinced there is one good common standard—the one set forth by the Baldrige contest. "If our suppliers will make themselves worthy to compete for that award," he says, "then they will move at the same level of quality that we will." How to get the suppliers to make that commitment? "I guess by edict," Galvin says with a wistful smile. "That wasn't the most pleasant thing to conclude or for suppliers to hear. But we had to get at the problem right away."

For those like Bendhoff who made the commitment, things have worked out well. His company is on a short list of preferred suppliers—ones Motorola can trust to deliver a quality product. Long gone are the days when Motorola purchases were put out to bid among long lists of suppliers, each trying to win mainly on price.

With the preferred supplier arrangement has come an almost familylike feeling between Craftsman and Motorola people. "One way they accomplish this is to have monthly meetings of not only their own employees but the suppliers as well," says Bendhoff. Now issues between suppliers and Motorola get resolved more swiftly and with less bureaucratic fuss. "If production control at my company has an issue with production control at [Motorola] cellular, they will just call one another up," Bendhoff reports. "Or if a designer at Motorola wants to talk with my programmers about how they are developing a new part, [again] they will just pick up the phone and call."

A final surprise for Motorola has been how much various administrative functions have benefited from the total-quality program. When the finance organization, for example, first approached total quality, they expected their role would be to measure everyone else. But deeper thinking led them to conclude that they were just as volume-driven, error-prone, and cycle-slow as manufacturing. The only difference is that they process pieces of paper, not electronic parts. One of their greatest successes is in closing the books, a process that used to take twelve working days from the end of the month and is now done in two. Motorola's finance department estimates that the combination of error and cycle-time reduction in just that one area—closing the books—is saving the company $20 million annually.

Another seemingly unlikely group who benefitted was Motorola's legal staff. They found that they were often tardy in filing patent applications. They studied their process and learned they could dramatically improve both the quality and number of filings if they organized as a team rather than dividing the patent applications among individual lawyers. In three years, Motorola's legal department increased its capacity to file patents by a factor of two without adding lawyers.

CONTINUOUS LEARNING

One reason the Motorola program works so well gets right back to where we started this book. People like Hossain Rasoli are, to use today's overworked word, empowered. As we saw with Rasoli, a vibrant quality program means putting a fair amount of power into the hands of people who are pretty low in the traditional command-and-control structure.

Motorola people are the first to explain, however, that you can't just empower. You can't approach people who have been working under the old management gestalt and tell them, "You're empowered!" Chances are they won't know what to do. Contend most Motorolans, you must both empower *and enable*. By "enable" they mean learning—lifelong education.

As with total quality, the roots of education go deep into Motorola history. Going way back, if you took a course that was even remotely connected to Motorola business, you got reimbursed 100 percent. Some of Motorola's top scientists and engineers got their bachelor's, master's, and doctoral degrees entirely on company sponsorship.

Motorola's total-quality program, however, shifted Motorola's commitment to education into high gear. In 1979, the same year that Sundry identified Motorola's pungent quality, Galvin commissioned an outside group to study and advise Motorola's on its long-term educational needs. The team came back with a five-year plan for training managers. Galvin was not pleased. He wanted a five-year education plan for the *company*, not just for managers.

The project had to be redone. This time over 300 Motorolans participated in the study. Their team's conclusion was that the company should invest $35 million and build a Motorola University. The team was prescient, but the only executive who bought the result was Galvin. The rest of the executive group supported the idea of more education but not the idea of founding a university or making such a large investment.

Frustrated by the lack of real support, Bill Wiggenhorn, who had been recruited from Xerox and put in charge of something called the Motorola Training and Education Center (MTEC), commissioned a nine-month study of the value of sales training. The result seemed amazing, almost implausible: For every dollar the company put into sales training, it earned $29 in increased sales effectiveness. Encouraged, Wiggenhorn decided that learning ought to be something central to the business.

He formed an MTEC board made up mainly of top execs, heads of operating divisions, and—of course—Bob Galvin to convince higher ups that the project was worthwhile and, at the same time, to show operational personnel to whom the program was geared initially that the company was committed to the project. And he urged at first, "Let's not call it Motorola University. If we do it will seem too far outside the mainstream of the business. We'll never get the operating people to buy in."

Even more significantly, he decided that for the program to work it couldn't be done off-line. (In 1990 Wiggenhorn said of the project begun in the 1980s, "At a typical plant with 2,500 workers, MTEC was using 50,000 hours of employee time—a lot of time away from the job for what some people [still] considered to be a pretty esoteric program."[8]) Finally, he made sure that the curriculum was designed to be taken straight to the plants.

An early goal was to help get that tenfold improvement in five years. So MTEC's core curriculum centered on the total-quality program. Through MTEC students first got training in the standard quality tools. (These days *every* Motorolan starts with a course called "Understanding Six Sigma.") Then they learned about industrial problem solving. Of particular interest, they got training on how to make presentations on conceptual material. Bill Wiggenhorn calls it, "a tricky assignment for an hourly worker presenting a technical solution to an engineer."[9]

Teaching managers was just as tricky. MTEC staff figured that managers—quick studies around Motorola—would need only some exposure to the total-quality concepts.

Wrong.

Managers needed, if anything, more training than down-line

employees. Old habits die hard and when push came to shove, the habit of getting products out the door tended to prevail even at Motorola and even if it meant shipping substandard quality. Meanwhile, the factory workers who had been "thoroughly indoctrinated" weren't practicing what they'd learned. What good does it do to keep meticulous control charts if manufacturing management never looks at them? Employees read the signals instantly.

In 1984, frustrated, but still optimistic, Wiggenhorn charged ahead. It was at this point that he called in two separate university study teams. Their findings verified and amplified the findings of the earlier study on sales training. The study teams divided Motorola's plants into three groups. In the first group was the small number of plants that had completely embraced the training they had received on total quality. They had learned the tools and techniques. They were applying process skills, like how to empower people to shut down a line if it was misbehaving, how to form teams to isolate quality problems, how to find the causes of quality problems, and how to run team meetings effectively. These were sites where support for total quality by plant management was palpable. The second group was half on board. These were plants that might have had tools and techniques in place but weren't using the process skills. Some management support was there, but it was not strongly felt. The last group of plants had been through the training program on quality, but had not followed up. If some of the plants in this group were using the new tools and process skills, they were doing so on a strictly hit-or-miss basis. Management at these plants showed no true commitment to the program.

The university teams reported back with some truly astonishing results. The totally committed plants were returning $33 on every dollar spent on education (including the dollars spent on wages and salaries while people were "sitting around" in class)— not bad. What other investment gives you a low-risk 3,300 percent return on investment? The second group of plants, the ones only moderately involved, turned in about a break-even result on their investment in learning. The third, detached group, lost money on learning.[10]

What may be just as important as the dollar return was what Motorola learned about effective teaching. What workers are taught matters little if they aren't also shown that its taken seriously by those in management. This verified Wiggenhorn's earlier assumption about involvement.

Knowing how to make education work, Motorola now seemed home free. Well, not quite. In 1988, armed with their increasing knowledge of how to make a quality product, Motorola decided to build a major new cellular facility in the United States. The company figured that with the right tools and training, an American workforce could match or beat a plant built anywhere in the world.

Motorola started from scratch at Arlington Heights, Illinois—not a low-cost area—with a new factory and new, automated equipment. Bill Weisz contends that the original idea was basically correct. "Today we think we make the highest quality, lowest cost cellular unit of anyone in the world." But there was one thing they hadn't planned on. "We began to evaluate people to work there, people we wanted to transfer in from our communications sector in Schaumburg, Illinois." Part of the evaluation was "a very simple test on math and reading [e.g., 10 is what percent of 100?]" A big fraction of would-be applicants couldn't pass. As Motorola dug into the problem, it found that the root cause was an inability to read. It wasn't that the people couldn't do simple math so much as they couldn't read the questions. It turned out that first line supervisors had been acting as *de facto* interpreters for those who used control charts and computer equipment. In a future that contemplated less supervision and far more empowerment, reading and math skills would be mandatory.

Something major had to be done. Motorola had a brand new role—remedial teaching. They didn't want it, but there it was. As the Director of External Education Systems Ed Bales says, "Motorola will never achieve Six Sigma quality without Six

Sigma . . . people. The education system in the United States
(our *supplier* of people) is providing Motorola with a 3 to 4 sigma
workforce. The forecast for the nineties is that the sigma level of
our labor supply will worsen."

Motorola launched several initiatives, the first at the plant
level. With MTEC's help, managers all over the company took
responsibility for organizing remedial classes, which employees
were encouraged to attend. In some cases the results were surprisingly positive. Says Wiggenhorn: "At a plant in Florida, we
offered English as a second language, thinking that maybe sixty
people would sign up, and we got six hundred—one out of three
employees."

Such skills have enabled employees to keep up with the ever
more demanding jobs in a factory where they are responsible for
making many of the tough decisions about production. But it has
also made life easier for them off the job. Charles Sengstock, an
old hand at Motorola, smiles: "There are some really heart-
warming stories that have come out of these remedial programs.
Mothers have come in with tears in their eyes after having taken
the course for six weeks. They'll say, 'Last night I had the most
wonderful experience in my life; I was able to help my son do his
math homework for the first time.' Others have said, 'I am able
to read the newspaper now.' In helping them on the job, you
help them in their personal lives too. There is this real rich,
warm, reward for all of us. You feel you are not only helping
Motorola but helping them significantly in their own lives."
Motorolan Alicia Gonzales is a good example. She left her native
Guatemala fifteen years earlier but still didn't feel comfortable
speaking English before taking the Motorola instruction. Now,
she says, "I don't need help when I go to the store. I don't have
to ask my children for help."

Not all the stories have been positive. To many employees, the
idea that they needed remedial training was painful or insulting.
Still, from Motorola's perspective the workforce simply had to
have such basic competencies if the company was to compete
effectively in the 1990s. Motorola also took the position that,
while it had a responsibility to train and retain workers as new

competition and technology demanded it, it was also the responsibility of the individual to get trained. If the course was offered
and an individual refused to take it, he or she could be fired.
(This has happened with fewer than twenty employees.)

Meanwhile, the people at MTEC concluded that, despite the
current situation and its demands, Motorola shouldn't be in the
business of remedial education, at least not indefinitely. So, the
company started working with schools at all levels. As they did,
they discovered other problems. One problem was a mismatch
between what schools taught and what Motorola needed. It was
as if university courses on manufacturing, for example, were
being taught out of Frederick Taylor's handbook, not from the
lessons learned on empowerment and total quality that characterized Motorola and other top companies. With rare exception,
the schools and universities that were supposed to be preparing
their graduates for the future, were in fact training them for the
past.

At that point Motorola decided it needed an aggressive approach to reshaping American education, starting with the K–12
grades. Motorola's president, Gary Tooker, has taken this issue
on as one of his top priorities.

In 1990 MTEC, (now called Motorola University) once more
expanded its role. Says Wiggenhorn (now Motorola University's
president): "Our charge . . . is not to just train Motorolans, and
not to just train our suppliers, . . . but also to make a positive
impact on the school districts from which we draw people." In
characteristic fashion, Motorola has launched a carefully
planned education initiative. It's multipronged, involving lobby-
ing at the federal and state levels, working with colleges that train
teachers, and interacting extensively with selected school districts in the five states with the most Motorolans—Illinois, Ari-
zona, Texas, Florida, and Massachusetts. Motorola even sent its
62,000 U.S. employees a company-prepared pamphlet entitled
"The Crisis in American Education," which urges them to get
involved with their local schools. If 1980 to 1985 was the era of
quality products and 1985 to 1990 the era of quality service, then
the decade of the 1990s, Motorola officials say, is the era of

quality people. They've even coined an expression for their objective—world-class "mindware."

— — —

FROM "QUALITY STINKS" TO Six Sigma, the mindware to go with it, and total customer satisfaction, the journey has been long and difficult but very rewarding. And Motorola is not there yet. Quality gurus have always urged the notion of "continuous improvement." Motorola's people clearly agree. On that famous benchmarking trip to Japan in 1986, Japanese officials told the Motorola group that it had taken them forty years to reach their current quality levels. They told Motorola it would take them at least twenty. By the end of 1992, the company had been at it thirteen years, an eternity by the standards of most American managers, but a source of true, sustainable advantage for Motorola.

12.

MATCH

The Potential Within

Apple Computer's Marci Menconi graduated from high school in 1961. Back then she, like many women in America, saw only three real career choices: being a nurse, going into teaching, or becoming a secretary. She settled on the latter, became good at it, and served as executive secretary for a number of company presidents, winding up at Apple in 1987. There she worked as secretary—or "area associate" as Apple calls the job—for Betsy Pace, who was then in marketing as director of K–12 educational programs.

Despite Menconi's obvious talent in the secretarial role, she never much liked the job and almost quit to work as a Federal Express courier. Today Menconi still works for Apple. But since October 2, 1990, her business card has read: Marcella Menconi, Electrician. She says she's never been so happy. These days, she exudes: "God! I get to go to work today."

TRAPPED IN A BOX

One of my strongest impressions from all my years consulting with various organizations is how many people seem mildly to wildly dissatisfied with what they do but don't know what to do about their lot, even though in small companies, the right job may be as close as an elevator ride or the office next door. Moreover, chances are that whoever is next door could use a little change or renewal, too. Even in the best companies and nonprofit organizations, a significant number of people feel bored or burned out, or they feel as if something is missing. Despite good things going on around them, these individuals feel boxed in, and they long to get themselves out. Some remain where they are, putting in time, sputtering along like an engine firing on half its cylinders. Others leave to go back to school, to move to a new company, or to change to a new profession.

Companies lose people all the time. The bad companies chalk it up to turnover, a staple of the organizational diet. The good ones are concerned and try to find out through "exit interviews" what's wrong with the organization—or more typically, one suspects, what's wrong with the individual. Sometimes the reason for leaving is obvious: better offer, new horizons, bad boss. Quite often, however, employees leave because something that they can't quite put their finger on is lacking.

In this book so far, we've talked about general categories of things that motivate us, like feeling in control and that what we do matters. But as much as we have in common, we have at least as much that's different. Personality traits are different, skills are different, interests are different, and—of singular importance—some of what motivates each of us is different. Aside from an example here or there, I have yet to see an organization unleash the powerful force of individuality. Some will. It's as inevitable as the year 2000.

The secret to unlocking phenomenally improved personal and corporate performance is something I call matching—matching individual values, skills, motivations, and interests to job needs. It's the process of nudging, prodding, awakening, and galvanizing the process by which square pegs and round pegs find their way into the right holes. Most organizations still overlook this need, and I'm convinced that it's costing them dearly. It costs in what's spent to recruit and train employees to replace those who have left. It costs in the loss of experience and institutional knowledge. But by far the biggest cost to companies, although impossible to measure, is having employees who aren't rowing with both oars.

There's no reason that an organization cannot and should not help its people find career renewal while *remaining with the firm.* I'll admit that at first blush, the idea presents a few practical and logistical challenges. But I'd argue that organizations that find a way to facilitate the matching process will discover huge payoffs, just as they did when employee assistance programs (EAPs) were started a couple of decades ago to help workers struggling against addiction. I'm sure that cost-conscious human resource managers worried about the expense of hiring a counseling staff and figured that firing people with unsavory addictions was the cheapest way to go. Today, it's widely accepted that salvaging an employee through an EAP is a good investment, and morally, it's also the right thing to do.

Remember that Motorola estimates it gets a return of $33 for every $1 the company invests in education. More organizations ought to think, as Motorola does, in terms of return on dollars put into human investments like education—or matching. If we invest $1 million in a new machine, we'd have the investment analyzed six ways from Sunday. We regularly invest at least that much in a human being over the course of his or her career. But our typical approach to that investment is to cross our fingers and hope.

Basic matching is, of course, fairly routine in company hiring programs. Remember Fred Smith's comments on the service business, where over the years Federal Express has developed a profile of the kind of person who is likely to be good in a customer contact job? Airlines do the same kind of screening for flight attendants, a job that demands exceptional interpersonal skills and a motivation to be of service. On the other side of the coin, applicants usually look into fields and jobs that interest them; they self-select. As in a new marriage, there's usually a surfeit of lusty enthusiasm when people start a new job.

Over years and decades, however, in relationships and at

work, enthusiasm levels off, and interests can wane and change. And all the irrelevant things that go into an initial career choice—including parental pressure, what peers are doing, and the expediency of simply finding a job, any job, to cover rent, food, and car insurance—don't do much to assure long-term job satisfaction. These expediencies may get us into a job but these very expediencies can be detrimental over the long haul. Often people don't reassess initial choices or, even when they do, act on that reassessment. It's no wonder that many feel dissatisfied.

Currently, when workers feel trapped and can no longer stand their jobs, if they can afford the service—*and if they know about the service*—they seek the help of an independent career counselor. And by and large, they get the direction they need. I've had a front row seat in watching the success of career counseling. My wife is a career counselor and has spent sixteen years helping people match their skills and interests to the right job. Time after time, a little professional guidance has enabled disenchanted people to find a new and more rewarding path through life.

Effective matching requires finding a person's subtle and often subconscious needs and motivations, which may only emerge through a battery of sophisticated tests* and other tools that go by such names as FIRO-B, the Strong Interest Inventory, the MBTI (Myers-Briggs Type Indicator), the 16PF, and the SIMA (System for Identifying Motivated Abilities).† After taking many of these tests, I learned a lot of things about myself that I'd only slightly sensed, and I've seen how revealing they can be about others.

---

*People in the counseling profession don't like to call them "tests." The reason is that the word implies that there are right and wrong answers. They often use the word "instrument," which to me sounds more menacing than "test." Most of us who aren't working day-to-day in the profession refer to them as tests, so with apologies to the counselors, I use "tests" instead of "instruments" throughout most of the chapter.

†SIMA is a structured interview process for discovering what motivates individuals.

The tests give clues to how you prefer to interact with others, and the kinds of people you interact with best. They show whether you have a strong need to lead in some fashion or prefer to let others do so. The tests might suggest that one person performs best in chaos, while another person needs a logical, orderly environment. When someone naturally suited to detail and follow-up work is placed in a job that demands developing broad strategies, then you've got a fish crawling across the prairie. That these complex but fairly distinct personality traits influence happiness at work, *and most especially job performance,* is to me highly obvious.

None of these tests, however, reveal everything about a person. If a person has had a bad week, gets a speeding ticket on the way to the counselor's office, or is temporarily elated after making a big sale at work, the test results can be markedly skewed. Correctly interpreting these various tests—which should be done in conjunction with interviews by the counselor so that an individual's background and circumstances can be put in context—is a demanding discipline.

TRUE RENEWAL

Currently, the few companies engaged in the kind of matching I'm talking about—those midstream shifts in direction that can invigorate an individual and an organization—are tackling this issue only in a small way; And the effort isn't usually very systematic. That was the case at Apple computer, where Menconi's dissatisfaction with her job prompted her to seek out help.

When Marci Menconi found out that Betsy Pace, her boss at Apple, had been promoted to another job and that she might not be able to go along, she decided to have a hard look at her career. She definitely wanted out of the secretarial role. Through a friend she had heard about Carol Dunne, one of several career counselors who staff Apple's Career Resource Center. At that time Dunne was putting on a variety of career development seminars for Apple employees and, on a more or less ad hoc basis, working with people in the middle of a career dilemma—people like Menconi.

Menconi contacted Dunne, who asked her to take a fairly standard battery of tests. On completing these, she and Dunne met for a series of extended discussions. A number of clues pointed the two toward Menconi's current job as electrician. Her score on the MBTI (Myers-Briggs Type Indicator) was one early indicator. In Myers-Briggs code, Marci is an "ISTP,"* People who fall in this category often like hands-on work, working independently, operating equipment, using tools, and troubleshooting. ISTPs don't usually like routine or being stuck inside one office. That test result roughly aligned with Menconi's past experiences: In high school, she took at least as much interest as the boys in souping up '57 Chevies; since high school one of her big time avocations had been working on and piloting small airplanes. She clearly had a strong mechanical bent.

The confirming evidence came from her scores on the Strong Interest Inventory. That pencil-and-paper exercise put her in the "very high" category in general occupational motifs such as agriculture, nature, and mechanical activities. More specifically, her interests ranked "similar" to such job categories as Air Force officer, horticultural worker, carpenter, engineer, photographer, and chef. But of all the categories her interests put her closest to the work of an electrician.† "I was floored with that result," she says.

Dunne then helped Menconi put together a list of next steps. The first was to read the book *Please Understand Me,* a detailed description of the MBTI. This would give Menconi real understanding of her MBTI results, the typical needs of ISTPs, and why she would always be unfulfilled in a secretarial or assistant

---

*This stands for: Introversion, Sensation, Thinking, Perceiving.
†Note that this ranking by itself didn't mean she should be an electrician. The Strong Interest Inventory doesn't even begin to list all possible job categories. It does mean that she probably would the kind of work that electricians do.

role. The second was to put together an "informational interview" outline—a set of questions that she could use in talking
with various people in Apple (or elsewhere) to learn about the
work they do and find out for herself whether their jobs matched
her own interests, and whether she stood a reasonable chance of
acquiring the necessary skills for such jobs. Her outline reminded
her to ask questions like: What are the educational and experien-
cial requirements for this job? What skills do you need for the
job? What are the job's basic duties and responsibilities.? What
do you like best about your work? And least? To what other
positions might this work lead? What problems or challenges
does your department face now? Who else should I contact
about this type of work? What kinds of pressure do you feel on
the job? And of no small importance to Menconi: What does the
job pay? What are the normal working hours? Is flextime a possibility?

Armed with her outline, Menconi first met with Jack Krause,
manager of electricians in Apple's facilities maintenance division. Next she arranged a tour of several Macintosh factories to
see whether jobs at these sites might be appealing. None of the
manufacturing activities caught Menconi's fancy, but facilities
maintenance looked intriguing. Questions in hand, she arranged
for a number of further interviews there. Her talks confirmed the
test results—the work done by the electricians seemed exactly
right for her. Right, that is, except for one small problem: She
didn't have the education, skills, or experience to be an Apple
electrician. Krause suggested that she take some electrical
courses, which she began in March 1990, going part-time in the
evenings. In October 1990, Menconi made a lateral move from
Apple's grade 27 area associate to grade 27 maintenance technician. She continues her education with Apple's blessing and financial support, having enrolled in a three-year program for
electricians at a county vocational school. These days she says:
"I'm incredibly happy. I wear jeans; I'm outdoors a good part of
the time; I'm doing something different every day in my own
van."[1]

Menconi's story illustrates several points. First, without out-

side help, she might never have found her way to a career she
loves. Second, those personality tests that seem little better than
reading palms to most of us are far more sophisticated than most
people assume. The trick is to pull them out of the realm of pop
psychology and use them only in conjunction with skilled professionals who've spent years understanding the validity, strengths,
weaknesses, and interpretation of various instruments. Third, no
one test contains the answer, that a group of tests is almost always needed, and that even a battery of tests won't substitute for
the kind of personal interaction and discussion that Menconi
had with people like Dunne and Krause.

Of paramount importance, *interest* can be a more powerful key
to personal motivation than skill. Menconi was skilled in her old
job yet initially had few skills relevant to her new pursuit. But her
interests, once she understood them, inspired action. With help
and training she could acquire the requisite skills for what has
proved to be her real passion.*

Think of the potential that could be unlocked in most organizations if people like Menconi had access to the right counsel.

RETURNING TO YOUR ROOTS

For many people, a change less radical than Menconi's is
sufficient to recharge their batteries. In some cases all that's
needed is finding a new hobby or community activity outside of
work to add stimulation that's not happening on the job. Or, for
some, returning to their roots does the trick. That's the case with
a man I'll call Sanford Neely, a project manager at Hewlett-
Packard (HP) who was very unhappy in his work and personal
life. He had just been through a divorce and was on the verge of
chucking it all, moving to the Northwest, and settling down to an
easier life, "perhaps," he said, "as a forest ranger." The clincher
was that Neely's department at HP was being thinned out, and

---

*This isn't always possible. Most people have interests well outside their apti-
tudes. I'd love to play jazz piano. No way.

he was asked to find another position that he wanted within HP.

Neely started interviewing for other project management posts, but his heart wasn't in it. "I realized the jobs made me very hesitant, and it came across loud and clear in the interviews, too," he recalls. The experience started him thinking about different career paths. To their credit, HP management supported his idea of consulting with an outside career counselor. He turned to long-time career counselor Maureen Shiells. Using tests and discussions, Shiells and Neely discovered several keys to the difficulties of the past and to what might make a brighter future.

Being a project manager in charge of software development was exceptionally draining for Neely because it required constant interaction with people. Moreover, Neely was something of a perfectionist. The duality was wearing him out: having to do a job through others on the team and having to do it extra well to meet his own standards. At the end of his typical twelve-hour day, he was completely stressed. At home he just wanted to curl up in a corner and read. "When I got home I just didn't want to be with people," he says, feeling that this contributed to his divorce.

As Shiells and Neely discussed his favorite past experiences, almost every one of them went back to before he was a project manager, back to the five years he was an HP engineer. One thing he remembered with particular joy was the satisfaction he got from writing software. The tangible accomplishment and direct feedback he got in that job were lacking in his management position. After some soul searching, Neely realized that "project management wasn't the best place for me" and that "I enjoy dealing with the nitty-gritty level of technology."

Yet he had been away from software engineering for six years and would have to go back to school to catch up. With the company's full support, Neely embarked on several educational refresher programs over the course of a year. Now back in engineering circles, he reports that he is far happier. And HP benefited too: It kept a valued employee and one who learned an important lesson, at that. "One of my goals," Neely says, "is every couple of years to go through a revaluation of where I am and where I'm headed."

Neely's realization is more important than it might sound at first. In an ideal world, a partnership between an employer and an employee should last only as long as it is beneficial for both sides, so long as the employee is contributing to the company and in turn feels challenged and satisfied. But, of course, this world is not perfect—employees cling to their old posts for security, or because they assume that unhappiness at work is "normal"; employers are loath to lose workers who have proved themselves, in whom they've already made a substantial investment in training. Unfortunately, there's still a widespread tendency to get stale in one's job and do nothing about it. Slowly, however, people are realizing, as Neely and others already have, that it's largely their responsibility to manage their own career paths in ways that make them happy. And slowly, ever-so-slowly, a few companies are realizing that it's to their benefit, too, to support that process.

RAYS OF HOPE

Unfortunately, there are all too few success stories like those of Menconi and Neely. Few companies have been willing to institutionalize career change by setting up a system for matching people with jobs. But two companies that are moving in that direction are Coors, the famed Colorado brewery, and Sun Microsystems, the fast-growing workstation manufacturer in California's Silicon Valley.

Coors has taken the step toward impartial career counseling for its employees through a partnership with Regis University, a private Denver-based educational institution that is one of the best in America at tending to the needs of adult learners. The idea of a corporate-academic partnership was unusual in 1987, when Regis and Coors linked up as a way for Regis to evaluate Coors' in-house training programs and remains unusual today. The two institutions took note of the uniqueness in their statement of purpose, which described their goals as "parallel but distinct." It said in part that the relationship "respects the uniqueness and integrity of both organizations. These principles will be vigorously guarded and compromises will be unacceptable."

Mary Lou Nugent, former director of the partnership, upheld these principles. Although she was a Regis employee in residence at Coors, she saw her role as one of a "neutral" counselor, helping employees with their educational needs. If employees needed or wanted particular skills, she could refer them to Regis programs—but she didn't have to: She could send them to whatever programs best suited their needs.

In 1990 the relationship expanded to include a second Regis professional, Kathy Bartlett, also housed at Coors. A career counselor, and Nugent's successor as director of the partnership, Bartlett set up a career development center that offers a library, confidential individualized counseling, and courses in such topics as assertiveness skills, team-building, and plateauing (that is, finding a new job at the same level in an organization when the opportunities to move upward are limited). By the time the partnership celebrated its five-year anniversary in 1992, private counseling sessions had been provided to 1,700 Coors employees, helping them find jobs and careers in a company that by then was turning slowly away from its paternalistic past.

One of those 1,700 employees was Jerry Ford. After having worked at Coors for six years as a bottle-line operator, Ford contacted Bartlett. He had always wanted to go to college. He explained that not only did he want the prospect for advancement that a college degree might bring him but that he also wanted to be a good role model for his children. But he had been in constant trouble in high school and the prospect of going back to school terrified him. Over the course of three sessions, Ford and Bartlett worked out a plan for Jerry to dip a toe into the educational waters. He would start with a communications course at a local community college. As registration day approached, however, Bartlett got a call from a thoroughly traumatized Ford. Just the prospect of entering the lobby to register triggered all his past fears. He was starting to back out.

Bartlett says, "A part of our philosophy is absolute commitment to take the extra steps to support our clients. I met Jerry at the front door of the college. I walked with him down the halls and helped him register." Now, she reports with obvious delight, Ford has completed three semesters, his last one with a straight A average. For Ford, with a jail record and as he describes, a "lousy work history," the partnership program has given him a new outlook on life and a confidence that benefits everyone.

The Coors partnership served as a role model for two similar relationships Regis has since formed, one with Storage Technology and another with an entity that in itself is a partnership between AT&T and the International Brotherhood of Electrical Workers. The company and the union both fund the pioneering effort at an AT&T manufacturing site to provide training and career development at a time when the company is requiring its employees to expand their portfolio of skills greatly.

In contrast to Coors, Sun Microsystems is a relative newcomer to the ranks of America's largest corporations. Started in 1982 by a foursome of young college graduates and Ph.D. candidates, the firm mushroomed beyond expectations to reach $3.2 billion in sales and 12,500 employees by 1991. It did that by staying on top of the latest nuances in the fast-paced computer world.

So it's not surprising that the company's avant-garde approach to human resource planning reflects its ongoing struggle to keep pace with technological change. Top managers at Sun know they walk a fine line. Technology is evolving so rapidly that they need consistently to attract new college graduates with skills on the cutting edge of computer know-how. On the other hand, Sun wants to keep the good people it already has on board provided, that is, that they, too, stay on top of change. The way to make that happen, Sun is discovering, is to infuse the organization with the understanding that employees are in charge of managing their own career development and then back that message up with action. "We're trying to have people prepare today for tomorrow," says John Cope, a Sun human resources manager.

Marianne Jackson, human resources director for Sun's U.S. operations, expresses the goal well. "We didn't want people to ride the sea of change like weightless victims waiting for the big swell to come. If it took them up and over the crest—great. If it drowned them, they'd be angry. We wanted to teach people to be really good navigators." Jackson refers to the concept as career fitness. It is much like what Sanford Neely did for himself at Hewlett Packard. The idea is keep your skills in shape, be proactive, control your own destiny, reinvent yourself, manage your career. In this age of corporate downsizing, employees all over the country hear admonitions like this every day. But Sun is one of the few firms I've found that is supporting its words with actions. The most tangible sign of the company's commitment is its Career Development Center, housed amid Sun manufacturing facilities in Milpitas, California. The comfortable center functions as Grand Central Station for career planning at the company.

The initial need for the center stemmed from the ongoing "redeployment" process at Sun. This company, like many these days, is constantly reorganizing and reassessing its activities, and in the process a handful of people at any one time find themselves on the redeployment list. At Sun, that means that while their precise job will be disappearing, they have the option of either leaving the company with a financial package in hand or finding another job inside Sun. In the beginning, the Career Development Center was mostly helping those folks on redeployment.

It was the brainchild of John Cope, whose fifteen years of experience in counseling and psychology convinced him of the importance of career management. Cope joined Sun in May 1990 after leaving another firm that was too stodgy to empower employees with the skills they needed to refocus their careers. Given the go-ahead to do just that at Sun, Cope met in the summer of 1991 with the director of the Career Action Center in

Palo Alto, California, a nonprofit career counseling center that
had evolved over twenty years from a tiny home-based operation
into a full-fledged, highly respected career center serving thousands of Silicon Valley job-seekers. Cope asked the center's director of programs, Betsy Collard, if the center could possibly
open a satellite facility at Sun. It was a novel idea, but within
weeks, amazingly, the deal was done. The Palo Alto center
agreed to clone itself.

The result is the Sun Career Development Center, a combination library, counseling center and general hub for career support and guidance. The center has plenty of private cubicles
where job-seekers can make telephone calls, prepare their
resumes, and set up a temporary home while their search is on. It
also is stocked with lots of books and materials about how to
search for a job. It has local newspapers and several long shelves
full of binders listing, on average, 5500 jobs available at other
companies in the San Francisco Bay Area. There are computer
terminals by which to access lists of openings across the country.
And there are lists of hundreds of positions open within Sun
itself. But those listings aren't the heart and soul of the center,
and anyway the center isn't really there to help people find a
specific new job. More often than not, new positions are found
through networks of acquaintances and co-workers. What the
center does do, though, is prepare people for a fruitful search.
"We teach them how to do it, and they do it themselves," Cope
says.

The teaching happens in a number of ways. For example, the
center sponsors regular brown bag lunches, on a wide range of
topics, open to anyone at Sun. Some samples include: managing
personal finances during times of employment uncertainties, tips
on starting a new business, navigating Sun's internal job-
selection system, using the telephone to market yourself, and
interviewing do's and don'ts. All seminars are subsequently
made available on videotape.

The center is also equipped with all sorts of tools for helping
people discover their hidden talents and interests. One self-
guided computerized system—many Sun people feel most at

ease when they're sitting in front of a computer terminal—is so complete that users can spend as many as ten hours completing career-assistance exercises. The system includes the Myers-Briggs test, as well as two others on-line. Unfortunately, while the users are encouraged to seek interpretation from a professional at the center, they may choose the more risky path of interpreting their results themselves.

Still, the center does have a staff of trained human resource specialists and career counselors on contract from the Palo Alto Career Action Center. Importantly, the primary responsibility of the Career Development Center's staff is serving their client—the employee. The center is under no obligation to counsel workers to stay at Sun, no matter how valued the employee might be. "The center's position is we don't help people stay or leave. We help people make good career decisions," Cope says.

Here's another way Cope looks at Sun's responsibility. "I think there is a commitment to every employee's employability—not necessarily to employment security."

All Sun employees are entitled to a limited amount of individual career counseling with no charge back to their departments. In situations where a more intense counseling program is needed, a program can be tailored to the situation with a nominal charge back to the employee's department—typically to the training budget. While technically there is a plan for the number of counseling hours a "redeployee" will receive, as a practical matter redeployees receive all the individual assistance they need and want.

One person who benefited from what the center has to offer is Kevin O'Loughlin. A political science major in college, O'Loughlin unexpectedly found himself in the computer industry, which isn't hard to do in Silicon Valley. He spent five years at Sun, advancing to a supply analyst's post in manufacturing. Though others might cherish that post, the heavy emphasis on statistics and process didn't suit O'Loughlin. He longed for a career in marketing or music. He yearned to find out where he might go next.

O'Loughlin had helped himself to many of the services at the career development center, but he wanted more. Fortunately for him, his supervisor agreed to foot the bill for a series of individualized counseling sessions. His early meetings with his counselor, which included analyzing results from standardized tests, confirmed his hunch that his main interests were in philosophy, music, teaching—almost anything that wasn't technical or mechanical. To help him figure out where to go next, his counselor helped arrange informational interviews at other companies, one in the music industry and another in the apparel industry. The interviews gave O'Loughlin a chance to chat openly with people in other firms and industries without the pressure of an actual job interview.

Throughout his search, O'Loughlin was convinced there was a payoff to Sun. He was a happier and better employee, knowing he was working towards making a change, and he felt better about Sun because the company was helping and supporting him.

O'Loughlin's and Sun's efforts paid off. Landing a position as a program manager in Sun's Intercontinental Operations Group, O'Loughlin is now traveling to points as far and diverse as Japan and Russia, specializing in getting new products into these countries. He loves the challenge of working in foreign countries, where he has to adapt to different customs and regulations. "I find myself in all kinds of interesting situations," he comments, with obvious delight.

Sun's top management probably wouldn't be very happy if too many O'Loughlins navigated their way right out of Sun. But, to their credit, it seems to be a chance that they've been willing to take. And it's probably a pretty safe bet that they won't be disappointed because the Career Development Center is just the kind of resource that will make good people want to stay at Sun, not leave it.

The efforts at Sun and Coors are clearly on the leading edge of human resource management. Countless corporations have jumped on the "partnership" bandwagon, typically forming partnerships with suppliers or customers—arrangements that are long-term and flexible and designed to change with changing needs. But how many try to build equally adaptable partnerships with their employees? How many make commitments where both sides agree to work to keep the relationship alive as long as its fruitful for both? Sun's model offers a chance to alter a troubling paradigm in America, where change most often occurs as a reaction to a crisis rather than as a result of thoughtful planning and preparation. Maureen Clark, who started the Career Action Center in Palo Alto and is the liaison between the center and Sun sums up the greater significance of their efforts. "Companies haven't figured out what to do besides add and subtract [hire and fire]." The Sun center, she says, offers "a real chance of breaking into the hiring-firing model."

THE PERFECT FIT

The examples I've used here only hint at the potential of matching. Companies and individuals ought to press forward in this important area in the same way that Motorola approaches education. Bill Wiggenhorn, the president of Motorola University, explains: "When we hire you, we hope you'll be part of our community for forty years. But it's a two-way street. Our obligation is to provide you with an opportunity to learn the skills you need today and tomorrow. It's your responsibility to learn and apply those. If either one of us breaks the [implicit] contract, then our investment in education won't work."

Similarly both companies and individuals have responsibilities in the job-matching process. The company has an obligation to:

- Make the kind of thoroughly professional career counseling I've talked about very accessible to all employees either by making outside counselors available and paying the cost or by establishing an internal career action center.
- Keep discussions and test results between employee and counselor confidential unless the employee wants to share that information with others.
- Keep a very complete job posting and information system

current and to make it available and fair. (Too often candidates get picked before a job is posted.)
- Make professional training easily available.
- Give ample warning and career planning support if jobs are likely to be phased out.

The individual has an obligation to:

- Accept responsibility for staying renewed. If that person is burned out and doesn't do something about it, that's the individual's problem—not the "system's."
- Make use of the career center or outside sources of help, when appropriate.
- Press the organization to support the idea of career planning and job matching.
- Accept the idea that careers need not always move up. Moving ahead, in many cases, may mean taking several steps backward in order to acquire skills and experience.
- Grasp the idea that the norm these days is change; changing interests, changing jobs. Don't expect the one right career for life.

A long time ago, Thoreau told us that most men live in quiet desperation. His words are as apt today as when he first uttered them, and they apply to both men and women in the workforce. Changing this situation has always seemed crucial. It now seems eminently possible.

EPILOGUE

Looking back over the years of research that went into not only this book but the others that preceded it—*In Search of Excellence, The Renewal Factor,* and *Adhocracy: The Power to Change*—one irritating and tough question persists. Why do some great companies, like IBM, stumble badly while others, like Procter & Gamble, remain vibrant? My flip answer has been that I'm not sure anyone knows—in one sense, I'm not sure I care. My whole message has been: Learn from the best while they're good and move on when they lose their edge. Like top athletes, it's reasonable to expect that even the best companies will get old and thick around the middle. Still the question is a good one, and though it may in some general sense be unanswerable (What would *you* tell GM?), I'll give it a shot. There are, it seems to me, some patterns that we see in the companies discussed here and that have emerged in earlier research, and these patterns help explain long-term success.

First, and maybe most important, is the fact that the companies that remain successful break themselves into small, fairly autonomous units. This has the effect of shoving the market mechanism for making decisions down into the hierarchy and keeps the upper echelons from doing dumb things. General Mo-

tors started this way. Way back when, they were the first big
company after du Pont (which then controlled GM) to decentral-
ize radically. As time went by, however, they maintained only
the form—not the fact—of decentralization.

In this book I've talked about small units mainly in connection
with product innovation. But small units keep companies innovative in another sense as well: They keep companies reinvent-
ing themselves. This probably occurs for two reasons. Small
units—think of Rubbermaid's business teams—stay much more
closely in touch with their customers than any companywide
department can do. Further, small units, organized to be relatively independent, have more *will* to succeed. If they hold themselves accountable for their own profit, cost, or both, they are not
inclined, say, to fly first class just because the parent company
seems relatively big and wealthy. Radical decentralization, and
these days that includes farming out activities that some other
company can do better, is a means of breaking big companies
into small, independent, market-driven units. It pulls the market
mechanism inside the hierarchy.

The second factor that seems to distinguish the noble survi-
vors parallels, but is different from, breaking the company up
into small, semi-independent units. It's the will and the ability to
organize "downward" rather than "upward." In a way it's what
this whole book is about. Organizing in conventional ways says
one thing to most people in companies: "Please the boss." The
companies that stay healthy organize to please their customers
and to motivate their people.

When it comes to consumer marketing there is only one business school in the world, and it's called Procter & Gamble. I
think it's safe to say that through the years no organization has
understood consumers better than P&G. Few pour as much
money, time, or energy into trying to understand them. Judging
from the Lima, Ohio, example, few companies understand the
needs of their own people as well as P&G either.

To be sure, they haven't got everything right. P&G would be
the first to admit that they could do a better job marketing to
powerhouses like Wal-Mart that are coming to dominate distri-

bution channels. And from the outside (and probably to many inside) the company seems very stiff, formal, and tough, not at all the human enterprise that I've described at Lima. But its 150-plus-year history suggests that it is doing something very right. My belief is that it's P&G's historic focus on the needs of its customers and its own people. This combines neatly with its version of independent units: relatively independent, sometimes competing brand and category* managers.

A third factor is the ability to switch smoothly and easily from normal bureacracy (using that word in its nicest sense) to what I've called "adhocracy."† The problem is this: Bureaucracy, our historic form of organization, is set up to handle the recurring problems of everyday life in organizations. Sales departments do the selling, manufacturing makes things, and so on. As long as the business world isn't changing very fast, bureaucracy works fine. But things are changing fast. Since change has a nasty habit of cutting across organizational lines, some other form of organization is needed to mirror the change. Usually this is the cross-functional project team or task force, but it can be any group coming together from different departments to solve common problems. It's adhocracy, and it's our main way of organizing for change.

Most organizations see the need for adhocracy but manage it poorly. Organizations that have staying power will be those that manage adhocracy as well as most do bureaucracy. The companies I've talked about here are pretty good models. Take Federal Express and its "quality action teams," AES with its plant-level "family" and "honeycomb" structure, Motorola with its quality teams, Levi's with the way it has organized to make Aspirations happen. Merk and Rubbermaid—with their cross-functional teams for innovation, which get replicated in other parts of their organizations—are also wonderful examples. P&G's Lima plant, with its seamless ability to move from on-line to off-line work, and then back again, is another. If I'd been smart enough to

*Collections of similar brands.
†Following Alvin Toffler's lead in his book *Future Shock*.

imagine it when I wrote *Adhocracy*, Lima would have been just
what I had in mind.

The last factor is sheer staying power and the will to commit
to long-term plans. Think of the thirty years that P&G has put
into making self-direction a way of life. Think of the fourteen
years Motorola has labored at making total quality a reality.
Think of the seventeen years it took Merck to bring Proscar to
market. Think of the massive effort Levi's has put into their
Aspirations program. Haas has persisted in pushing this program over the years. And the company has made great progress,
but Levi's would be the first to admit they have a long way to go.

In this do-it-yesterday society few executives have the patience
for that kind of commitment. They want total quality now, self-
direction a year later, and incidentally "let's change our culture." Inability to commit to the time it takes to make big things
happen is precisely why most "leaders" won't make big things
happen. The companies I researched seem to understand this.
It's one reason they are so open. They know that most others
won't be able to match their example even if they understand it
completely.

———

SO FAR I'VE TALKED about the good news pouring out of
America and about some select American organizations. We
need to understand these companies. Just as Abraham Maslow
started to revolutionize psychology when he began looking at
healthy people, those of us who worry about life in organizations
need to know what the healthy ones look like. That has been the
thrust of my own research for over a decade, starting with *In
Search of Excellence*.

One crucial question, however, remains unanswered by this
kind of research: If we're doing so well, why does it feel so bad?
One reason is captured neatly by a story Lamar Alexander, former U.S. secretary of education and former governor of Tennessee told me: "In the Southeastern Conference, Kentucky would
win every year in basketball. Then suddenly Vanderbilt won,
then Alabama, and then Tennessee. Everybody in Kentucky

thought their team had gone to hell. But, in fact, nothing had happened to Kentucky; the league had just gotten better. So Kentucky had to practice harder and stay on its toes. It was a shock to have to compete for the championship every year and sometimes lose it." The obvious economic parallel is that in industries America used to own—such as automobile and consumer electronics—having to compete and losing regularly has been a shock. But having to compete seems precisely why we are producing better goods now. Look at Motorola's response to Japanese competition or the quality in American automobiles now versus a decade ago.

The deeper reason behind our unease seems to me to be that we quite probably are in the midst of a revolution—call it the knowledge revolution or the information revolution—that is as dramatic as the one that took people off the farms and into the factories. Before that revolution 70 percent of the American workforce tilled the soil so that all of America could eat. These days we eat better (many would say too much) with less than 3 percent of our workforce tending the farms. Today's revolution is changing the nature of work and will change the structure of society.

A large part of our disquiet is in the nature of revolution itself. It creates enormous change and uncertainty. Most people don't do well with massive uncertainty. Another source of unease is the impact the information revolution seems to be having on disparity of pay for American workers. We barely noticed the effect of knowledge, information, and the computer on income in the 1960s and 1970s. But we sure are feeling it now: From 1965 to 1975 real incomes for all levels of education in America rose by 20 percent; from 1975 to 1985, though, real income for high-school dropouts dropped by 4 percent, while real income for college graduates went up 48 percent! If that pattern persists, (as many, including Secretary of Labor Robert Reich, think it will), we are in serious danger of becoming a splintered, have-versus have-not society. It will sorely test the egalitarian American dream.

The most serious problem the knowledge revolution presents

could well be in job creation. Consider the meaning of productivity: more work with fewer people. There is nothing wrong with replacing human beings doing boring, dirty, dangerous work with machines. Besides, mechanization is the source of the wealth of nations. So far we have been able to make up for the inevitable job losses with economic growth,* but this is unlikely to continue.

Today, what you don't see in most advanced factories is lots of people. The great bulk of the cost of most manufactured goods is indirect overhead—supervision, coordination, accounting, research, design, engineering, selling—everything but direct labor. In fact, as management guru Peter Drucker is fond of pointing out, if direct labor is much more than 5 percent of a manufactured product's cost, something must be wrong with the manufacturing process. (This is why, as one part of the McKinsey Global Institute study shows, we haven't lost manufacturing employment to foreign competitors. Lower labor costs in foreign countries don't make that much difference.)

Work systems like P&G's self-direction, AES's families and honeycombs, Motorola's Six Sigma dramatically reduce the number of people needed to get the work done. Self-direction takes direct aim at indirect cost—first and second line supervision and many staff support services. A true total-quality system takes a huge slice out of indirect overhead—the cost of rework and the people it takes to do it. It's not hard to imagine long and continuous growth in the manufacturing base coupled with a persistent decline in manufacturing employment.

But manufacturing is only 20 percent of the economy. What about services? Precisely the same phenomenon is occurring

---

*Taken as a whole the companies talked about in this book have been job creators. In the decade ending 1992, these companies added 110,000 jobs, growing from a base of 222,000 in 1982 to 332,000 in 1992. However, large companies in general have not been job creators, and there is no reason to expect the companies talked about here to keep creating jobs. From 1982 to 1992 the sales of these companies grew a lot faster than jobs, so that sales per employee—one measure of productivity—went up by 90 percent.

there. For big hunks of the economy, manufacturing and services aren't that much different: Levi's processes jeans, and FedEx processes mail; P&G processes consumer goods, and banks process checks and electronic transactions. In fact, McKinsey managing director Fred Gluck suggests that the distinction between manufacturing and services is increasingly irrelevant. "If you write software, call on customers, or do bookkeeping at a manufacturing plant, then your job counts as a manufacturing job. On the other hand . . . all of Microsoft's employees are counted as service jobs despite the fact that the software they make is as tradable as any machine tool."[1]

Dartmouth professor James Brian Quinn also drives a big nail in the coffin of the manufacturing/services distinction. His studies show that service businesses now typically employ just as much capital as manufacturing (and their rate of capital employment is growing faster than manufacturing). Often service businesses are more capital intense—for example, think about Federal Express and its investment in aircraft.[2]

Until recently productivity in the American service sector scarcely grew at all. Now it seems to be burgeoning. As Alan Greenspan, chairman of the Federal Reserve Board, recently told Congress, "A new synergy of hardware and software applications may finally be showing through in a significant increase in labor productivity." If true, then in the words of the *Wall Street Journal,* "this is real man-bites-dog stuff," so negligible had been the impact of computerization before.[4] The *Wall Street Journal* went on to cite numerous examples—almost all in the service sector—of recent big corporate gains in productivity through computerization.

Consider that the whole of the McKinsey Global Institute's 1992 study of productivity focused almost exclusively on the service sector and demonstrated major differences in productivity between countries. The commonly held view that service businesses resist productivity gains must be wrong. I find no reason to believe that the service industry will not, in the future, experience the same productivity gains as manufacturing.

In the past we have greeted such news with a big bear hug.

Today, I'm not so sure what to make of it. The rub, it seems to me, is that we don't now have the equivalent of farm-to-factory job replacement in either manufacturing or services. The potential social problem in the service sector is the same as in manufacturing: job loss.

This ought not to be. We are a rich nation and are not in much danger of losing that distinction. My belief is that we ought to use our wealth to be rich twice—rich in spirit, as well as rich in material goods. My view comes from one of the hardest questions I get asked when I'm lecturing abroad, especially in countries that are struggling to make a market system work, most recently for me Brazil, Russia, Chile, Argentina, and Ecuador. It goes something like this: Why in a wealthy nation like America can't you solve your problems in education, the environment, drugs, violence, homelessness, health care . . . ? The list goes on.

Why indeed? The broad answer is that we have no mechanism for effectively directing our economic might toward solving those problems. The efficient problem-solving mechanism in our society is the free-enterprise system. It's not perfect, but any other system, most especially government intervention, works far less well. But the problem that our free-enterprise system solves is the problem of creating material wealth. We do that very well. The trouble is that most of the problems that now confront us lie outside our conventional definition of wealth.

The real problem, then, is not lack of work. Potentially . . . potentially, there is plenty of work. Our society is replete with problems that people could be put to work solving. But how to connect our spectacularly successful economic system with the problems at hand? That is the issue that ought to come near the top of our national priorities. I have no ready answer, though in a book that will follow this I'll discuss how some organizations, private and public, are coming to grips with various facets of the general problem.

One big part of the problem, and one that will continue to get in our way even in business, is our system for distributing wealth. We rely on our old system for thinking about organizations. We are entombed in the pyramid. Up to now, in most organizations the pyramid defined who you were. If the title on your business card signaled that you managed something, then few questioned your importance. The only question was one of degree. Better to be a vice-president than merely a manager, better yet to be group vice-president, maybe even vice-chairman. Better still to be chairman. And the real royals in America: chief executive officers.

The pyramid did, and still does, much more than define your symbolic importance. If you are among its denizens, the pyramid gives you a daily fix of what many consider the ultimate aphrodisiac—power. If people report to you, well then you have control over them. At least that's the way it was supposed to work. Never mind the fact that most people pretty much do things their own way no matter what managers tell them to do.

The pyramid also determined, and determines, how much you get paid. With most institutions there is still a direct correlation bctwccn how many bodies sit below you on the pyramid and how much cash and how many stock options you get. This curious fact of life has a curious side effect: it spawns managers. Wcll-meaning supervisors who can't get more money to their subordinates through the normal system of merit increases have found a simple way to beat the system. They promote them. In this interesting variant on Parkinson's Law, managers and organizational layers get created, not by the need for more managers but by the need to get more money into the hands of decent, hard-working folks who deserve it.

Now, most of this pyramid system, though we still cling to it, is obsolete, the inevitable result of self-direction and empowerment. These two things make delayering possible and also that terrify middle managers: Their jobs have become obsolete.

While I don't know what should be done to reorganize our system for distributing wealth and creating jobs, I do think I know where to start. A real solution will recognize the following:

Our wealth per individual American continues to rise. While productivity threatens jobs, it also creates continuing growth in

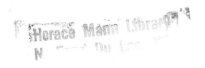

gross domestic product per capita. On paper, at least, each of us has more money. The trouble is that it seems to be distributed less and less equitably.

We must find ways to use pay systems to encourage flexibility. What we need in these fast-changing times is widespread recognition and use of what the P&G people at Lima call off-line work and what I label adhocracy—the widespread equivalent of P&G's work- and skill-based pay systems, extending well beyond technicians, would be a good start.

We must look for market-based solutions to societal problems. I have no idea how they will work, but I know what other approaches do and don't work. Government intervention doesn't work: Part of the reason we outstrip other nations in productivity is that other governments own more of what we deem private enterprise, and other governments protect jobs and industries at the consumer's expense. Such intervention doesn't work because highly central-ized decision making, in big government or big business, doesn't work.

Tax incentives do work, though perhaps too well—look at how we built, then over built, real estate when we granted that business favorable tax treatment. And they create their own seemingly unstoppable momentum, a momentum that has con-tributed to their lack of popularity. But they work because they are part of a market system.

A well-regulated* market system works for the economy as a whole, and it works for big businesses that divide themselves into small units—it certainly works better than hierarchy. With thought we ought to be able to come up with market mech-anisms that we can aim at the social problems of the day.†

*I choose the modifier "well-regulated" carefully. We abandoned almost all sensible regulation of the thrift institutions in order to bring this industry into the market system. But removing sensible oversight attracted an irresponsible, often criminal, element, costing all of us taxpayers hundreds of billions of dollars.

†The AES Corporation is one striking example of what I have in mind. The social issues are energy conservation and pollution. Legislation favoring co-generation made AES possible.

We should aspire to be rich twice. To do so means redefining what we mean by wealth. We are not a wealthy nation until our measure of wealth includes progress at easing social problems that trouble us all. Given our mighty domestic product per capita, should we be satisfied with the way we educate? With our slumping infrastructure? With the state of our environment? With the level of drug use? With the violence? With large and growing pockets of poverty?

If we are really to be a rich nation, spiritually as well as materially, we must find a way to put money behind our talk. We wax eloquent about the need for education—and don't pay our teachers. We decry our sagging infrastructure—and vote down measures to fix it. We abhor pollution—and waste billions on superfunds. We bemoan violence—and take policemen off the streets (and let the market system for drugs and handguns go wild).

The profound irony of our times is that all the ingredients of the solution are there: The work systems and technology that make us enormously productive; plenty of problems to solve to make America and the world a better place; the wealth to address at least some of these problems; the need to create jobs in the areas where these problems are most felt; the societal concern that would make these jobs meaningful. What we need, however, is the imagination and the will to turn these ingredients into a vibrant reality.

Appendix I

SURPRISE— AMERICA'S ECONOMIC STRENGTH

In late 1991 some figures began trickling out of the Paris-based Organization for Economic Cooperation and Development (OECD) that whacked convention on the side of the head by showing that in 1990 America still had a commanding lead in productivity over Japan—and Germany—and France—and Britain.

Specifically, the OECD study showed that per capita wealth production in America was 16 percent higher than in West Germany, 23 percent higher than in both Japan and France, and 36 percent higher than in Britain[1]—astonishing. Could these figures be right?

Perhaps, for other researchers were finding similar results. Dirk Pilat and Bart van Ark, both economists at the University of Groningen in the Netherlands, published a paper in early 1992 that looked only at manufacturing productivity in the United States, Germany, and Japan.[2] In 1987 (the latest date for which the figures they used were available) value added per working hour in the United States was 27 percent ahead of that in West Germany and 32 percent ahead of that in Japan. What's more, German productivity, which had been close to that of the United States in 1980, had slipped badly since, and Japanese productivity, which had been rapidly catching up with that of the United States in the 1970s, stagnated (relative to the United States) in the 1980s.

The most in-depth and thoughtful look at the situation came from a study by the McKinsey Global Institute, an arm of the consulting firm McKinsey & Company.[3] Their starting point was the OECD study. The

OECD results puzzled not only the McKinsey researchers but also the outside brain trust that had joined them—such notables as Nobel laureate Robert Solow of MIT, Martin Bally of The Brookings Institution and the University of Maryland, and Francis Bator of Harvard University. The puzzle: It has been nearly fifty years since the end of World War II. Given the quicksilver flow of capital across international boundaries, the mobility of technologies, and comparably educated and healthy work forces, shouldn't highly industrialized nations produce goods and services with equal efficiency? If they don't, why don't they.

The team launched this year-long project by asking these sorts of questions: What about the widespread belief that America is falling behind? What about the wild swings in currency exchange rates between countries? What's the effect of spending by government in different countries? How about productivity in the very difficult to measure service sector? Of most importance, if the differences are real, what causes them?

First, the team eliminated currency aberrations as an explanation. The OECD, it turned out, had already taken this into consideration by making comparisons on the basis of purchasing power, so they looked not just at yen per capita in Japan, marks per capita in Germany, and so on, but, as they had done in 1980 and 1985, they adjusted for what a person could really buy with his or her yen, marks, francs, pounds, or dollars.

Next the team looked at employment patterns. It could be, they reasoned, that wealth per capita is the wrong measure of productivity, since there are more working couples in the United States than in the other countries. Further, not all workers contribute directly to wealth creation. So they decided to leave out people employed by government, education, health services, and real estate, and include only those working in what the team called the "market economy."

Measuring wealth produced per person employed in the "market economy," America still led. By this measure the United States led France by 19 percent, West Germany by 25 percent, Britain by 39 percent, and Japan by a mind numbing 64 percent. In an unusual burst of rhetoric for the staid firm, McKinsey asked: "How can this be, given that the Japanese juggernaut seems to be continuing to gain market share abroad [for example, autos] and even dislocating whole industries [for example the formerly U.S.–based consumer electronics industry]."[4]

A part of the answer is the wide disparity among industries in Japan. The best Japanese manufacturing firms do dominate the rest of the world. But as anybody who has studied the Japanese know, these firms are only a small fraction of the economy. Japanese productivity, especially—as we will see—in the service sector, is very low.

Another part of the answer lies in hours worked. Americans take less vacation than the Europeans. Adjusting for that brings France and West Germany closer to the United States. Adjusting for hours worked, however, puts the Japanese even further behind, since the number of hours put in by Japanese workers beats the rest of the industrialized world by a considerable margin (but cuts their score in terms of wealth created per hour worked). No matter what the criteria used, McKinsey found that the United States leads Europe, and Europe leads Japan. Why?

To understand the reasons the researchers decided to focus on the service sector, which accounts for 60 to 70 percent of the employment in industrialized nations. (The real figure is probably higher since a fair amount of value added in the manufacturing sector is service, but this gets counted as manufacturing). Service-sector productivity numbers are notoriously flaky, so the team went to work on in-depth case studies of representative service industries: airlines, banking, restaurants, retailing, and telecommunications.

Their findings for each segment of the service sector ran parallel to the figures for industry in general except in the restaurant business (where there is very little productivity difference between countries) and except in Japan. In Japan service productivity seems to be only half that of the United States. But again the question: why should there be differences at all?

Where they could get data the team probed each service sector in each country in depth. While the team found peculiarities in each industry, they also found a general pattern across the service industry. Differences in productivity could not generally be attributed to differences in technology, capital availability, the marketplace, degree of unionization, economies of scale, production processes, capital intensity, or differences in employee skill.

The difference is in what the report called "division of labor," "management behavior," and government "policy and regulation." What this means is that across the industries they studied, America is better organized to earn superior returns on its investment in human capital. Labor is more mobile and flexible. Management attitudes are less rigid, partly because managers are less protected from competition and partly because they are more willing to experiment with new organizational forms. Government policy and regulation is less confining.

At the time of this writing, the McKinsey Global Institute had just completed a similar, in-depth study of the manufacturing industry in industrialized nations. The findings were a little different. For example, they found that technology did make a difference in a few industries, the most notable of which was processed food, where Japan and other countries simply do not use modern technology. The same is true for beer production in Germany and steel production in countries that don't use minimills. The study did verify that the Japanese are ahead in certain manufacturing segments, though their lead is diminishing in the auto industry; according to the researchers, the Ford Motor Company may well be the most productive auto company in the world. (For more on the turnaround at Ford see the sections on that company in *Adhocracy* or *The Renewal Factor*.)

In general, however, the findings on the manufacturing sector parallel those on the service sector: the United States is ahead and the differences are mainly attributable to differences in organizational arrangements in the different societies.

Appendix 2

DON'T PUT
PROFIT FIRST

In Chapter 1 I mentioned that recent research coming out of business schools strongly supports the idea that putting profits first isn't necessarily the best strategy for enhancing profitability. But this idea is not really a new one. In fact, the work by Kotter and Heskett, Porras, Collins, and Hansen has strong historical roots. Not long after the end World War II, a young brigadier general left his position as head of the Small War Plants Board, traded his stars for mufti, and returned to head his family's business. He wrote: "Institutions, both public and private, exist because the people want them, believe in them, or are at least willing to tolerate them. The day has passed when business was a private matter—if it ever really was. In a business society, every act of business has social consequences and may arouse public interest. Every time business hires, builds, sells or buys, it is acting for the people as well as for itself, and it must accept full responsibility for its acts. . . ."[1]

His name: Robert Wood Johnson. His company: Johnson & Johnson. He wrote that statement as the preamble to the now famous Johnson & Johnson credo, the corporate philosophy that puts people, customers, and community ahead of profits.

James E. Burke, chief executive of Johnson & Johnson from 1976 until 1989, echoes General Johnson's sentiments: "I have long harbored the belief that the most successful corporations in this country—the ones that have delivered outstanding results over a long period of time—were driven by a simple moral imperative—serving the public in the broadest possible sense better than their competitors."

Burke's staff worked with the Business Roundtable's Task Force on Corporate Responsibility and the Ethics Resource Center in Washington, D.C., to compile a list of socially responsible companies. The group found twenty-six that fulfilled two very rigid criteria: First, they had to have a written, codified set of principles stating that serving the public was central to their being. Second, there had to be solid evidence that these ideas and principles had been promulgated and practiced for at least a generation.

The thirty-year performance of fifteen of these companies was carefully studied. (Eleven had to be dropped from the list. Some hadn't been in business that long. Others, like Hewlett-Packard, Levi Strauss, and Johnson's Wax, were private during part or all of the studied period and so performance figures weren't available.)

The group found that the return to shareholders for this group of fifteen companies beat the typical Dow Jones company by 7.6 times over the thirty-year period. (They happened to pick a period when the Dow underperformed it's long-term average. If the Dow had performed up to par, the number would "only" be 3.4 times the Dow).[2]

Appendix 3

EXCERPT FROM *FEDERAL EXPRESS MANAGER'S GUIDE*

LEADERSHIP DIMENSIONS AT FEDERAL EXPRESS

Charisma: Makes others proud to be associated with him/her. Instills faith, respect, and trust in him/her. Makes everyone around him/her enthusiastic about assignments. Has a special gift of seeing what it is that is really important for subordinates to consider. Transmits a sense of mission to subordinates.

Individual Consideration: Coaches, advises, and teaches subordinates who need it. Treats each subordinate individually. Expresses appreciation for a good job. Uses delegation to provide learning opportunities. Lets each subordinate know how he/she is doing. Actively listens and gives indications of listening. Gives newcomers a lot of help.

Intellectual Stimulation: Gets subordinates to use reasoning and evidence, rather than unsupported opinion. Enables subordinates to think about old problems in new ways. Communicates ideas that force subordinates to rethink some of their own ideas which they had never questioned before.

Courage: Willing to persist and stand up for his/her ideas even if they are unpopular. Does not give in to group pressures or others' opinions to avoid confrontation. Able and willing to give negative feedback to his/her subordinate or superior. Has confidence in his/her own capability and wants to act independently. Will do what is right for the company and/or subordinates even if it causes personal hardship or sacrifice.

Dependability: Follows through and keeps commitments. Meets deadlines and completes tasks on time. Takes responsibility for actions and accepts responsibility for mistakes. Able to work effectively with little contact with the boss. Keeps boss informed on how things are going, will take bad news to him/her, and is not afraid to admit mistakes to boss.

Flexibility: Maintains effectiveness and provides stability while things are changing. Able to see what is critical and function effectively within varying/changing environments. Able to remain calm and objective when confronted with many different situations or responsibilities at the same time. When a lot of issues hit at once, able to handle more than one problem at a time, and still focus on the critical things he/she must be concerned about. Able to "change course" when the situation dictates or warrants it.

Integrity: Adheres firmly to a code of business ethics and moral values. Does what is morally and ethically right. Behaves in a manner consistent with corporate climate and professional responsibility. Does not abuse management privileges. Gains and maintains the trust and respect of others. Is a consistent role model demonstrating and supporting corporate policies/procedures, professional ethics, and corporate culture.

Judgment: Reaches sound and objective evaluations of alternative courses of action through logical and skillful intellectual discernment and comparison. Puts facts together in a rational and realistic manner to come up with alternative courses of action. Bases assumptions on logic, factual information, and consideration of human factors. Knows his/her authority and is careful not to exceed it. Makes use of past experience and information to bring perspective to present decisions.

Respect for Others: Honors and does not belittle the opinions or work of other people regardless of their status or position in the organization. Demonstrates a belief in the value of each individual regardless of their background, etc.

Appendix 4

LEVI'S MANIFESTO

LEVI STRAUSS & CO.

Mission Statement   The mission of Levi Strauss & Co., is to sustain profitable and responsible commercial success by marketing jeans and selected casual apparel under the Levi's® brand.

We must balance goals of superior profitability and return on investment, leadership market positions, and superior products and service. We will conduct our business ethically and demonstrate leadership in satisfying our responsibilities to our communities and to society. Our work environment will be sage and productive and characterized by fair treatment, teamwork, open communications, personal accountability and opportunities for growth and development.

Aspiration Statement   We all want a Company that our people are proud of and committed to, where all employees have an opportunity to contribute, learn, grow and advance based on merit, not politics or background. We want our people to feel respected, treated fairly, listened to and involved. Above all, we want satisfaction from accomplishments and friendships, balanced personal and professional lives, and to have fun in our endeavors.

When we describe the kind of LS&CO. we want in the future what we are talking about is building on the foundation we have inherited: affirming the best of our Company's traditions, closing gaps that may exist between principles and practices and updating some of our values to reflect contemporary circumstances.

What Type of Leadership is Necessary to Make our Aspirations a Reality?

New Behaviors: Leadership that exemplifies directness, openness to influence, commitment to the success of others, willingness to acknowledge our own contributions to problems, personal accountability, teamwork and trust. Not only must we model these behaviors but we must coach others to adopt them.

Diversity: Leadership that values a diverse workforce (age, sex, ethnic group, etc.) at all levels of the organization, diversity of experience, and diversity in perspectives. We have committed to taking full advantage of the rich backgrounds and abilities of all our people and to promote a greater diversity in positions of influence. Differing points of view will be sought; diversity will be valued and honesty rewarded, not suppressed.

Recognition: Leadership that provides greater recognition—both financial and psychic—for individuals and teams that contribute to our success. Recognition must be given to all who contribute; those who create and innovate and also those who continually support the day-to-day business requirements.

Ethical Management Practices: Leadership that epitomizes the stated standards of ethical behavior. We must provide clarity about our expectations and must enforce these standards through the corporation.

Communications: Leadership that is clear about Company, unit, and individual goals and performance. People must know what is expected of them and receive timely, honest feedback on their performance and career aspirations.

Empowerment: Leadership that increases the authority and responsibility of those closest to our products and customers. By actively pushing responsibility, trust and recognition into the organization we can harness and release the capabilities of all our people.

NOTES

CHAPTER 1

1. John Gardner, *Morale* (Toronto: George J. McLeod, Ltd., 1978), p. 58.
2. Michel Foucault, *This Is Not a Pipe* (Berkeley: University of California Press, 1983), jacket.
3. John P. Kotter and James L. Heskett, *Corporate Culture and Performance* (New York: Free Press, 1992), p. 11.

CHAPTER 2

1. Herbert M. Lefcourt, *Locus of Control: Current Trends in Theory and Research*, 2d ed. (Hillsdale, N.J.: Lawrence Erlbaum Associates, 1982), pp. 3, 5.
2. Edward Lawler, "The New Plant Revolution Revisited," *Organizational Dynamics* (Autumn 1990): 7.
3. John Hoerr, Michael A. Pollock, and David E. Whiteside, "Management Discovers the Human Side of Automation," *Business Week*, Sept. 29, 1986, p. 74.
4. Brian Dumaine, "Who Needs a Boss?" *Fortune*, May 7, 1990, p. 52.
5. Dumaine, "Who Needs a Boss?" p. 52.

6. Douglas McGregor, *The Human Side of Enterprise* (New York: McGraw-Hill, 1960).

_____

CHAPTER 4

1. James Traub, "Hernandez Takes Charge," *New York Times Magazine,* June 17, 1990, p. 23.
2. George Anders, "Million Dollar M.D.," *Wall Street Journal,* Apr. 8, 1993, p. 1.
3. J. R. Steadman, "Rehabilitation after Knee Ligament Surgery," *The American Journal of Sports Medicine,* 8, 4 (1980): 294.

_____

CHAPTER 5

1. Federal Express *Manager's Guide,* p. 1-1.

_____

CHAPTER 6

1. Roger Sant, Dennis Bakke, and Roger Naill, *Creating Abundance* (New York: McGraw-Hill, 1984), p. viii.
2. Thomas Watson, Jr., *A Business and Its Beliefs* (New York: McGraw-Hill, 1963), p. 11.
3. Watson, *A Business and Its Beliefs,* p. 5.

_____

CHAPTER 9

1. James Gleick, *Chaos* (New York: Viking, 1987), pp. 11–31.

_____

CHAPTER 10

1. Jared Diamond, "Turning a Man," *Discover,* June 1992, p. 74.
2. Quoted in "Keeping the Pipeline Filled at Merck," *New York Times,* Feb. 16, 1992, p. 3-1.
3. Roy P. Vagelos, "Are Prescription Drug Prices High?" *Science* 252 (May 24, 1991): 1083.

4. *Values and Visions: A Merck Century* (Rahway, N.J.: Merck & Co., Inc., 1991), p. 166.
5. Pharmaceutical Manufacturers' Association, *Good Medicine: A Report on the Status of Pharmaceutical Research* (Washington, DC: Pharmaceutical Manufacturers' Association Foundation, 1992), p. 6.
6. Pharmaceutical Manufacturers' Association, *Good Medicine,* p. 16.
7. Quoted in Thomas A. Stewart, "Brain Power" *Fortune,* June 3, 1991, p. 44.
8. Stewart, "Brain Power," p. 54.

CHAPTER 11

1. Roger Slater, *Integrated Process Management: A Quality Model* (New York: McGraw-Hill, 1991), p. 54.
2. Slater, *Integrated Process Management,* p. 54.
3. *Creating the Environment for Total Quality Management* (Chicago: A. T. Kearney, 1991), p. 3.
4. *Creating the Environment,* p. 4.
5. *Creating the Environment,* p. 4.
6. Lois Therrien, "The Rival Japan Respects," *Business Week,* Nov. 13, 1989, p. 108.
7. Alexandra Biesada, "Benchmarking," *Financial World,* Sept. 17, 1991, p. 50.
8. William Wiggenhorn, "Motorola U: When Training Becomes an Education," *Harvard Business Review* 4 (July-Aug. 1990): 74.
9. Wiggenhorn, "Motorola U," p. 73.
10. Wiggenhorn, "Motorola U," p. 75.

CHAPTER 12

1. "From Area Associate to Apprentice Electrician," *5-Star News Local* (Apple Computer, Inc.) Sept. 24, 1991, pp. 1, 8.

EPILOGUE

1. Frederick W. Gluck, "Recreating the American Dream," lecture presented in the John J. Horan Endowed Lecture Series, Oct. 21, 1992, at Manhattan College.
2. See James Brian Quinn, *Intelligent Enterprise* (New York: Free Press, 1992), pp. 9, 10.
3. "Computers Start to Lift U.S. Productivity," *Wall Street Journal*, Mar. 1, 1993, p. B10.

APPENDIX 1

1. *OECD in Figures* (Paris: Organization for Economic Cooperation and Development, 1992); McKinsey Global Institute, *Service Sector Productivity* (Washington, D.C.: McKinsey Global Institute, 1992), Exhibit 1-1.
2. Dirk Pilat and Bart van Ark, *Productivity Leadership in Manufacturing, Germany, Japan, and the United States, 1973–1989* (Groningen: Economics Faculty, University of Gronigen, 1992), p. 2.
3. McKinsey Global Institute, *Service-Sector Productivity*.
4. McKinsey Global Institute, *Service-Sector Productivity*, p. 4.

APPENDIX 2

1. Robert Wood Johnson, quoted in James E. Burke, "The Leverage of Goodwill," Speech to the Advertising Council, Nov. 16, 1993, p. 2.
2. Burke, "The Leverage of Goodwill," p. 2.

Index